Chipping Away at Public Debt

Chipping Away at Public Debt

Sources of Failure and Keys to Success in Fiscal Adjustment

EDITED BY

PAOLO MAURO

WILEY

John Wiley & Sons, Inc.

Library of Congress Cataloging-in-Publication Data

Chipping away at public debt: sources of failure and keys to success in fiscal adjustment/ edited by Paolo Mauro.

p. cm.

Includes index.

ISBN 978-1-118-04338-7 (hardback)

ISBN 978-1-118-11304-2 (ebk);

ISBN 978-1-118-11305-9 (ebk);

ISBN 978-1-118-11306-6 (ebk)

Printed in the United States

1. Debts, Public. 2. Fiscal policy. 3. Budget deficits. 4. Government spending policy. I. Mauro, Paolo.

HJ8015.C47 2011

336.3'435–dc22   2011014255

Printed in the United States of America

10 9 8 7 6 5 4 3 2 1

Contents

Foreword

"A plan is nothing, but planning is everything." A quote from U.S. President Dwight D. Eisenhower in 1957, referring to a military context where a shifting situation can rapidly make a plan obsolete and worthless, yet the process of thinking ahead through all possible contingencies and the appropriate response to them is extremely valuable. The former general's wisdom carries through, if appropriately adapted, to the context of economics and public finance.

Ever since the beginning of the global financial and economic crisis that broke out in the late 2000s, my colleagues and I at the IMF have consistently called for the announcement of credible medium-term fiscal adjustment plans. In the early stages of the crisis, when a new Great Depression loomed as a real possibility, we called for fiscal stimulus (in those countries with sufficient fiscal space to afford it), but simultaneously advised the announcement and publication of fiscal adjustment plans that would gradually restore the state of the public finances to a more sustainable situation. As the world economy began to recover, we called on countries to begin implementing fiscal adjustment plans.

To us, not just planning, but also plans are everything, if they are well designed. Plans to adjust the public finances are a way to commit to the long and hard task ahead, to explain to the public at large how the government intends to ensure the solidity of the public finances, and to anchor market expectations. In the absence of plans and their implementation, market participants would become more concerned about fiscal sustainability and would, sooner or later, demand high-risk premia on government bonds, thus causing an increase in borrowing costs for the government and perhaps interest rates more generally.

But the important point implicit in Eisenhower's observation—that the situation often changes—applies just as forcefully to the economics context. The list of possible types of surprises that may imply costs for the fiscal deficit is vast: in particular, it includes shocks to macroeconomic variables, such as economic growth or interest rates; occasionally, banking crises or natural disasters also inflict a major toll on the public finances.

In view of these possible surprises, fiscal adjustment plans must thus be designed in a way that makes them sufficiently flexible to accommodate the impact of shocks, but also sufficiently resilient so as to preserve their medium-term fiscal consolidation objectives even when the underlying economic environment turns out differently than initially expected.

This book tells the stories of many fiscal battles of the past and the shifting situations that influenced the course of events. Some of these battles were fought almost without a plan; some with plans that were drawn up in greater detail but had to be abandoned; and some where plans proved resilient and instrumental to ultimately bringing the public finances under control. The stories are important, informative, and interesting in themselves, and thus deserve to be written and read. The book records the motivation, objectives, and ultimate success or failure of the plans and of the people—capable civil servants and politicians—who designed them and sought to implement them. The lessons are valid today and will continue to be relevant for a long time to come, not only because the fiscal implications of this most recent crisis will take many years to resolve, but also because no doubt further crises and new fiscal challenges will emerge in the future.

One of our main tasks at the International Monetary Fund—and its Fiscal Affairs Department in particular—is to help countries design and implement fiscal policies that promote strong, sustained, and balanced growth. We do so through policy advice and technical assistance grounded in decades of collective operational experience as well as research, such as the work reported in this book. Our counterparts and everyday interlocutors are primarily country officials. Yet, one of the key findings in this book is that, ultimately, for fiscal adjustment to succeed, it has to be supported by the public at large. Thus the stories in this book are relevant not just for technical experts, but also for taxpayers, investors, and voters who want to be better informed about how the lessons of the past can guide the fiscal policies planned by their governments today and in the years to come. I hope you find this work interesting and helpful.

Carlo Cottarelli

Director, Fiscal Affairs Department,
International Monetary Fund.

Acknowledgments

This book is the outcome of a large team effort. Although the individual chapters bear the main authors' names, the team that produced this book met numerous times to establish and consistently apply its common approach, exchange ideas, compare notes, and share feedback. In addition to the authors listed in the individual chapters, several people deserve special mention and warm thanks. Carlo Cottarelli, Director of the International Monetary Fund's (IMF's) Fiscal Affairs Department, was highly supportive throughout the project. Ricardo Velloso and Mauricio Villafuerte played a key role in shaping the overall project and providing guidance and detailed comments to several of the country case study teams. Our assistants' team, consisting of Patricia Quiros, Katia Chen, and Alica Dzelilovic, provided excellent editorial and logistical support and was of great help in conducting archival searches. The project was initiated and led by Paolo Mauro. Many colleagues in the IMF, other institutions, and academia provided insightful and constructive comments: in particular, Masatsugu Asakawa, Alan Auerbach, Roel Beetsma, Benoît Coeuré, Carlo Cottarelli, David Heald, Paul-Henry Lapointe, and others acknowledged in the individual chapters. Sean Culhane and Patricia Loo of the IMF's External Relations department liaised effectively with our publisher. Natasha Andrews-Noel, Timothy Burgard, and Stacey Rivera of Wiley were helpful and efficient throughout the editorial and production process.

The opinions expressed in this book are those of the authors and editor alone and should not be attributed to the International Monetary Fund, its Board of Directors, its management, or any of the institutions with which they are affiliated.

Introduction

General public interest in government debts and their consequences is now at an all-time high in the advanced economics. Indeed, with the global financial and economic crisis that began in the late 2000s, the state of the public finances in the advanced economies has experienced its most pervasive and pronounced worsening since the Second World War.[1] Government debts as a share of gross domestic product (GDP) in the G-7 countries are now higher than they were in the early 1950s, that is, in the immediate aftermath of the Second World War (see Figure I.1). Spending pressures in aging-related areas—pensions and, especially, health care—will add to the challenge in the years ahead.

Until the "Great Recession" of 2008–09, developments in public debts and deficits had seldom been the stuff of high drama in the advanced economies. Occasionally, budget negotiations had led governing coalitions to fall apart or even governments to shut down. Austerity measures had sometimes triggered public demonstrations or strikes, and even severe violence. But as fiscal variables such as overall revenues and expenditures usually change slowly from year to year, the perception by and large had been that public debts were a bit like cholesterol: high levels would increase the chances of serious trouble, but there was no guarantee that trouble would occur, at least not in the near term. It was well understood that high levels had to be gradually brought down at some point: ultimately, fiscal adjustment is motivated by the need to avoid debt reduction through disruptive means such as default or inflation. However, the temptation to postpone adjustment was strong, implying that (as shown later in the book) fiscal adjustment plans often lacked ambition in their design or implementation. Fiscal crises precipitating fiscal adjustment—those associated with sharp increases in interest rates, refinancing difficulties, support by international financial institutions, or sovereign defaults—were the domain of developing and emerging countries.[2]

With fiscal crises having recently begun to affect some advanced economies (albeit relatively small ones, thus far), there is now greater realization that the need for fiscal adjustment in the years ahead is at its highest and will no doubt remain a key issue for a long time to come. In response, many

(In percent of GDP)

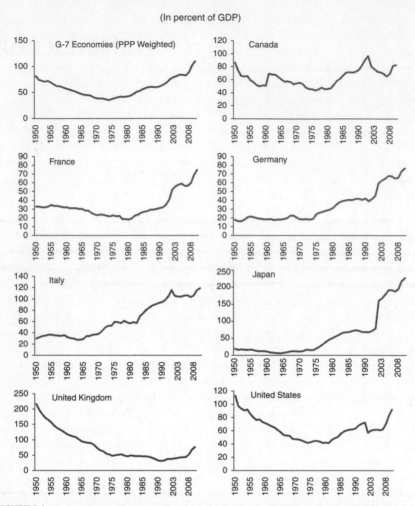

FIGURE I.1 General Government Gross Debt Ratios in G-7 Economies, 1950–2010

Sources: Data are drawn mainly from the International Monetary Fund's (IMF's) Fiscal Affairs Department Historical Government Debt database supplemented by the following: Canada (1950-60)—Federal Gross Government Debt (Haver Analytics); France (1950-77)—National Debt (Goodhart, 2002); Germany (1950-75)—Credit Market Debt and Loans (Statistisches Bundesamt Deutschland); Italy (1950-78)— National Government Debt (Banca d'Italia); Japan—Central Government Debt (Ministry of Finance of Japan); United Kingdom (1950-79)—National Debt (Goodhart, 1999); United States—Gross Federal Debt (Office of Management and Budget; and U.S. Census Bureau). G-7 average is weighted by gross domestic product at purchasing power parity.

governments have prepared and are still refining medium-term fiscal adjustment plans for the period ahead. Academic research on fiscal policy, after languishing for several years, is experiencing a revival.

The objective of this book is to inform the public debate on how to ensure successful fiscal adjustment in the period ahead, through systematic analysis of past adjustment plans and their outcomes.[3] Our belief is that although today's circumstances may be different from those experienced in the past, history may nevertheless provide useful guidance. Our hope is that the design and implementation of today's plans may be improved by avoiding the pitfalls that plagued the plans of the past, and by learning from past successes. In some ways, our work is especially motivated by today's difficult challenges. But we think the lessons to be drawn will be relevant for many years to come. It will take years, if not decades, of fiscal adjustment to place the public finances of the advanced economies back on a sustainable path: we are in this for the long haul. Moreover, fiscal adjustment has had to be undertaken on many occasions throughout history, and it is safe to expect that the issue will come back to the fore many times in the future.

Indeed, high and growing government debts have long been a recurring concern for policymakers and the public at large, calling for periodic attempts at fiscal adjustment, and this is the past experience we leverage in this book's analysis. The extent to which the issue has come to the fore in public debate has varied over time and across countries, depending on economic developments, financial market conditions, and perhaps even social and cultural norms and attitudes vis-à-vis public savings. Nevertheless, it is fair to say that, for a good part of the past four decades, most advanced economies have sought to grapple with increasing government debts and deficits, as fiscal revenues often failed to keep pace with rising government expenditures, which in turn largely stemmed from the expansion of social spending on welfare benefits, pensions, and health care.

In particular, the 1980s and early 1990s saw rapidly rising debts in many advanced economies, leading to the design and implementation—with varying degrees of success—of several large fiscal adjustment plans. In the mid- to late 1990s, attempts at fiscal adjustment were a frequent topic of household discussion in many European countries, as part of the drive toward meeting the prerequisites for European Monetary Union. Concerns were temporarily alleviated in some other advanced economies by economic and asset price booms in the late 1990s and the early to mid-2000s, as revenues rose, government deficits shrank, and economic growth reduced debt/GDP ratios. In hindsight, however, it is now clear that public debts remained an important policy challenge all along. Public concern with the issue has been reflected in myriad debates on the appropriate fiscal stance and policy measures to attain it, as well as attention-grabbing initiatives such as the billboard-sized "United States national debt clock" in Manhattan, along with various similar clocks and debt-tracking resources online for the United States and other countries.

From an analytical perspective, this book seeks to change the way in which we look at large fiscal adjustments, by shifting the focus of empirical analysis to large fiscal adjustment *plans,* and a comparison of plans versus outcomes. Previous studies focused on ex-post successes, identifying successful fiscal adjustment episodes on the basis of the largest observed improvements in the government debt or the fiscal balance.[4] That traditional approach asked important questions—such as whether fiscal adjustments are longer lasting and more successful when they rely on expenditure cuts rather than on tax hikes—and yielded useful information. However, important pieces of the puzzle were still missing. In our view, useful lessons can be drawn not only from successes, but also from failures. Moreover, it is important to understand not just outcomes, but also whether the outcomes turned out as intended. In this regard, our results will shed further light on the interpretation of some of the findings that had been obtained through the traditional, outcomes-based approach.

Our project takes an alternative, complementary approach. It starts from ex-ante, fiscal adjustment plans, rather than actual, ex-post outturn data. It identifies large fiscal adjustment plans on the basis of large *planned* reductions in debts and deficits. The empirical analysis then tracks ex-post outcomes compared with ex-ante plans. It looks at the extent to which macroeconomic variables (growth, interest rates, etc.) deviated from those projected at the time when the plans were drawn up. It also looks at whether spending exceeded expectations, or revenues fell short of expectations, and why, as well as whether planned debt reductions proceeded faster or slower than projected in the plan.

In light of the book's emphasis on the benefits of an ex-ante approach in analyzing large fiscal adjustments, we selected the sample of countries for the case studies solely on the basis of ex-ante criteria. We wanted the experiences described in the book to resonate especially with readers in advanced economies, which at the time of writing face the most acute need for fiscal adjustment. We also wanted the countries to be analyzed in the case studies to have two or more large medium-term fiscal adjustment plans, with a reasonable degree of specificity, available to the public, and with a horizon of at least three years. Finally, and perhaps most importantly, we wanted to bring back to life the motivation for fiscal adjustment, the constraints faced by policymakers, and the real-world choices they had to make given the information that was available to them at the time. In other words, to inform today's choices, we wanted the readers (and today's policymakers) to be able to put themselves in the shoes of their predecessors, so as to be able to learn from their experience. To permit that in-depth treatment, our country sample thus had to focus on a relatively small number of case studies. This led us to choose the G-7 countries (Canada, France, Germany, Italy, Japan, the United Kingdom, and the United States), a long-established and well-known group of the largest advanced economics.

For each country, we had to identify the largest, or most significant, fiscal adjustment plans to be analyzed in the case studies, again, solely on an ex-ante basis. The broad criteria we used are the following:

- Large size of fiscal adjustment, measured by the improvement of the fiscal balance (or the cyclically adjusted fiscal balance, or the cyclically adjusted primary balance, the fiscal measure that is most closely under the control of the government)
- Public announcement of the plans and their visibility in the media
- Formal and detailed presentation of the plans
- Medium-term orientation of the plans

Within these broad criteria, the teams for individual case studies adopted more specific ex-ante criteria to selecting the plans, tailored to country-specific circumstances and availability of information. Each case study explains its approach in detail, but in a nutshell:

- *Canada*. Although fiscal adjustment was a recurring policy objective, only two medium-term fiscal adjustment plans were presented to the public.
- *France*. The case study briefly analyzes two austerity packages of the 1970s and 1980s, and then delves into the details of the two most ambitious plans, both undertaken in the context of European initiatives linked to Euro membership: the plan aimed at meeting the Maastricht criteria for Euro entry and the plan to correct the fiscal deficit under the European Union's Excessive Deficit Procedure.
- *Germany*. Medium-term fiscal adjustment plans have long been prepared each year (on a rolling basis). The authors of the case study computed the ambition of each plan (measured by the *targeted* improvement in the cyclically adjusted primary balance, where the cyclical adjustment was computed by the authors using only real-time data that would have been available to contemporaries), They then analyzed the four plans displaying the most ambitious fiscal adjustment according to that ex-ante measure.
- *Italy*. Here, the public debt has been chronically high and medium-term fiscal adjustment plans have been published every year, but governments have been short-lived. The case study analyzes (i) the most important and ambitious fiscal adjustment plan (to meet the Maastricht criteria for Euro entry); and (ii) the only plan designed and fully implemented by the same government.

- *Japan*. Formal medium-term fiscal adjustment plans were introduced as recently as the late 1990s, and only two plans were sufficiently detailed and well publicized to merit analysis.
- *United States*. There has traditionally been little emphasis on, and formality in, medium-term fiscal adjustment plans. Nevertheless, three initiatives combining efforts by both the administration and Congress to contain fiscal deficits stood out as especially relevant: the Gramm-Rudman-Hollings in the mid-1980s and the two Omnibus Budget Reconciliation Acts (OBRA) of the early 1990s.
- *United Kingdom*. The four chosen medium-term fiscal adjustment plans are those presented by new chancellors of the exchequer at the beginning of the legislature and government cycle. Each of these plans displayed significant ex-ante ambition with respect to improving the fiscal balance.

The main features of the large fiscal adjustment plans analyzed in detail by the case studies are summarized in Table I.1. Although the plans are selected entirely on the basis of ex-ante considerations, the table also briefly gives a sense of the wide range of outcomes, in terms of ex-post performance, with respect to meeting the plans' initial objectives. This is to whet the reader's appetite for the analysis in the case studies, which will compare ex-ante objectives with ex-post outcomes and will seek to identify the factors underlying such discrepancies.

To complement the case studies, we cast the net to a wider set of countries and undertake a systematic *cross-country statistical analysis* of large fiscal adjustment plans. Again, we are careful to select our sample on an ex-ante basis and analyze the countries of the European Union (EU), which have to produce fiscal adjustment plans as part of their obligations as EU members. Specifically, we use a comprehensive database that we assembled, consisting of all the three-year "convergence" or "stability and growth" programs produced by each EU country for every year over the past couple of decades.[5] In addition to fiscal variables (revenues, primary and interest expenditures, etc.) for the next three years, the programs include underlying macroeconomic assumptions (growth, inflation, etc.). This permits a comparison of expectations and outturns not only for the fiscal variables, but also for the macroeconomic variables. Using real-time data, we thus analyze plan implementation errors and ratios (actual adjustment versus planned adjustment) and their economic and political determinants.

Throughout the remainder of this book, one finding is clear: all plans encountered large surprises. In particular, differences in economic growth compared with expectations embedded in the plans had a sizable, direct impact on the fiscal accounts, and also an indirect impact by altering policymakers' and the public's perceptions of the relative merits of fiscal adjustment versus stimulus. In addition, other macroeconomic shocks,

TABLE I.1 Summary of Large Fiscal Adjustment Plans

Country	Large Fiscal Adjustment Plan	Objectives/Design	Comments/Outcome
Canada	1985–91	▪ Reduce overall deficit by 3.5% of GDP over 6 years. ▪ Across-the-board cuts and freezes.	Overall deficit objectives met, but not sufficiently ambitious to halt the rise in debt.
	1994–97	▪ Reduce overall deficit by 3% of GDP over 3 years. ▪ Major restructuring of spending, including reforms of unemployment insurance, transfers to provinces, and pensions.	Successfully met objectives and attained long-lasting reversal of debt dynamics.
France	Plan Barre, 1976–77	▪ Austerity packages to curb inflation and current account deficit. ▪ Not set in multi-year frameworks.	Effective in reducing deficits and containing aggregate demand, but impact short-lived.
	Virage de la Rigueur, 1982–84	▪ Combination of tax hikes and spending curbs. ▪ Reforms in 1982–84.	
	1994–97 Plan aimed at meeting the Maastricht criteria	▪ Introduced multi-year framework. ▪ Quantitative objectives aimed at meeting Maastricht criteria.	Met Maastricht criteria, partly through last-minute revenue measures. Difficulties in controlling expenditures.
	2003–07 Consolidation under the Excessive Deficit Procedure	▪ Fiscal adjustment focused on expenditure control. ▪ Legally binding zero real growth rule for central government spending; health and pension reforms.	Some expenditure slippages, partly offset by revenue developments.

(continued)

TABLE I.1 (*Continued*)

Country	Large Fiscal Adjustment Plan	Objectives/Design	Comments/Outcome
Germany	1976–79 Plan	■ Cut deficit by 2.75% of GDP. ■ Back-loaded; focus on expenditures (generalized cuts; cuts in labor market expenditures; wage restraint).	Weak economic growth led government priority to shift from fiscal adjustment to stimulus.
	1981–85 Plan	■ Cut deficit by 1.25% of GDP. ■ Front-loaded expenditure cuts (reduction in entitlement and wage bills).	Largely successful.
	1991–95 Plan	■ Cut deficit by 1.5% of GDP while minimizing tax increases needed to finance unification. ■ Mainly expenditure-based (defense, social spending). Revenue package from 1990 plus Value Added Tax (VAT) rate hike.	Did not meet objectives.
	2003–07 Plan	■ Cut deficit together with "Agenda 2010" structural reforms (labor market, pensions). ■ Back-loaded. All on expenditure side: reducing unemployment insurance, transfers to pension system, firing benefits, and subsidies.	Largely successful. Higher-than-expected costs of labor market reforms. Increase in VAT made it possible to meet objectives while reducing the tax burden on labor.
Italy	1994 Economic and Financial Program Document (EFPD) for 1994–97	■ Reduce the debt/GDP ratio beginning in 1996. ■ Strong interest in joining European Monetary Union (EMU). Initial plan	Attained lasting reduction in debt/GDP ratio, albeit at high levels. Maastricht criterion met through last-minute efforts.

		did not aim at meeting Maastricht criterion of 3% deficit, but objectives made more ambitious in mid-course.	
	2002 EFPD for 2002–05	▪ Planned limited improvement in fiscal balance (by 1% of GDP); together with a 2% of GDP reduction in the revenue ratio, thus implying the need for a 3% of GDP expenditure cut.	Revenue ratio remained unchanged. Large expenditure and fiscal balance overruns.
Japan	1997—Fiscal Structural Reform Act	▪ Reduce deficit to 3% of GDP by fiscal year (FY) 2003. ▪ 3-year expenditure ceilings on initial budget by major policy area. ▪ No revenue-enhancing measures announced. Future policy decisions needed to achieve targets.	Immediately derailed by Asian crisis and domestic banking crisis.
	2002—Medium-Term Fiscal Adjustment Plans. (Two sub-periods: 2002– and 2006)	▪ Aim for primary surplus by early 2010s. ▪ Introduced 5-year rolling frameworks. ▪ 5-year expenditure cut plans by major policy area introduced in FY 2006. ▪ No revenue-enhancing measures announced. Future policy decisions needed to achieve targets.	Partially successful in the initial stages. Ultimately derailed by the global crisis.
United Kingdom	Howe's 1980 Medium-Term Financial Strategy (FY 1980–1983)	▪ Curb government borrowing to rein in the money supply and inflation. ▪ Envisaged 5.5% of GDP cut in the deficit, through lower spending and an expected rise in oil revenues.	Expenditure overruns in social security, public wages, and support to public enterprises.

(continued)

TABLE I.1 (*Continued*)

Country	Large Fiscal Adjustment Plan	Objectives/Design	Comments/Outcome
	Lawson's 1984 Budget (FY 1984–1988)	■ Rebalance the tax burden from direct to indirect taxes and reduce marginal tax rates. ■ Shrink the State (Thatcher government agenda).	Expenditure cuts beyond what was envisaged. Privatization of large public enterprises.
	Clarke's November 1993 Budget (FY 1994–1998)	■ Reduction in public sector manpower. Eliminate the 8% percent of GDP deficit by 1998. ■ Increases in national insurance contribution rate and excises, broadening of the VAT base. Freezes on running costs combined with zero-based budgeting "fundamental expenditure reviews."	Delivered a steady reduction in the fiscal deficit.
	Darling's 2007 Pre-Budget Report and Comprehensive Spending Review (FY 2008–2012)	■ Planned modest reduction in the deficit, by reducing the growth of spending.	Derailed by global crisis: revenue underperformance, expenditure overruns, capital injections to banks.
United States	1985 Gramm-Rudman-Hollings (GRH) (Balanced Budget and Emergency Deficit Control Act)	■ President to submit budgets consistent with GRH targets each year, and balanced budget by 1991. ■ If legislated policy was projected to result in higher deficits, automatic "sequestration" with spending cuts would apply.	Did not achieve targets but deficit would have been larger in absence of GRH.

OBRA—1990	■ Reduce deficit by cumulative US$500 billion (equivalent to 8.5% of 1991 GDP) in 1991–95.	Unable to restrain the unexpected growth in spending for entitlement programs (notably, Medicare and Medicaid).
	■ Introduced discretionary spending caps and pay-as-you-go (PAYGO) mechanism. Included some tax increases.	
OBRA—1993	■ Reduce the deficit by 1.75% of GDP, relative to the no-policy–change baseline, by 1998.	Deficit reduction well in excess of targets, with stronger-than-expected economic growth and revenues, but also effective spending caps.
	■ PAYGO continued and discretionary spending caps extended, with 5-year nominal spending freeze. Some tax increases and measures to close loopholes.	

revisions to past fiscal data, and political developments all presented significant challenges. This general finding highlights the importance of designing and implementing plans in a way that makes them sufficiently flexible to respond to shocks while credibly preserving their medium-term consolidation objectives.

The busy policymaker who is looking for a quick summary of the main policy implications of our work may now wish to go straight to our conclusions chapter. However, we believe that the devil is in the details and that the in-depth treatment of the case studies in Chapters 1 through 7 should prove not only entertaining, but also informative, by providing some important nuances and country-specific considerations. Chapters 1 and 2 analyze the cases of Canada and the United States, respectively, which present substantial differences in approaches and outcomes, despite similarities in timing of attempted consolidation and underlying macroeconomic developments. Chapters 3 through 5 consist of the cases of France, Germany, and the United Kingdom. Again, underlying cyclical/macroeconomic developments present similarities among these three European countries, with greater commonalities between France and Germany resulting from Euro qualification and adoption. Chapters 6 and 7 focus on two countries "living with" high debt and relatively low economic growth over the past two decades, Italy and Japan. Chapter 8 consists of our cross-country statistical analysis. Chapter 9 summarizes and concludes.

Notes

1. The International Monetary Fund's *Fiscal Monitor* (published twice a year) reports on developments in fiscal variables and estimates fiscal adjustment needs for a large sample of countries. Throughout the book, the term "fiscal adjustment" refers to a combination of government expenditure cuts and revenue increases that improves the fiscal balance and halts or reverses the growth of public debt as a share of GDP.

2. Highly disruptive reductions in debt/GDP ratios have not occurred in the advanced economies since the 1940s. Hyperinflations occurred in the aftermath of major wars. Partial defaults occurred during the interwar period, for example, in Italy in the late 1920s (Alesina, 1988) and in the United States in 1933, when the abrogation of "gold clauses" in debt contracts prevented a 25 percentage point increase in the government debt/GDP ratio (Kroszner, 2003). The history of most advanced economies over the previous centuries is of course littered with frequent debt crises (Reinhart and Rogoff, 2010).

3. More specifically, our focus is on how to ensure that fiscal adjustment plans meet their intended fiscal objectives. We do not analyze the impact of fiscal adjustment on economic performance. (For a recent study and a review of previous studies on that issue, see International Monetary Fund, 2010).

4. Previous studies include, for advanced economies, Alesina and Perotti, 1995; Alesina and Ardagna, 1998, 2009; and von Hagen et al., 2001; and, for broader samples of countries, Giavazzi et al., 2000; Gupta et al., 2005; Tsibouris et al., 2006; Baldacci et al., 2006.

5. To assemble our database, which consists of 229 three-year plans for 25 countries, covering 1991–2007, we gathered the pre-1998 plans from various archival sources, entering the data from hard copies, and drew the post-1998 plans from an existing EU database (see Chapter 9 for details).

CHAPTER 1

Canada: A Success Story

Cemile Sancak
Lucy Qian Liu
Taisuke Nakata

Introduction

As in most advanced economies, the fiscal pressures in Canada started in the 1970s and became most pronounced in the mid-1980s. Canada stands out among the G-7 countries, however, as it successfully responded to these pressures in the subsequent decades through large and sustained fiscal adjustment. The ex-ante approach adopted in this chapter reveals that the adjustment was underpinned by two substantially different plans in terms of speed and nature of adjustment measures. The chapter compares and contrasts these two plans, based on both ex ante design and ex post performance.

The plans are analyzed with regard to:

- The scale of planned adjustment, in particular, whether the scale of the planned adjustment was sufficiently large to stabilize debt
- The comparison of plans vis-à-vis outcomes
- The nature of adjustment measures
- Whether adjustment was sustained in the aftermath of the episode

The main analysis in this chapter focuses on the federal government budget, because fiscal adjustment plans were formulated only at the federal government level, rather than the consolidated general government level including the provinces, territories, and local governments. However, for completeness, a separate section also discusses the consolidation efforts of the subnational governments.

The identification of the federal government adjustment plans is based on an examination of federal budget documents covering 1961–2010. We use three criteria to select an adjustment episode: (i) the adjustment plan is clearly announced to the public (in the budget); (ii) it specifies explicit medium-term fiscal targets involving substantial fiscal adjustment; and (iii) it is formulated in a medium-term framework. Based on these criteria, we identify two adjustment plans in which the federal government announced medium-term fiscal targets against the background of large and increasing debt levels: the 1985 Plan covering 1985–91 and the 1995 Plan covering 1994–97.[1]

The actual overall balance, the main fiscal target, outperformed plans in both adjustment episodes. In fact, the extent to which ex-post performance conformed to ex-ante design was exceptional in Canada compared to other G-7 countries. That said, the 1985 Plan was criticized both domestically and internationally for not being sufficiently ambitious: it did not make enough effort to reduce the deficit and eschewed tough measures on major spending programs. The 1995 Plan, on the other hand, scored better, building on the lessons learned from the 1985 Plan. The 1995 Plan was highly ambitious in terms of both speed and nature of planned adjustment measures, as it aimed to introduce major changes to government programs and services. Indeed—to give a preview of outcomes—debt stabilization, the main objective of both adjustment plans, was achieved only during the 1994–97 episode. The overall balance improved by almost 5 percent of Gross Domestic Product (GDP) over 1994–97, moved to a surplus in 1997–98, and remained in surplus until 2007–08 (see Figure 1.1). The federal net debt declined to 34 percent of GDP by 2007–08, compared to 74 percent in 1995–96 (see Figure 1.2).

The following elements were key in ultimately bringing about a lasting improvement in Canada's fiscal position:

- Broad-based public support
- A repositioning of the role of government and profound structural reforms
- Prudent macroeconomic and fiscal assumptions
- Fiscal consolidation at the subnational level

Background

Canada's debt problems started to emerge in the mid-1970s (see Figure 1.2). Debt accumulation was driven by both the global environment and domestic policies. The main global factors were: (i) the 1973–74 energy price surge, which reduced economic growth through a negative supply-side shock; (ii) higher interest rates in advanced economies; and (iii) the 1973 move to floating exchange rates following the collapse of the Bretton Woods

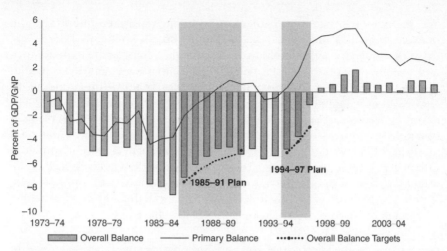

FIGURE 1.1 Federal Government Primary/Overall Balance, 1973–2008

Source: Fiscal Reference Tables 2009, Budget 1985 and 1995, Department of Finance Canada.

Note: Balances between 1984–85 and 1990–91 are in percent of GNP.

system, which removed domestic financing discipline. These factors together contributed to an increase in the differential between interest rates and growth—a key determinant of the debt/GDP ratio dynamics.

The impact of these global factors was compounded by Canadian policies. In 1973–74, Canada indexed to inflation several expenditure programs

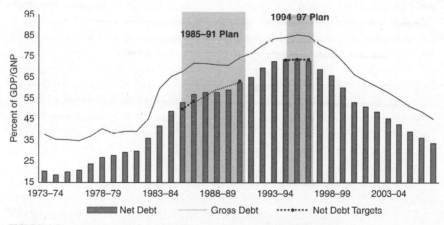

FIGURE 1.2 Federal Government Gross and Net Debt, 1973–2008

Source: Fiscal Reference Tables 2009, Budget 1985 and 1995, Department of Finance Canada.

Note: Debt ratios between 1984–85 and 1990–91 are in percent of GNP.

and the personal income tax system—both the basic exemptions and the brackets were fully indexed. In the high inflation environment of the 1970s, these new indexing systems led to a sharp increase in program expenditures and a weakening of revenue growth.[2,3] As the economy entered into stagflation in the mid-1970s, the government consistently relied on spending increases and revenue reductions to provide short-term stimulus. There was a strong consensus among politicians and the public in favor of such stimulative policies during this period, partly because the productivity slowdown after the 1973–74 energy price shock was seen as a cyclical phenomenon rather than a structural change. The large primary deficits, combined with increasing cost of debt service, soon led to a rapid increase in public debt. Within less than ten years, the federal net debt more than doubled, reaching 42 percent of Gross National Product (GNP) in 1983–84.

The 1985 Plan (Covering 1985–91)

A new Conservative government, led by Prime Minister Brian Mulroney, recognized that further pursuing expansionary fiscal policy would damage the Canadian economy in the long term. To restore fiscal responsibility and control the growing debt, Mulroney set up the Nielsen Task Force in 1984 to review all federal departmental programs. In November 1984, the government outlined the "Agenda for Economic Renewal," with the goal of reducing the fiscal deficit in an orderly manner. The essence of this Agenda was incorporated in the 1985 Budget—henceforth "the 1985 Plan."

The 1985 Plan consisted of two distinct, yet interrelated, elements. The first element and the primary focus of the Plan was a set of structural reforms aimed at improving the competitiveness of the Canadian economy, including the Canada-U.S. free trade agreement, which came into effect in 1989, and the reform of the federal sales tax system in 1991. These structural reforms provided long-lasting, important foundations for economic growth and fiscal adjustment. The second element—the focus of our analysis—emphasized the need to curb overall deficit to stabilize public debt. The 1985 Plan viewed these two goals as interrelated: economic growth supported by structural reform would help fiscal adjustment by increasing the tax base; a sound fiscal stance would foster economic growth, with increased confidence in the economy promoting investment.

Given the high levels of inherited public debt and expected real interest rates in the medium-term, the 1985 Plan aimed to stabilize debt at 65 percent of GNP by 1990–91. This was equivalent to an overall deficit reduction of 3.6 percent of GNP over six years (from 8.5 percent of GNP in 1984–85 to 4.9 percent in 1990–91). Four-fifths of the adjustment would be achieved through expenditure measures, with the remainder attributable to revenue measures. The 1985 Plan's adjustment in expenditures relied primarily on across-the-board cuts and freezes, and efficiency gains. Details on the revenue and expenditure measures of the 1985 Plan are provided in the "Nature and Composition of Adjustment" section.

The 1995 Plan (Covering 1994–97)

Benefiting from the 1985 Plan, the government initially made good progress in reducing the deficit. By 1988–89, it achieved a small primary surplus for the first time in almost 20 years. However, with increasing interest rates due to growing inflationary pressures, the government consistently underestimated the interest bill. As the recession hit in 1990, the overall deficit once again started to rise, reaching 5.6 percent of GDP and the federal net debt increased to an unprecedented 70 percent of GDP in 1992–93.

Public polls in the early 1990s revealed that reducing the fiscal deficit had become the primary economic issue for Canadians. The 1993 Decima Research polls reported that Canadians' concern for the deficit reached an all-time high. An April Gallup poll showed that 70 percent of Canadians would cut spending to reduce the deficit, rather than increase it to stimulate the economy (Bourgon, 2009). This is in sharp contrast to the level of public awareness prior to the 1985 Plan. Less than 2 percent of respondents to a 1984 Decima Research poll had cited the federal deficit and national debt as Canada's most important economic problem.[4]

How did public awareness of the fiscal challenges increase over time? International institutions, international rating agencies, Canadian research institutions, and the media had been stressing the urgency to address Canada's unsustainable debt for some time. With the federal government net debt at 73 percent of GDP by 1993, Canada had the second worst standing in the G-7 after Italy. In October 1994, the government published its report "A New Framework for Economic Policy" to educate the public about the importance of fiscal adjustment.[5] It shared the key messages of this report through an intensive communication strategy, including national and regional conferences organized by Finance Minister Paul Martin and substantive public debates across the country.[6] Furthermore, contrary to the tradition of holding consultation meetings separately with each interest group, the government held meetings mixing interest groups from different backgrounds. The government "wanted the public to understand long before the budget was presented that there were tough choices to be made, that there was no perfect answer and that everyone had to bear their fair share of the burden in the greater good, which meant that everyone had to give" (Martin, 2010). Canadians thus became increasingly aware of the implications of high debt levels for growth and intergenerational equity as well as of the opportunity cost of debt service, which consumed 35 percent of government revenues in the early 1990s.

During the 1993 federal election campaign, the election platforms of most political parties included deficit reduction. A new Liberal government, led by Prime Minister Jean Chretien, was elected in November 1993. The Liberal election commitment was to reduce the overall federal government deficit to no more than 3 percent of GDP by 1996–97 (from 5.9 percent in 1993–94). The 1994 Budget reaffirmed this commitment, but it was not explicit about the supporting measures except for announcing a review of the federal government's programs and services—called the Program Review.[7] This budget was criticized by financial markets at the time for not being ambitious enough.

Following the Mexican peso crisis in late 1994, the *Wall Street Journal* ran an editorial in January 1995 arguing: "Mexico isn't the only U.S. neighbor flirting with the financial abyss. . . . If dramatic action isn't taken in next month's federal budget, it's not inconceivable that Canada could hit the debt wall."[8] This editorial sent shockwaves across Canada, increasing pressure on the government to deliver a more ambitious budget. Furthermore, shortly before the 1995 Budget, Moody's put Canada on a "credit watch." With these developments, debt stabilization became the number-one priority for the government.

The 1995 Plan introduced a major restructuring of federal department spending, including a reform of the unemployment insurance program, revisions to transfers to provinces, and pension reform.[9] The government launched a Program Review (i.e., expenditure review) in May 1994 to "review all federal programs in order to bring about the most effective and cost-efficient way of delivering programs and services that are appropriate to the federal government's role in the Canadian federation (1995 Budget, p. 11)." Program Review decisions were included in the 1995 Budget. The measures in the 1995 Budget aimed to secure the achievement of the government's interim deficit target of 3 percent of GDP for 1996–97, with the ultimate goal of a balanced budget. The government's strategy was to adopt two-year rolling targets, that is, each budget laid out the targets only for the next two years and did not make promises for the longer term. The objective of this approach was to help increase political accountability by putting pressure on program managers to deliver promised savings and ensure that targets were not missed due to economic uncertainties. Consistently meeting the targets would in turn help build public confidence in the program.[10] Although the 3 percent target was announced in the 1994 Budget, credible measures to attain it were introduced only in the 1995 Budget (hence, this chapter calls the adjustment plan "the 1995 Plan"). About 90 percent of the adjustment focused on expenditure measures, with the remainder expected from revenue measures.[11] The main reason for focusing on expenditure reduction in both plans—and especially in the 1995 Plan—was that the tax burden was already high relative to the United States, although lower than the Organization for Economic Cooperation and Development (OECD) average. Given the close integration of the economies of Canada and the United States, especially after the North-American Free Trade Agreement (NAFTA) in 1994, the United States was a more relevant comparator for tax burden. Details on the revenue and expenditure measures of the 1995 Plan are discussed in the "Nature and Composition of Adjustment" section.

Plans versus Outcomes: Macroeconomic Factors

In assessing the implementation of a consolidation plan, it is important to understand the role of the underlying macroeconomic developments. For instance, revenue developments are linked to an economy's cyclical position. We decompose revenues into cyclical and structural components to examine how much of the difference between plans and outcomes can be attributed to cyclical effects. We also decompose expenditures into primary expenditures and interest payments.[12]

Structural and Cyclical Components

Tables 1.1 and 1.2 present the headline and structural fiscal aggregates scaled to nominal income.[13] The columns of $\Delta a - \Delta p$ present the actual improvement compared to the planned improvement. Several interesting findings emerge from Tables 1.1 and 1.2.

In both adjustment episodes, the outcomes for the overall and primary balances were better than planned. However, the overperformance of the overall balance was much greater over 1994–97, despite the 1995 Plan's ambitious target over a short period. The actual overall balance outperformed the plan by 1.7 percent of GDP, compared to 0.3 percent over 1985–91.

The 1995 Plan was more ambitious, especially in terms of the speed of its primary expenditure adjustment: it aimed to reduce primary spending by 3.7 percent of GDP within three years, whereas the 1985 Plan envisioned a reduction of 3.5 percent of GNP over six years. Despite its shorter duration, the 1995 Plan delivered a larger cumulative primary spending adjustment compared to the 1985 Plan. Actual primary spending reduction amounted to 4 percent of GDP over 1994–97, compared to 3.6 percent of GNP over 1985–91. The 1985 Plan was widely criticized at the time for moving too slowly to reduce the deficit, even when the overall deficit target was more than met and before the government started backsliding in its efforts to keep the deficit under control, mainly due to the 1990–91 recession. For example, a 1990 editorial in the *Globe and Mail*, a national newspaper, stated, "On virtually every major spending program, the tough decisions have been deferred," and criticized the government's measures for being temporary, piecemeal, and insufficient.[14] International institutions also

TABLE 1.1 Structural versus Cyclical Decomposition—1985 Adjustment Plan

(As percent of GNP)

| | Plan (p) | | | Actual (a) | | | Overperformance (actual relative to plan) | Of which: | |
| | | | | | | | | | |
	FY 1984-85 p	FY 1990-91 p	Δp	FY 1984-85 a	FY 1990-91 a	Δa	1990-91 actual *minus* 1990-91 planned	Δa − Δp = Actual improvement *minus* planned improvement[a]	1984-85 actual *minus* 1984-85 preliminary estimate from plan ("base effect")
Revenues	15.2	15.9	0.7	14.6	16.3	1.7	0.4	1.0	−0.6
Cyclical	−0.2	0.0	0.2	−0.2	0.4	0.6	0.4	0.4	0.0
Structural	15.4	15.9	0.6	14.8	15.9	1.1	0.0	0.5	−0.6
Expenditures	23.7	20.8	−2.9	23.4	21.2	−2.3	−0.4	−0.6	0.3
Primary	18.4	14.9	−3.5	18.3	14.7	−3.6	0.2	0.1	0.1
Interest	5.3	5.9	0.6	5.1	6.5	1.4	−0.6	−0.8	0.2
Overall balance	−8.5	−4.9	3.6	−8.8	−4.9	3.9	0.0	0.3	−0.3
Primary balance	−3.2	1.0	4.2	−3.7	1.6	5.3	0.6	1.1	−0.5
Memo items (in percent of potential GNP):									
Structural primary balance	−3.0	1.0	4.0	−3.4	1.3	4.7	0.2	0.7	−0.5
Structural revenues	15.2	15.9	0.7	14.6	16.3	1.7	0.4	1.0	−0.6
Primary expenditure	18.1	14.9	−3.3	18.0	15.0	−3.0	−0.1	−0.2	0.1

[a]For expenditures, the formula is −(Δa − Δp).

TABLE 1.2 Structural vs. Cyclical Decomposition—1995 Adjustment Plan

(As percent of GDP)

| | Plan (p) | | | Actual (a) | | | Overperformance (actual relative to plan) | Of which: | |
| | | | | | | | 1996-97 actual *minus* 1996-97 planned | $\Delta a - \Delta p$ = Actual improvement *minus* planned improvement[a] | 1993-94 actual *minus* 1993-94 preliminary estimate from plan ("base effect") |
	FY 1993-94 p	FY 1995-97 p	Δp	FY 1993-94 a	FY 1996-97 a	Δa			
Revenues	16.3	15.7	0.4	15.9	16.8	0.9	0.1	0.5	-0.3
Cyclical	-0.5	-0.2	0.4	-0.6	-0.5	0.1	-0.3	-0.3	0.0
Structural	16.8	15.9	0.1	16.5	17.3	0.8	0.4	0.7	-0.3
Expenditures	22.2	19.3	-2.9	21.7	17.9	-3.8	1.4	0.9	0.5
Primary	16.9	13.1	-3.7	16.5	12.5	-4.0	0.7	0.3	0.4
Interest	5.3	5.2	0.8	5.2	5.4	0.2	0.8	0.7	0.1
Contingency Reserve	0.0	0.4	0.4	0.0	0.0	0.0	0.4	0.4	0.0
Overall balance	-5.9	-2.9	3.0	-5.8	-1.1	4.7	1.9	1.7	0.1
Primary balance	-0.6	3.6	4.2	-0.6	4.3	4.9	0.7	0.7	0.0
Memo items (in percent of potential GDP):									
Structural primary balance	0.0	3.7	3.8	0.0	4.7	4.6	0.9	0.9	0.0
Structural revenues	16.3	15.7	0.4	15.9	16.8	0.9	0.1	0.5	-0.3
Primary expenditure	16.3	13.0	-3.3	15.9	12.2	-3.7	0.8	0.4	0.4

[a]For expenditures, the formula is -(Δa−Δp).

viewed a more rapid pace of fiscal consolidation as desirable, especially given the strong economic growth in the late 1980s.[15] In retrospect, it is clear that it would have been preferable to take advantage of the favorable economic circumstances in the second half of the 1980s.

The difference in the overall balance performances of the two episodes is explained by differing performances on the spending side. In the 1985–91 episode, expenditures were higher than planned by 0.6 percent of GNP, due to the underestimation of interest payments by 0.8 percent of GNP—a sizable adverse surprise. As a result, despite the better than planned revenue and primary expenditure performance, the overall deficit reduction exceeded the plan only by 0.3 percent of GNP. By contrast, in the 1994–97 episode, total expenditure reduction was better than planned by 0.9 percent of GDP, with 0.3 percent of GDP coming from the additional reduction in primary expenditure and 0.7 percent of GDP due to prudent assumptions for nominal interest rates.

Learning from the 1985–91 episode, the government adopted prudent assumptions for nominal interest rates and other key macroeconomic and fiscal variables in the 1995 Budget. This helped achieve a strong overall balance performance over 1994–97. From an ex-ante point of view, prudent assumptions in the 1995 Plan also helped set tighter limits on planned primary spending. The 1995 Budget was transparent about its prudent assumptions about key macroeconomic variables, highlighting that they were more cautious than the average private sector forecast. Short- and long-term interest assumptions were higher than the private sector outlook by 60 and 70 basis points, respectively, during 1995 and 1996. Relative to the government's assumptions, long-term interest rates turned out to be 180 basis points lower, and the short-term interest rates almost 240 basis points lower, partly as a result of public confidence in the government's adjustment plan and the Bank of Canada's price stability strategy (see Figure 1.3).[16] The overall fiscal deficit was reduced by 4.7 percent of GDP over three years, outperforming the plan by 1.7 percent of GDP.

An additional factor that contributed to a higher than planned overall balance over 1994–97 was a contingency reserve (of 0.4 percent of GDP) included in the deficit projection to cover the risks of unpredictable events and forecasting errors. The reserve was added to expenditures but was not to be used as a source of funding for new initiatives; and if it was not needed, it had to be used to pay down the debt.

Revenue increases also played a role in both episodes even though both plans emphasized expenditure reduction as the major adjustment tool. This is particularly true for the 1985–91 episode, when actual revenues outperformed plans by 1 percent of GDP. This episode benefited from a positive growth surprise—leading to a cyclical revenue overperformance of 0.4 percent of GNP—and additional income tax policy measures not foreseen in the 1985

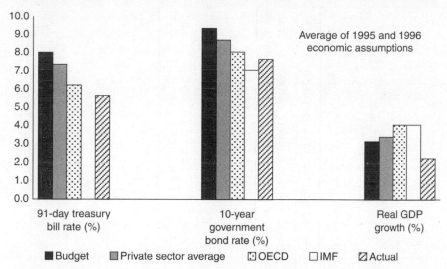

FIGURE 1.3 Comparison of the Economic Assumptions with Other Forecasts (As of February 1995)

Budget—leading to a structural revenue overperformance of 0.5 percent of GNP. In 1994–97, actual revenues outperformed plans by only 0.5 percent of GDP, because the negative output gap eroded 0.3 percent of GDP of revenue improvement. Structural revenue overperformance, at 0.7 percent of GDP, was actually higher than in the earlier adjustment episode.

Growth (Denominator) and Inflation Effects

In the comparison between planned and actual expenditure cuts, a deviation from the planned reduction in the expenditure-to-GDP/GNP ratio results from either a higher- or lower-than-expected expenditure cut in nominal terms (i.e., the numerator effect), or a higher- or lower-than-expected nominal GDP growth (i.e., the denominator effect). To examine the extent to which the government adhered to its original expenditure reduction plans, we decompose the planned adjustment in the expenditure-to-GDP ratio into (i) inflationary effect; (ii) the nominal GDP growth (or denominator) effect; and (iii) expenditure changes in real terms.[17] Applying the same decomposition to the actual reduction in the expenditure-to-GDP ratio, we examine the extent to which each factor contributes to the deviation between planned and actual adjustment.

During the 1985–91 episode, actual expenditure reduction in real terms turned out to be 0.8 percent of GNP greater than planned, even though the overall cut in primary spending was only 0.1 percent of GNP greater than planned (see Table 1.3). This unexpected real cut was largely due to the

TABLE 1.3 Sources of Greater-Than-Expected Expenditure Cuts

	1985 Adjustment Plan (as percent of GNP)				1994-95 Adjustment Plan (as percent of GDP)			
	Over-performance	Denominator effect	Inflation effect	Real changes	Over-performance	Denominator effect	Inflation effect	Real changes
Primary expenditures	**0.1**	**−0.4**	**−1.0**	**0.8**	**0.3**	**0.1**	**0.0**	**0.4**
Transfers to persons	−0.4	−0.2	−0.3	−0.3	0.1	0.1	0.0	0.2
Transfers to other levels of gov't	0.0	−0.1	−0.3	0.2	0.1	0.0	0.0	0.1
Defense	0.1	0.1	−0.1	0.3	0.2	0.0	0.0	0.2
Other[a]	0.4	−0.1	−0.4	0.7	−0.1	0.0	0.0	−0.1

[a]Other spending includes spending by departments (other than defense), agencies, and Crown corporations, and transfers other than major transfers to persons and other levels of government.

underestimation of inflation (1.0 percent of base-year GNP). In addition, the denominator effect contributed to another 0.4 percent of base-year GNP difference. In the 1994–97 episode, by contrast, actual reduction for most expenditures was greater than planned. The contributions of GDP growth and inflation effects were both marginal.

Nature and Composition of Adjustment

The previous analysis showed that the compositions of expenditure adjustments in the 1985 and 1995 Plans were different. This section further decomposes revenues and expenditures in order to investigate the differences in the nature of adjustment measures introduced in the two consolidation plans. (For the 1985 Plan, disaggregated revenue projections are available only for the first two years.)

Revenues

In both plans, revenue increases were expected to make only a small contribution to deficit reduction. Ex-post, revenue increases outperformed projections in both episodes. As discussed earlier, revenue overperformance was entirely structural over 1994–97, and more structural than cyclical over 1985–91.

In the 1985 Plan, revenues were expected to increase by 0.7 percent of GNP from 1984–85 to 1990–91, accounting for about 20 percent of the total adjustment effort. Key revenue increasing measures were to:

- Change the indexation factor of personal income tax exemptions, deductions, and tax brackets from full indexation to the consumer price index (CPI) to a partial indexation of CPI minus 3 percentage points.
- Impose temporary surtaxes on higher-income individuals and large corporations.
- Eliminate the federal personal income tax "reduction" (a sizable tax deduction).
- Broaden the sales tax base by reducing exemptions.
- Increase the sales tax rate by 1 percent.
- Increase automotive fuels tax.

In the 1995 Plan, revenues were expected to increase by 0.4 percent of GDP from 1993–94 to 1996–97. The contribution of revenue to the adjustment effort, at 13 percent of total adjustment, was lower than in the 1985 Plan. The key revenue measures were to:

- Eliminate tax deferral on business income.
- Limit tax assistance for contributions to registered retirement savings plan by high-income earners.

■ Introduce an additional tax on investment income of private corporations.
■ Increase the large corporation tax rate and the corporate surtax.
■ Increase excise taxes on tobacco and gasoline.

The excise tax on gasoline would be the largest contributor.

Tables 1.4 and 1.5 present the basic features of the revenue plan and outcome, and the contribution of each disaggregated revenue item to the overall revenue overperformance in the two episodes. The numbers in Table 1.4 are calculated as the two-year difference of the budget projections and outturns, because a six-year projection for disaggregated revenues is not available for the 1985 Plan. For example, the second column of the third panel in Table 1.4 represents the difference between the planned and actual changes over 1984–85 and 1986–87.

Actual revenues outperformed plans by 1 percent of GNP in the 1985–91 episode (see Table 1.1) and 0.5 percent of GDP in the 1994–97 episode (see Table 1.5), with a different set of overperforming revenues in each episode. More specifically, personal income tax revenues consistently outperformed the budgets in the 1985–91 episode, owing to tax policy measures not foreseen in the 1985 Plan and introduced to compensate for higher than planned public debt charges. (Specifically, the surtax on personal income tax was increased from 3 to 5 percent and an additional 3 percent surtax was levied on high-income earners in 1989.) An additional contributing factor to the overperformance was the restriction of indexation of brackets to increases in CPI in excess of 3 percentage points. The so-called "bracket creep" was estimated at 0.2 percent of GNP annually. Sales and excise taxes and duties underperformed budget projections dramatically over 1988–89 to 1990–91, likely due to the introduction of the Value Added Tax (VAT)— called the Goods and Services Tax in Canada, which while intended to be revenue neutral in actuality caused a temporary revenue decline. The corporate income tax revenue outcome also tended to be lower than planned. In the 1994–97 episode, personal income tax revenues slightly underperformed while other revenues marginally overperformed, due to the prudent revenue elasticities in the 1995 Plan (see Table 1.5).

Expenditures

The entire approach to expenditure adjustment differed markedly between the two plans. The main measures in the 1985 Plan included: (i) rationalization and improved efficiency of government programs; (ii) privatization and rationalization of the activities of Crown Corporations; and (iii) reduction in transfers and subsidies to various sectors. The 1985 Plan's adjustment in nonstatutory expenditures relied primarily on across-the-board cuts and

TABLE 1.4 Disaggregate Revenues (Two-year Rolling Changes)—1985 Adjustment Plan

(As percent of GNP/GDP)

	1984–85 (Base-year level)	1984–85 to 86–87	1985–86 to 87–88	1986–87 to 88–89[a]	1987–88 to 89–90	1988–89 to 90–91	1990–91 (End-year level)
2-year *projected* changes							
Budgetary revenues	**15.2**	**0.8**	**0.8**	n/a	**-0.4**	**0.5**	**17.9**
Tax revenues	**13.4**	**0.9**	**0.9**	n/a	**-0.2**	**0.8**	**16.7**
Personal income tax	6.9	0.7	0.9	n/a	-0.4	0.5	8.2
Corporate income tax	2.3	0.2	0.0	n/a	0.1	0.2	2.2
UI contributions[b]	n/a	n/a	0.0	n/a	-0.3	0.0	1.8
Sales and excise taxes and duties	4.3	-0.1	0.0	n/a	0.3	0.2	4.5
Other revenues	**1.8**	**0.0**	**-0.1**	n/a	**-0.1**	**-0.3**	**1.2**
2-year *actual* changes							
Budgetary revenues	**14.6**	**0.8**	**1.7**	n/a	**-0.2**	**0.6**	**17.6**
Tax revenues	**13.0**	**0.9**	**1.5**	n/a	**-0.2**	**0.4**	**15.9**
Personal income tax	6.7	0.9	1.3	n/a	-0.2	1.0	8.5
Corporate income tax	2.2	-0.2	0.1	n/a	0.0	-0.2	1.7
UI contributions[b]	n/a	n/a	0.1	n/a	-0.2	0.0	1.9
Sales and excise taxes and duties	4.2	0.1	0.1	n/a	0.2	-0.4	3.8
Other revenues	**1.5**	**0.0**	**0.1**	n/a	**0.0**	**0.1**	**1.6**
Overperformance (actual relative to plan)							
Budgetary revenues	**-0.6**	**0.0**	**0.9**	n/a	**0.2**	**0.0**	**-0.4**
Tax revenues	**-0.4**	**0.0**	**0.6**	n/a	**0.0**	**-0.4**	**-0.8**
Personal income tax	-0.2	0.2	0.4	n/a	0.2	0.4	0.3
Corporate income tax	-0.1	-0.4	0.0	n/a	-0.1	-0.4	-0.4
UI contributions[b]	n/a	n/a	0.1	n/a	0.0	0.1	0.0
Sales and excise taxes and duties	-0.1	0.2	0.1	n/a	-0.1	-0.5	-0.7
Other revenues	**-0.2**	**0.0**	**0.3**	n/a	**0.2**	**0.4**	**0.4**

[a]The 1987–88 Budget was not published.
[b]The 1985 Budget recorded and projected the net unemployment insurance expenditure (benefits minus contributions).

15

TABLE 1.5 Disaggregate Revenues—1995 Adjustment Plan

(As percent of GDP)

	Plan (p)			Actual (a)			Greater-Than-Expected Increase
	1993–94 (p)	1996–97 (p)	Δp	1993–94 (a)	1996–97 (a)	Δa	$\Delta a - \Delta p$
Budgetary revenues	**16.3**	**16.7**	**0.4**	**15.9**	**16.8**	**0.9**	**0.5**
Tax revenues	**14.9**	**15.6**	**0.7**	**14.5**	**15.4**	**0.9**	**0.2**
Personal income tax	7.2	7.9	0.7	7.1	7.6	0.5	−0.2
Corporate income tax	1.4	2.0	0.6	1.3	2.0	0.7	0.1
UI contributions	2.6	2.3	−0.3	2.5	2.4	−0.1	0.2
Sales and excise taxes and duties	3.8	3.5	−0.3	3.7	3.5	−0.2	0.1
Other revenues	**1.4**	**1.1**	**−0.3**	**1.4**	**1.4**	**0.0**	**0.3**

freezes, and efficiency gains, rather than a fundamental review or change in mandate.[18] The 1986 Budget Papers stated that a general cut averaging 2 percent of nonstatutory expenditures (excluding defense and foreign aid) would be implemented by 1986–87, and funding for operations and maintenance would be allowed to grow by only 2 percent per year from this reduced base over the remainder of the decade. Departments were expected to use efficiency gains. Although the 1985 Budget recognized that reduction of the deficit over the medium-term would require a reduction in transfers to persons and other levels of government (which accounted for half of primary expenditures), measures in these areas were limited.[19]

Having learned from the 1985–91 episode and backed by unprecedented public support, the government introduced in the 1995 Plan major initiatives centered around four pillars:

  i. A Program Review encompassing a comprehensive review of federal department spending, excluding only major statutory programs
 ii. A reform of the unemployment insurance program
iii. Major revisions to the system of transfers to the provinces
 iv. Pension reform

This section will focus on the Program Review, leaving the discussion of the latter three initiatives to the section on structural reforms.

The Program Review, announced in the 1994 Budget and incorporated in the 1995 Budget, aimed to "ensure that the government's diminished resources are directed to the highest priority requirements and to those areas where the federal government is best placed to deliver services" (1995 Budget, p. 11). It stressed that fiscal adjustment could not be the only element to a strategy to promote growth and employment. The Program Review, consequently, helped refocus the role of government by examining the mandates for the federal government as a whole and for each department.[20] It encompassed all program spending, except major statutory spending, such as unemployment insurance, old age security, and major transfers to the provinces.[21] Ministers were asked to assess their own programs and activities by applying six criteria:

  i. Serving the public interest
 ii. Necessity of government involvement, as opposed to the private sector
iii. Appropriateness of federal role, as opposed to other levels of government
 iv. Scope for public and private sector partnerships
  v. Scope for increased efficiency
 vi. Affordability

The Program Review suggested a "long-lasting structural change in what the government does" and a "fundamental change in how the government delivers programs and services" (1995 Budget, pp. 11–12). The main changes included:

- Elimination and substantial reduction of subsidies
- Redesign of programs to make them more efficient
- Merger and consolidation of programs
- Transfer of programs to other levels of government
- Privatization of activities

The program review exercise was politically challenging, including within the government. Many ministers initially found it difficult to accept the extent of the cuts expected of them. Nevertheless, Finance Minister Paul Martin fostered their support, with the firm backing of Prime Minister Jean Chretien.[22] "The [program review] process was disciplined by a firm requirement that the individual spending cuts had to add up to a predetermined level of savings needed to meet the budget targets" (Martin, 1996). "If a minister did not identify the cuts necessary to reach the target, the [program review] committee would do it for him. . . . [The committee] was told they could alter the specific targets for cuts to each department, but it was a zero sum game: if they wanted to lower the target on one department from 20 percent to 10 percent, they could; but then they had to cut deeper elsewhere" (Martin, 2008). After the committee ratified the departmental amounts, individual ministers established priorities within their own areas of responsibility.

As a result of the reduction or elimination of government programs, expenditures of some departments would be cut in half. There would be a reduction in the number of federal civil servants by 14 percent compared to the 1994–95 level over three years. In addition, there was an extension of the civil service wage freeze.[23] Other major cuts in spending included a reduction in defense spending by 0.4 percent of GDP.

Tables 1.6 and 1.7 show that the primary (program) expenditure outcome was better than planned in both episodes. In terms of the composition of expenditure adjustment, the 1995 Plan put somewhat more emphasis on cuts in transfers compared with the 1985 Plan: 55 percent of planned primary expenditure adjustment in the 1995 Plan was in transfers to persons and other levels of government, compared to 45 percent in the 1985 Plan. Ex-post, transfers were lower than planned over 1994–97 and higher than planned over 1985–91. This reflected the lack of structural reforms in the 1985 Plan, which relied primarily on a change in the indexation scheme, in contrast with a major structural reform of the unemployment insurance program in the 1995 Plan. Similarly, other spending, the primary focus of the

TABLE 1.6 Disaggregate Expenditures—1985 Adjustment Plan

(As percent of GNP)

	Plan (p)			Actual (a)			Greater-Than-Expected Cuts
	1984-85 p	1990-91 p	Δp	1984-85 a	1990-91 a	Δa	$-(\Delta a - \Delta p)$
Budgetary expenditures	**23.7**	**20.8**	**-2.9**	**23.4**	**21.2**	**-2.3**	**-0.6**
Program spending	**18.4**	**14.9**	**-3.5**	**18.3**	**14.7**	**-3.6**	**0.1**
Transfers to persons	4.0	3.1	-0.9	3.8	3.3	-0.4	-0.4
Transfers to other levels gov't	4.2	3.5	-0.7	4.3	3.5	-0.8	0.0
Defense	2.1	2.0	-0.1	2.0	1.8	-0.2	0.1
Other spending[a]	8.1	6.3	-1.8	8.3	6.1	-2.2	0.4
Public debt charges	**5.3**	**5.9**	**0.6**	**5.1**	**6.5**	**1.4**	**-0.8**

[a]Other spending includes spending by departments (other than defense), agencies, and Crown corporations, and transfers other than major transfers to persons and other levels of government.

TABLE 1.7 Disaggregate Expenditures—1995 Adjustment Plan

(As percent of GDP)

	Plan (p)			Actual (a)			Greater-Than-Expected Cuts
	1993-94 p	1996-97 p	Δp	1993-94 a	1996-97 a	Δa	$-(\Delta a - \Delta p)$
Budgetary expenditures	**22.2**	**19.3**	**-2.9**	**21.7**	**17.9**	**-3.8**	**0.9**
Program spending	**16.9**	**13.1**	**-3.7**	**16.5**	**12.5**	**-4.0**	**0.3**
Transfers to persons	5.5	4.5	-1.0	5.2	4.1	-1.1	0.1
of which: UI benefit	2.5	1.7	-0.8	2.4	1.5	-0.9	0.1
Transfers to other levels gov't	3.8	2.8	-1.0	3.7	2.6	-1.1	0.1
Defense	1.5	1.2	-0.4	1.6	1.0	-0.5	0.2
Other spending[a]	6.0	4.6	-1.4	6.1	4.8	-1.3	-0.1
Public debt charges	**5.3**	**6.2**	**0.8**	**5.2**	**5.4**	**0.2**	**0.7**

[a]Other spending includes spending by departments (other than defense), agencies, and Crown corporations, and transfers other than major transfers to persons and other levels of government.

1985 Plan, overperformed over 1985–91. Furthermore, the reduction in most expenditure categories was greater than the target set by the 1995 Plan. The next section will further examine the structural reforms introduced in the 1985 and 1995 Plans.

Structural Reforms

The spending reduction in the 1994–97 episode was buttressed by a structural reform of major statutory spending programs associated with transfers to persons and transfers to other levels of government, whereas there was no major attempt to reform these programs during the 1985–91 episode.[24]

Most of the reduction in statutory spending over 1985–91 was carried out through a change in the indexation factor used for family allowances and old-age security payments, from full CPI adjustment to an increase in the CPI minus 3 percentage points—introduced in the 1985 Budget. The change in indexation for old-age security was later withdrawn in response to intense public criticism. Toward the end of the 1985–91 episode, there were also efforts to contain transfers to the provinces (through freezes and caps) and an unemployment insurance reform, but these were of relatively limited scope and implication. By contrast, the 1995 Plan aimed to reduce spending in the statutory programs through major reforms explained below.

Transfers to Persons: Unemployment Insurance

The Canadian unemployment insurance system was characterized as not only distortionary but also fiscally costly relative to other OECD countries in the early 1990s.[25] Two distortions stood out: (i) the system encouraged a high incidence of frequent users; and (ii) the regional differences in the benefits exacerbated the regional differences in unemployment.

An initial set of reforms was introduced through the 1994 Budget, including: (i) an increase in the minimum period of work required to qualify for unemployment insurance benefits; and (ii) a reduction in the maximum duration of benefits and the benefits rate, especially for the high-unemployment regions. A major labor market reform was introduced by the 1996 Employment Insurance Act, which overhauled the system of benefits as well as labor market policies and funding of the system.[26] Together, these reforms helped reduce the distortions and excessive cost of the unemployment insurance system.

Transfers to Provinces

In the 1995 Budget, the system of transfers to the provinces was changed, to increase cost-effectiveness and flexibility. Canada Assistance Plan, a shared cost

program for provincial social welfare programs, and Established Programs
Financing, a block grant from the federal government to finance provincial
post-secondary education and health, would be replaced by Canada Health
and Social Transfer, a full block grant. In addition to reducing federal transfers
to the provinces, the move from partial cost-sharing to full block grants was
designed to increase the incentive for provinces to limit additional social expenditure. The shared-cost program, under which the federal government covered
up to one-half of the provincial governments' spending on a broad range of
social services and social assistance, had grown at an unsustainable rate even
during periods of strong economic growth. The full block grant system would
also provide the provinces more flexibility in allocating social expenditures.

With these reforms, the provinces played an important role in the elimination of the federal government deficit. Actual transfers to the provinces
had already been reduced by 0.5 percent of GNP from 1984–85 to 1993–94.
They were further reduced by 1.1 percent of GDP by 1996–97—from
3.7 percent of GNP in 1993–94 to 2.6 percent of GDP in 1996–97. Despite
these cuts in transfers, the provinces improved their own finances, as
discussed below.

Both adjustment plans were at the federal government level, rather than
at the consolidated general government level. However, in view of the reduction in transfers to subnational governments, we augment the analysis
through an assessment of the consolidated general government overall
balance.[27] This assessment is done on an ex-post basis due to the constraint
in budget data availability at the subnational government level. Figure 1.4
depicts the overall balance paths at the federal, subnational, and consolidated

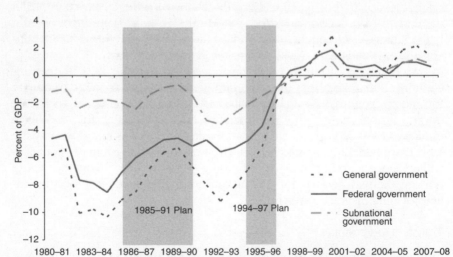

FIGURE 1.4 General, Federal, and Subnational Government Overall Balances

general government levels. The subnational government overall balance improved together with the federal government overall balance over 1986–87 to 1989–90. However, the former deteriorated to a much larger extent than the federal government overall balance after 1989–90, resulting in a fast deterioration of the consolidated general government balance. The deterioration in the subnational government overall balance is explained by the large increase in subnational government expenditure related to the 1990–91 recession. The financial markets reacted to these developments by downgrading provincial credit ratings, which in turn induced most provincial governments to take drastic adjustment measures in their 1993 Budgets. In response, most provincial governments introduced plans to balance their budgets within three years, with some passing balanced-budget legislation.[28] During 1994–97, the overall balance of subnational governments, the federal government balance, and the consolidated general government balance all improved.

Pension Reform

Consistent with the focus on long-term fiscal sustainability and following extensive debate, the federal government and the provinces also reformed the Canada Pension Plan (CPP) in 1998. CPP pensions are paid entirely by contributions made by employers and employees; hence, public pension accounts are not part of the federal government's budgetary accounts.[29] Nevertheless, as in several other advanced economies, pensions are a key long-run fiscal challenge for the government.

In the mid-1990s, it was clear that, owing to population aging, slower productivity growth, and generous benefits, action needed to be taken to ensure the sustainability of the pension system. The net present value of the unfunded liabilities of the CPP stood at 75 percent of GDP in 1995, a level comparable to the net federal debt at the time. Based on status quo trends, the contribution rate would have to increase from 5.6 percent in 1995 to 14.2 percent for pay-as-you-go sustainability. In 1998, the federal and provincial governments agreed to pre-fund the CPP by raising premiums over 1998–2003 from 5.6 percent to 9.9 percent, and to create an independent CPP Investment Board charged to invest the excess contribution income using a market-driven investment strategy (Courchene, 1997). Thanks to these measures, the CPP has since been assessed to be actuarially sound.

Extent to which Adjustments Were Sustained

The last element in our analysis examines the extent to which the adjustment gains accomplished by the plans were sustained in subsequent years. In

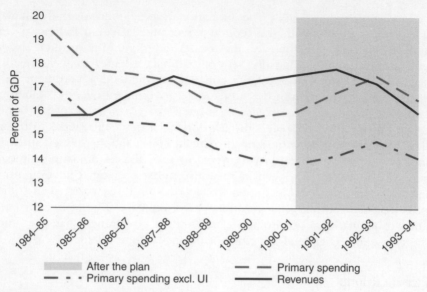

FIGURE 1.5 **Period after the 1985–91 Plan**

short, while both adjustment plans resulted in improved fiscal balances, the
1994–97 gains were better sustained, because they were accomplished
through durable, structural reforms. Figures 1.5 and 1.6 present the development of the headline fiscal aggregates after each adjustment episode.

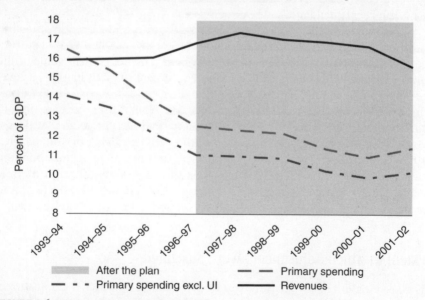

FIGURE 1.6 **Period after the 1994–97 Plan**

The 1985 Plan resulted in an improvement in the primary surplus to 1.6 percent of GDP in 1990–91. However, the primary balance deteriorated in the following three years, owing to a recession and subsequent moderate growth. Both declining revenues and increased spending contributed to this deterioration (see Figure 1.5). Spending increase was a result of both the automatic increase in the unemployment insurance benefits and other discretionary policies.

The 1995 plan firmly raised the primary surplus to above 4 percent of GDP in 1996–97, setting the debt-to-GDP ratio on a downward path. In subsequent years, this permitted some tax cuts in combination with a stabilization of the spending-to-GDP ratio.[30] Primary surpluses were maintained for 11 consecutive years until the economic crisis of 2008–09.

Conclusion

Canada, which currently has the lowest net general government debt–to-GDP ratio among the G-7 countries, stands out based on its successful response to fiscal pressures through large and sustained adjustment. This chapter's analysis of two fiscal adjustment plans in Canada finds that four elements brought about a lasting improvement in Canada's fiscal position:

   i. Broad-based public support
  ii. A repositioning of the role of government and deep structural reforms
 iii. Prudent macroeconomic and fiscal assumptions
  iv. Fiscal consolidation at the subnational level

In both adjustment episodes, the actual overall balance outperformed plans. The 1985 Plan, however, was not able to stabilize the public debt–to-GDP ratio. The 1985 Plan relied primarily on across-the-board cuts and freezes and was criticized both domestically and internationally for not being sufficiently ambitious. Indeed, throughout the 1985–91 episode, the general government overall deficit remained higher than all G-7 countries' except Italy's.

By contrast, over 1994–97, Canada's general government overall balance improved from the second worst to the top ranking in the G-7 countries and remained there until 2009 (see Figure 1.7).

Despite its shorter duration, the 1995 Plan was able to stabilize debt, benefiting from a repositioning of the role of government and profound structural reforms. A comprehensive review of federal departmental spending proposed and implemented major changes to what the federal government did and how it delivered its programs and services. In addition, structural reforms addressed inefficiency and sustainability issues with

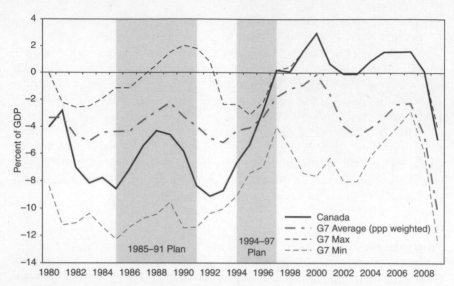

FIGURE 1.7 General Government Overall Balance Canada versus G-7

transfers to provinces, unemployment insurance, and the pension system. Prudent macroeconomic and fiscal assumptions helped the overall balance outcome to be consistently better than plans, raising public confidence in the plan. The subnational governments also helped to improve the general government balance, by increasing their fiscal balances despite cuts in transfers from the federal government.

The ambition of the 1995 Plan reflected a stronger public mandate for fiscal consolidation. While a small percentage of the public viewed the federal deficit and national debt as a major economic problem prior to the 1985–91 episode, 70 percent of Canadians were in favor of cutting spending to reduce the deficit, rather than increasing it to stimulate the economy, prior to the 1994–97 episode. The government's intensive communication strategy on the implications of high debt levels for growth and intergenerational equity helped to raise public awareness of the need for fiscal adjustment and supporting structural reforms.

Acknowledgments

We thank Mauricio Villafuerte and the editor for their guidance, and Paul-Henri Lapointe for very useful comments and discussions. The chapter has also benefited from discussions with Jocelyne Bourgon, Thomas Hockin, Dan Holmes, Glenn Purves, and Pierre St-Amant. Junhyung Park and Katia Chen provided efficient research assistance.

Notes

1. More specifically, the 1985 Plan was announced in the February 1985 Budget and covered fiscal years 1985–86 to 1990–91. The 1995 Plan was announced in the February 1994 and February 1995 Budgets and covered fiscal years 1994–95 to 1996–97. The fiscal year in Canada runs from April 1 to March 31.

2. Strong productivity growth before 1973 and tax bracket creep from inflation had resulted in strong personal income tax revenue growth in the 1960s and early 1970s.

3. Bank of Canada's policy switch toward greater emphasis on price stability in the early to mid-1980s further contributed to high short- and medium-term interest rates. (See Courchene, 2005, for a more detailed discussion.)

4. *Globe and Mail,* "Confronting the Debt," August 14, 1984.

5. Government of Canada, *A New Framework for Economic Policy,* Ottawa, 1994.

6. Another important document ("Creating a Healthy Fiscal Climate") presented the required fiscal actions to achieve the desired deficit reduction targets for 1995–96 and 1996–97; Government of Canada, *Creating a Healthy Fiscal Climate,* Ottawa, 1994.

7. This budget contained some expenditure reduction measures, primarily for defense spending and unemployment benefits.

8. *Wall Street Journal,* "Bankrupt Canada?" January 12, 1995.

9. The 1995 Plan launched the discussions with the provinces on the reform of the Canada Pension Plan (CPP). The pension reform was implemented in 1998.

10. The 1995 Budget proposed revenue and expenditure *measures* for three years (i.e., 1995–96 to 1997–98). However, medium-term revenue and expenditure *projections* were limited to the first two years.

11. A budget allocation of 0.4 percent of GDP was to be kept in a contingency reserve, and hence, was not recorded as part of planned deficit reduction (see Table 1.2).

12. Previous studies have shown that the elasticity of expenditures, and thus, the cyclical expenditure component is small in Canada.

13. To match the authorities' original presentation, we use GNP as a scaling variable for the 1985 Plan and GDP for the 1995 Plan. For simplicity, we scale the headline and structural variables to nominal GNP (or GDP) rather than potential GNP (or GDP). The equation we used for decomposition is

$$\frac{R}{Y} = \frac{R}{Y}\frac{Y^P}{Y} + \frac{R}{Y}\frac{Y - Y^P}{Y}$$

where R is nominal revenues; Y is actual GNP (or GDP), and Y^P is potential GNP (or GDP). For comparison, we also present major structural variables as percentages of potential GNP (or GDP) in memo items.

14. *Globe and Mail,* "[Finance Minister] Mr. Wilson Didn't Go Far Enough," February 21, 1990. For a similar comment a year earlier, see *Globe and Mail,* "Ottawa Urged to Halve $29 billion Deficit," February 22, 1989.

15. International Monetary Fund, "Staff Report for the 1988 Article IV Consultation," Washington, D.C., 1989; Organization for Economic Co-operation and Development, "OECD Economic Surveys: Canada," Paris, 1994.

16. The government's real GDP growth assumptions were also prudent compared to the private sector and OECD assumptions, however, the government's assumptions turned out to be more optimistic than the outcome.

17. Denote G as the planned nominal government expenditure, and Y as the nominal GDP. Subscript t refers to the year when the fiscal adjustment plan is announced, and $t+N$ is the target year. The adjustment (both planned and actual) in the expenditure-to-GDP ratio can be decomposed as follows:

$$\left(\frac{G_{t+N}}{Y_{t+N}} - \frac{G_{t-1}}{Y_{t-1}}\right) = \frac{P_{t-1}(g_{t+N} - g_{t-1})}{Y_{t-1}} + \frac{(P_{t+N} - P_{t-1})g_{t+N}}{Y_{t-1}}$$
$$- \left(\frac{Y_{t+N} - Y_{t-1}}{Y_{t-1}}\right)\left(\frac{G_{t+N}}{Y_{t+N}}\right)$$

Assuming that government expenditures are fully indexed to the consumer price index, P, the first term on the right-hand side of the above equation describes the contribution from expenditure changes in real terms, the second term the inflationary effect, and the last term the denominator effect coming from the nominal GDP growth. This analysis is especially important in periods of high inflation and output volatility, as in the 1980s.

18. Nonstatutory expenditures are those that Parliament approves annually through an Appropriation Act. Federal departmental expenditures fall under this category. Statutory expenditures are those that Parliament has approved through legislation (other than Appropriations Acts) setting out the purpose of the expenditures and the terms and conditions under which they may be made. Transfers to persons and to other levels of government fall under the latter category.

19. Major components of expenditures were (i) transfers to persons (28 percent of total primary expenditures); (ii) transfers to provincial governments (22 percent); (iii) defense (9 percent); and (iv) other expenditures (40 percent) in 1984–85.

20. See Bourgon (2009) for a detailed discussion on the distinct approach taken by the Program Review.

21. 1995 Budget in Brief, p. 8.

22. The political challenges of the program review process were discussed with the then–Finance Minister Paul Martin and Assistant Deputy Minister for Economic and Fiscal Policy Paul-Henri Lapointe. They are explained in detail in Paul Martin's memoirs (Martin, 2008).

23. Civil service wage freeze was first introduced in March 1991.

24. Transfers to persons consisted of old-age security benefits, family allowance and children's benefits, and unemployment insurance benefits. Transfer programs to other levels of government included the Established Programs Financing, the Canada Assistance Plan, and Equalization Payments.

25. See OECD Economic Surveys, Canada, 1994.

26. The main changes to the system of benefits included: (i) the basing of the eligibility requirement on hours worked rather than weeks; (ii) the basing of the benefit calculation on earnings over a fixed reference period; (iii) the introduction of a new intensity rule that reduced the replacement rate for frequent users; (iv) a reduction in the duration of benefits in higher unemployment regions; (v) a reduction in maximum insurable earnings; and (vi) a clawback of benefits for frequent high-income users.

27. The reduction in transfers to provinces was found to be too drastic in some cases. These transfers were later increased, although they never went back to the levels in terms of GDP prior to the 1994–97 adjustment.

28. The two largest provinces, Ontario and Quebec, were slower to adjust.

29. CPP is included in the general government accounts, which is relevant for international comparisons.

30. The 2000–01 recession was very mild in Canada compared to the United States or compared to the 1990–91 recession.

CHAPTER 2

United States: The Quest for Fiscal Discipline

Jiri Jonas

"In framing a government which is to be administered by men over men the great difficulty lies in this: You must first enable the government to control the governed, and in the next place, oblige it to control itself."

Alexander Hamilton (first Secretary of the U.S. Treasury).

Introduction

The recent sharp deterioration of the U.S. fiscal position and fiscal outlook brought the issue of fiscal adjustment to the forefront. This is not the first time that reducing fiscal deficit and public debt became a policy priority. The period after World War II until the early 1970s saw moderate and temporary deficits, and even during the 1974 recession, the federal budget was almost balanced. However, the deficit widened sharply in 1975, and stayed deep in the red until the late 1990s (see Figure 2.1). The federal debt rose steadily in the 1980s and the first half of the 1990s. While the operation of automatic stabilizers during economic slowdowns often led to higher expenditure and weaker revenues, the deficits were mostly structural (see Figure 2.2).[1] Widening budget deficits have led to repeated efforts to bring them under control over the past decades. How can the government be enabled and obliged to control itself—the challenge highlighted by Alexander Hamilton?

As is clear from Figure 2.1, attempts to restore fiscal discipline were largely unsuccessful until 1993, which marked a sharp reversal of the

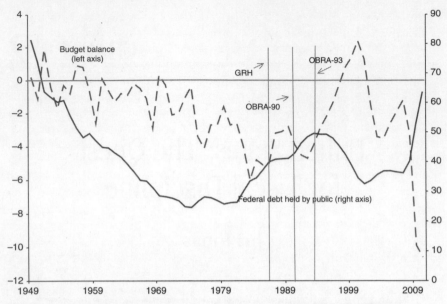

FIGURE 2.1 Federal Budget Balance and Debt, 1949–2009 (In percent of GDP)

Source: Congressional Budget Office (CBO) GRH:
Gramm-Rudman-Hollings; OBRA: Omnibus Budget Reconciliation Act.

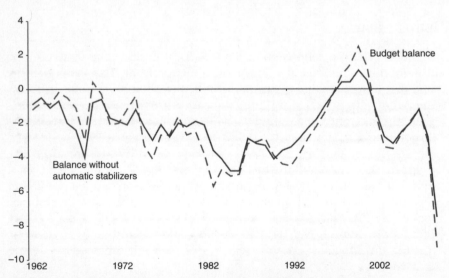

FIGURE 2.2 Federal Budget Balance, 1962–2009 (In percent of potential GDP)

Source: CBO (2010).

previous trend. But even this reversal was not sustained, and during the 2000s, the federal budget returned once again to sizable deficits.

In this chapter, we review three attempts at bringing the federal deficit under control: (i) the 1985 Balanced Budget and Emergency Deficit Control Act (Gramm-Rudman-Hollings Act (GRH)); (ii) the Omnibus Budget Reconciliation Act of 1990 (OBRA-90); and (iii) the Omnibus Budget Reconciliation Act of 1993 (OBRA-93).[2] We aim to answer the following questions. First, what were the objectives of these fiscal consolidation programs (the size and timing of deficit reduction) and what were the intended mechanisms (budgetary rules) of fiscal consolidation? Second, were the objectives achieved and what were the factors underlying success or failure? Third, were the envisaged rules adhered to and policies implemented, and were macroeconomic developments in line with the assumptions made at the time of formulation of the consolidation programs? Did other unforeseen factors affect fiscal outcomes?

We will see that the first two attempts (GRH and OBRA-90) failed to rein in the deficits as planned because macroeconomic developments turned out to be worse than projected, but also because the budgetary rules adopted did not really tackle the root causes of the deteriorating fiscal position, and adhering to them became politically unworkable. In contrast, the third fiscal consolidation attempt that started in 1993 produced a much more significant deficit reduction than envisaged. One important factor was the stronger than projected real Gross Domestic Product (GDP) growth in the second half of the 1990s. However, this alone does not explain the difference; other factors were at play that boosted revenues, reduced expenditures, and thus contributed importantly to shrinking deficits and eventual surpluses. Unfortunately, this rapid improvement in the budget balance may also have sowed the seeds of the reversal during the 2000s; in fact, subsequent policies may have been put in place on the erroneous assumption that the fiscal surpluses by the end of the 1990s reflected fundamental and lasting improvements in macroeconomic and fiscal performance. In hindsight, we know that better results stemmed partly from temporary factors.

First Attempt: Balanced Budget and Emergency Deficit Control Act 1985

During the first half of the 1980s, the federal deficit increased sharply, reaching levels then unprecedented in peacetime. The federal budget deficit peaked at 6 percent of GDP in 1983, and remained around 5 percent in 1984–86 even as growth picked up. The deficit excluding automatic stabilizers peaked in 1985 and 1986, when it reached almost 5 percent of GDP.

While Democrats blamed President Reagan's tax cuts and military buildup, Republicans blamed Congress's inability to control spending.[3]

The increase in fiscal deficits during the first half of the 1980s coincided with a widening current account deficit, from about zero in 1980 to 3.5 percent of GDP in 1985, triggering a debate about the perils of the so-called "twin deficits." The concern of many economists was that fiscal deficits were fueling current account deficits and the accumulation of external debt, raising the risk of financial instability or a collapse of the dollar. However, the concern of the Reagan Administration was that rising deficits reflected higher spending and an increasing role of the government in the economy, which would result in less effective resource allocation and lower growth.[4]

In response to the increase in deficits, Congress passed the 1985 Balanced Budget and Emergency Deficit Control Act (called Gramm-Rudman-Hollings Act—henceforth, GRH). GRH offered a compromise acceptable to both parties: defense spending was to be scaled back and tighter control of nondefense spending introduced. GRH established specific deficit targets for each year: the budget was to be balanced by fiscal year 1991, by cutting the deficit from a starting level of $180 billion in 1986 by $36 billion each year (see Figure 2.3).[5] The president was required to submit budgets each year consistent with the GRH deficit targets, and if legislated policy was projected to result in higher deficits, automatic "sequestration" would

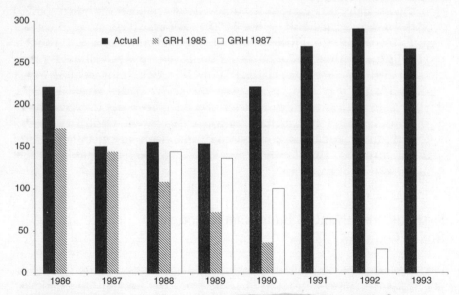

FIGURE 2.3 GRH Deficit Reduction Targets versus Actual Deficits, 1986–1993 (In billions of dollars)

Source: CBO.

be applied, with spending cuts equally divided between defense and non-defense spending (with the exemption of social security, interest payments, and some programs for the poor).[6,7]

In the end, the GRH targets were missed. Moreover, in 1987, in the context of revamping the GRH rules in response to legal challenges (see endnote 6), and as it became clear that the 1985 GRH deficit targets would require large spending cuts in coming years, the GRH deficit targets were eased and the target date for achieving budget balance was moved from 1991 to 1993. But even the revised target proved far too ambitious: rather than declining, the deficits began to increase again in the 1990s, as the recession reduced revenues. In both 1991 and 1993, the GRH's original and revised dates for balancing the budget, deficits reached 4-4.5 percent of GDP.

Why were the budget targets missed by such a large margin? One factor was weaker than expected economic growth. Although the Administration's macroeconomic assumptions were not out of line compared with those by independent forecasters (see Table 2.1), real GDP grew less than projected as a result of the 1990–91 recession. But the slowdown added only 1 percentage point of GDP to the deficits (see Figure 2.2). The main problem was the failure to control the spending. Although GRH did not prescribe how to reach the targeted deficit reduction, the Administration expected that this would be achieved through spending cuts. Between 1986 and 1991, noninterest expenditures other than social security were to fall from 15.7 percent of GDP to 12.5 percent, and net interest payments were to be reduced by at least 1 percentage point of GDP (Economic Report of the President, 1987, page 71). Tax increases were not explicitly envisaged (though revenue gains of about 1 percent of GDP from the 1986 Tax Reform Act contributed significantly to the deficit decline in 1987—see Reischauer, 1990).

In the end, net interest payments as a share of GDP increased slightly, instead of falling as envisaged.[8] More importantly, the reduction in noninterest expenditure other than social security did not happen: while social security outlays as a share of GDP remained constant as envisaged, the ratio to GDP of other noninterest expenditure fell only marginally—despite the

TABLE 2.1 Real GDP Growth (In percent)

Projections Published in 1986 for 1986–1991 and Outturns

	1986	1987	1988	1989	1990	1991
Administration	3.4	4	4	3.9	3.8	3.5
CBO	3.2	3.1	3.3	3.5	3.5	3.2
Actual	3.4	3.5	4.2	3.5	1.7	−0.2

Sources: CBO, *Economic and Budget Outlook, Fiscal Years 1987–1991,* February 1986; Economic Report of the President, 1986.

decline in defense spending by 1 percent of GDP. This was partly due to the recapitalization of deposit insurance, which temporarily boosted spending. Studies taking stock of GRH's impact find that GRH restrained outlays for nonexempt programs, but spending under the exempt programs grew briskly. One study estimates that GRH restrained outlays by $59 billion by fiscal 1989, not enough to achieve the targeted deficit reduction in the absence of higher revenues (see Hahm et al., 1992).

GRH rules suffered from several design weaknesses. First, targeting directly the budget deficit, which is influenced by many factors beyond government control, does not encourage accountability. Second, large spending items (e.g., social security) were exempted from sequestration and, as a result, deep cuts in nonexempted categories would have been required to meet the deficit targets. Third, while GRH contained an escape clause in case of severe recession, it mandated the resumption of spending cuts in the first year of the recovery, a challenging time for fiscal tightening. In all, meeting the GRH targets would have required more significant cuts in nonexempted spending than what the political process was able and willing to support, especially during the recession years of 1990–91. Yet despite these defects, there was a widely held perception that the deficit would have been even larger in the GRH absence.[9]

Second Attempt: Omnibus Budget Reconciliation Act of 1990

In the spring of 1990, it became clear that the 1990 deficit was going to exceed the (revised) GRH deficit limit by almost $100 billion. Containing the deficit as prescribed by the (revised) GRH targets would have required huge and politically unacceptable spending cuts. The Office of Budget Management estimated that a sequestration of $85 billion would be needed to achieve the 1990 deficit target. However, as some budget items had been exempted from the sequester, this would have required a 32 percent reduction in defense programs and a 35 percent reduction in non-defense programs.[10] Clearly, this was not a realistic option.

Instead, in May 1990, President Bush and the congressional leadership convened negotiations on the budget, and in November 1990, President Bush signed into law the Omnibus Budget Reconciliation Act of 1990 (OBRA-90), which included the Budget Enforcement Act (BEA). The BEA replaced the GRH deficit limits with two enforcement regimens: (1) discretionary spending caps on 1991–95 appropriations, with sequestration to ensure compliance; and (2) pay-as-you-go (PAYGO) mechanism, which required that legislation affecting mandatory spending and revenues does not increase the deficit (with a separate sequestration applied if needed). The BEA also provided for enforcement by the congressional and executive branches of the discretionary caps and the PAYGO requirement. Beside the BEA, OBRA-90 also increased tax rates on income and some excises.[11]

The goal of OBRA-90 was to reduce the budget deficits by cumulative $500 billion during 1991–95 compared to the baseline (unchanged policies and legislation). The main part of the deficit reduction was to come from lower expenditure growth: lower discretionary spending was to contribute about 40 percent to the deficit reduction relative to the baseline (mainly lower defense outlays), lower growth of entitlement spending another 20 percent, and higher tax revenue the remaining 40 percent.[12]

Table 2.2 summarizes the fiscal outlook before OBRA-90, its projected impact, and the actual outcome. The first row shows the CBO baseline projection from July 1990, before the OBRA-90 enactment. The deficit as a share of GDP was projected to peak at 4 percent in 1991 and to decline thereafter.[13] Yet it was still projected close to 3 percent of GDP in 1993, the year when it was supposed to reach zero according to the revised GRH target. The second row shows the CBO deficit projection including the BEA impact. Despite including the BEA impact, the January 1991 projections displayed larger deficits than the July 1990 pre-BEA projections, owing to lower projected economic growth and larger deposit insurance outlays related to the savings-and-loan crisis. To capture this, the third row shows the CBO January 1991 projected deficits excluding the estimate of BEA impact. The large difference between the first and third rows reveals a significant deterioration in fiscal outlook between July 1990 and January 1991. The final row— "implied BEA impact"—provides a measure of BEA impact: it compares the

TABLE 2.2 CBO Fiscal Projections, 1991–96

	1990	1991	1992	1993	1994	1995	1996
In $bn							
CBO July 1990 baseline	−195	−232	−239	−194	−146	−138	n.a.
CBO BEA January 1991	−220	−298	−284	−215	−160	−57	−56
CBO January 1991 ex BEA	−220	−332	−353	−303	−291	−217	n.a.
Actual balance outturn	−221	−269	−290	−255	−203	−164	−108
CBO estimate of OBRA-90 impact	n.a.	33	69	89	131	160	n.a.
Implied BEA impact[a]	. . .	63	63	48	88	53	
In percent of GDP							
CBO July 1990 baseline	−3.6	−4	−3.8	−2.9	−2.1	−1.8	n.a.
CBO BEA January 1991	−4.1	−5.3	−5	−3.7	−3.1	−1.8	−1.8
Actual balance	−3.9	−4.5	−4.7	−3.9	−2.9	−2.2	−1.4

Source: CBO, *Economic and Budget Outlook* (1990 Update and 1991 issue covering 1992–1996).
[a]CBO January 1991 projection excluding BEA less actual balance outturn.

TABLE 2.3 CBO Fiscal Projections for 1991–96

(In percent of GDP, different vintages)

	1991	1992	1993	1994	1995	1996
December 1990	−5.3	−5.0	−3.7	−3.1	−1.8	−1.8
January 1991	−5.3	−4.7	−3.4	−2.4	−0.8	−0.7
August 1991	−5.0	−6.1	−4.4	−3.5	−2.2	−2.1
January 1992	−4.8	−6.0	−5.2	−3.9	−2.8	−2.4
August 1992	−4.8	−5.4	−5.3	−4.1	−3.5	−3.5

Source: CBO, Economic and Budget Outlook, various issues.

CBO January 1991 projection excluding OBRA-90 with the actual deficits (which were affected by BEA, but also by other factors): cumulatively, the actual deficit was less by $300 billion, about two-thirds of the January 1991 CBO estimate of BEA impact.

The main objective of OBRA-90 was to lock in the political agreement reached during the 1990 negotiations on reducing the deficit, and to prevent future legislation and discretionary policy actions from undoing this achievement. However, the deficit continued to worsen despite the observance of the discretionary spending caps and the tax measures, for three reasons: (i) the 1990–91 recession and relatively slow recovery in 1992; (ii) additional costs of resolving the savings-and-loan crisis; and (iii) failure to control entitlement spending. The PAYGO limits discouraged new unfunded spending or tax initiatives, and constrained discretionary spending, but did not restrain the rapid growth in entitlement programs such as Medicare and Medicaid, which was not anticipated. Thus, BEA rules were not sufficient to prevent the rapid deterioration of the fiscal outlook (see Table2.3).

Third Attempt: Omnibus Budget Reconciliation Act of 1993

However, despite the above-discussed shortcomings, OBRA-90 and the spending constraint of BEA laid the foundation for improved fiscal performance later in the 1990s. To be sure, this was not yet obvious in 1992, when deficits were projected to persist at more than 3.5 percent of GDP in the medium-term (see the August 1992 CBO projection in Table 2.3). After taking office in January 1993, President Clinton made fiscal deficit reduction one of his main economic priorities, and proposed a five-year deficit reduction package that was supposed to reduce—relative to the baseline—budget deficits by $500 billion cumulatively in 1994–98, the same amount as OBRA-90. After an intense debate, the Omnibus Budget Reconciliation Act of 1993 (OBRA-93) was enacted in August 1993.[14]

TABLE 2.4 Projected Effect of OBRA-93 on 1998 Budget

(In billions of dollars)

	Without OBRA-93	After OBRA-93	Difference
Outlays	1,825	1,738	−87
Discretionary	584	548	−36
Mandatory	971	945	−26
Interest	270	245	−25
Revenue	1,492	1,551	+59
Projected 1998 deficit	333	187	−146

Source. Economic Report of the President, 1994.

OBRA-93 was to reduce the 1998 budget deficit by 1.75 percent of GDP relative to the no-policy-change baseline, from $333 billion to $187 billion (see Table 2.4). Two-fifths of the deficit reduction was to come from higher tax revenues, with the remaining three-fifths from lower outlays. The BEA 1990 discretionary spending caps were extended, with a five-year nominal spending freeze: the 1998 discretionary spending was capped at $548 billion, marginally below the 1993 level of $550 billion. Inflation was projected to average less than 3 percent during that period, implying a 13 percent real cut. In case of lower than projected inflation, nominal expenditures were to be reduced accordingly. Mandatory expenditures were projected to be lower by $26 billion relative to the baseline, mainly as a result of Medicare cuts. Revenue measures included corporate and income tax rate hikes, and steps to close tax loopholes. By fiscal year 1998, these measures were projected to raise tax revenues by almost $60 billion relative to the baseline. Finally, falling interest rates were expected to reduce the costs of servicing public debt by over $25 billion in 1998. A decision to shorten the debt maturity was also expected to contribute to lower interest costs.

The fiscal adjustment was projected to reduce structural or cyclically adjusted deficits from 3.5 percent of GDP in 1992 to 2.1 percent of GDP in 1995 and thereafter (see Table 2.5).

TABLE 2.5 Projected Structural Deficits, 1992–98

	1992	1993	1994	1995	1996	1997	1998
In billion $	206.0	214.7	190.8	149.1	156.1	162.8	171.4
In percent of GDP	3.5	3.4	2.9	2.1	2.1	2.1	2.1

Source: Economic Report of the President, 1994.

The Clinton Administration's decision to reverse past increases in the deficit was motivated by concerns about the perilous effects of the worsening state of the public finances on the U.S. economy. An important role in supporting this decision was played by Federal Reserve Chairman Alan Greenspan and Treasury Secretary Robert Rubin.[15] They were concerned that continued increases in budget deficits and public debt would push up interest rates, with harmful effects on economic performance. Fiscal discipline and adoption of specific and credible measures to reduce future deficits were seen as bringing significant long-term benefits: long-term bond yields would decline, private investment would be boosted, and economic growth would accelerate in a durable manner. OBRA-93 also aimed at *expenditure switching* from consumption (public and private) to investment. Lower interest rates resulting from deficit reduction were seen as the main instrument for this expenditure switching.

The size of the deficit-cutting measures was calibrated so as to achieve a tangible improvement in the fiscal deficit, while avoiding a sharp fiscal contraction that would hurt growth in the near-term. Although reduced spending and increased taxes would reduce aggregate demand, the stimulative effect of lower long-term interest rates was expected to compensate for this impact and to foster economic growth in the medium and long term.[16]

The CBO assessment of the fiscal impact of OBRA-93 is summarized in Table 2.6. The first and second rows show the CBO baseline projection (without OBRA-93), and the CBO's March 1993 preliminary assessment of the Administration's budget proposal (based on the proposals and

TABLE 2.6 Administration and CBO Estimates of the OBRA-93 Fiscal Impact

(In billions of dollars, unless noted otherwise)

	1994	1995	1996	1997	1998	Total
1. Deficit (CBO-baseline, March 1993)	286.7	284.4	290.0	321.7	359.7	1,542.5
In percent of GDP	4.4	4.1	4.0	4.3	4.6	. . .
2. Deficit (CBO, March 1993)	268.1	257.0	222.0	204.9	228.5	1,180.5
In percent of GDP	4.1	3.7	3.1	2.7	2.9	. . .
3. Deficit (CBO, Sept 1993)	253.0	196.0	190.0	198.0	200.0	1,037.0
In percent of GDP	3.9	2.9	2.6	2.6	2.5	. . .
4. Deficit (Administration)	262.4	241.6	205.3	206.4	241.4	1,130.1
In percent of GDP	4.0	3.1	2.9	2.7	3.1	. . .
5. OBRA-93 revenue impact	26.4	43.5	51.5	60.7	58.5	240.6

Sources: CBO, *The Analysis of the President's February Budget Proposals*, March 1993; *Economic and Budget Outlook Update*, September 1993; and *Economic and Budget Outlook*, Fiscal Years 1994–2004, January 1994.

estimates described in the Administration's document, "A Vision of Change for America"). The third row shows the CBO's revised assessment from September 1993—after OBRA-93 was passed by Congress. For comparison, the fourth row shows the Administration's deficit projection from March 1993 (as reported by the CBO).[17] The last row shows the CBO-projected cumulative revenue impact of OBRA-93 provisions during 1994–1998. Several observations are worth highlighting on the basis of these projections.

In the absence of the OBRA-93 (CBO baseline), deficits were projected to stay above 4 percent of GDP and gradually increase. This confirms the difficult fiscal outlook at the start of the Clinton Administration. A comparison of the CBO-baseline and CBO assessment of the Administration's proposal (rows 1 and 2) shows that the CBO estimated the total cumulative deficit reduction impact of the OBRA-93 to be $362 billion during 1994–98, equivalent to 4.6 percent of the projected 1998 GDP. The Administration projected about $50 billion lower cumulative deficits in 1994–98 than the CBO projection (row 4). However, the updated CBO projection following the August 1993 approval of OBRA-93 projected a more optimistic fiscal outlook, with cumulative deficits of $143 billion less than projected in March 1993, and $100 billion less than the Administration's projection.

A CBO breakdown of the projected deficit reduction stemming from OBRA-93 into the contributions of revenue increases and expenditure cuts is provided in Table 2.7. About three-quarters of the projected $362 billion cumulative deficit reduction were to come from higher tax revenues, and one-fourth from expenditure cuts, mainly lower mandatory spending and debt service. The Administration did not provide a year-by-year assessment of the revenue and expenditure contribution to deficit reduction, only the impact for 1998 (see Table 2.4). For that year, the Administration projected a larger contribution to deficit reduction from lower spending than higher revenues, the opposite of the CBO projection.

TABLE 2.7   CBO Estimates of the Administration's Policy Proposals' Impact on Deficit

(In billions of dollars)

	1994	1995	1996	1997	1998	Total
Total deficit changes	−18.6	−27.4	−68.1	−116.7	−131.2	−362.0
Revenues	−27.6	−39.1	−56.4	−72.2	−71.7	−267.0
Expenditures	9.1	11.6	−11.7	−44.5	−59.5	−95.0
Discretionary	9.6	14.9	−3.4	−16.8	−18.9	−14.6
Mandatory	−0.4	−1.6	10.8	−17.9	−23.5	−32.6
Debt service	−0.2	−1.5	4.2	−9.8	−17.1	−24.4

Source: CBO, *Analysis of the President's February Budget Proposals,* March 1993.

Actual versus Projected Fiscal Performance under Omnibus Budget Reconciliation Act of 1993

Actual fiscal performance under OBRA-93 was much stronger than foreseen in the original projections by the Administration and the CBO. The CBO's preliminary March 1993 assessment of the President's budget and the OBRA-93 measures foresaw temporary deficit reduction, from close to the 5 percent of GDP projected for 1993 to 2.7 percent of GDP by 1997, after which the deficit was projected to increase again in 1998. In the September 1993 update, the projection was for the deficit to stabilize at around 2.5 percent of GDP.

These projections suggest that the measures introduced under OBRA-93 were expected to cut the 1992 deficit of 4.7 percent of GDP by about half. Moreover, as the no-policy-change scenario (see the CBO baseline) foresaw that the 1998 deficit would be about the same as in 1992, the projected impact of OBRA-93 using comparison with the baseline was similar to the impact when comparing the projected deficits with the 1992 deficit.

Both the Administration's and the CBO's deficit projections turned out to be way off the mark when compared to the actual outcome (see Figure 2.4). Already in 1993, the actual deficit was almost 1 percentage point of GDP

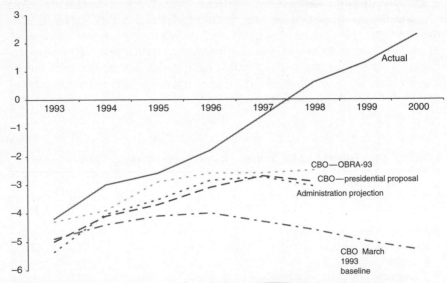

FIGURE 2.4 Projected and Actual Federal Government Balance, 1993–2000 (In percent of GDP)

Source: CBO.

lower than projected. In the next three years, the speed of deficit reduction was broadly as projected, with actual deficits about 1 percentage point of GDP lower than projections. But in 1997, instead of leveling off and eventually widening again, the deficit shrank further and in 1998, a fiscal surplus was attained for the first time since 1969—almost 4 percentage points of GDP stronger fiscal balance than the original projection by the Administration. In 2000, the federal budget surplus exceeded 2 percent of GDP.

As a result of the much lower than projected deficits, the federal government debt held by the public turned out significantly lower by the end of the 1990s than projected in 1993 (see Figure 2.5). It is noteworthy that in 1993 when assessing the Clinton Administration's plans, the CBO projected a moderate but persistent increase in the debt-to-GDP ratio for the whole five-year projection period.

What was the main driver of the faster than projected reduction in the deficit? Table 2.8 summarizes the results. The second column shows the Administration's projection of the OBRA-93 impact on the 1998 budget outcome (as published in the "Economic Report of the President" in 1994). The third column shows the CBO's projection for 1998 published in January 1994, which is almost identical to the Administration's projection. The fifth column shows the difference between the 1998 actual and the Administration's projection. Actual deficit turned out to be more than $250 billion lower than projected: higher revenues contributed about two-thirds to this outcome (mainly as a result of higher than projected individual income taxes),

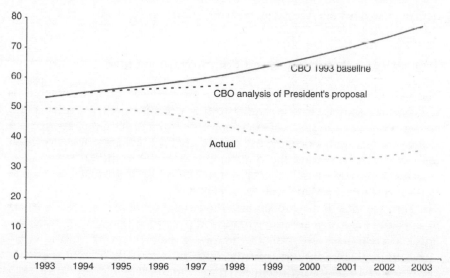

FIGURE 2.5 Federal Debt Held by Public (In percent of GDP)
Source: "Economic Report of the President," different issues.

TABLE 2.8 1998 Budget Outcome: Actual and OBRA-93 Projection

(In billions of dollars)

	1993 Actual	Administration's projection for 1998	CBO projection for 1998	1998 Actual	Difference between 1998 actual and Administration projection
Outlays[a]	1,409.4	1,738.2	1,736.0	1,652.0	−86.2
Discretionary		548.0	547.0	555.0	7
Interest	125.4	245.0	249.0	241.0	−4
Revenue	1,154.4	1,550.8	1,556.0	1,721.0	+170.2
Balance	−255.0	−187.4	−180.0	69.0	+256.4

Sources: "Economic Report of the President," 1994; CBO, *Analysis of the President's February Budget Proposal*, March 1994 and *Monthly Budget Review*, November 1999.

[a]Total outlays also include offsetting receipts and thus do not equal the sum of discretionary and mandatory outlays and net interest payment. Administration did not project separately offsetting receipts for 1998 but these are included in the total outlays.

with lower spending contributing the remaining one-third. Discretionary spending ceiling was observed as planned, and actual discretionary spending was close to the original 1993 BEA target. Interestingly, despite lower deficits, actual net interest payments were close to projected.

1990s Deficit Reduction: Good Policy or Good Luck?

The reduction of the fiscal deficit during the 1990s was unprecedented in U.S. history, and also unexpected as discussed earlier. What explains this reduction? Was it the political decision of the Administration to reduce the deficits for fiscal prudence, greater support for fiscal adjustment in Congress and society at large, and the policies pursued within the OBRA-93 constraints? Or was this more a matter of good luck and strong macroeconomic performance unrelated to fiscal policy choices?

First, we look at macroeconomic developments during 1993–98. When formulating the five-year budget reduction plan, the Clinton Administration adopted a realistic growth outlook, projecting real GDP growth below 3 percent and gradually declining, pretty much in line with the contemporary consensus forecast (though somewhat more optimistic than the April 1993 International Monetary Fund (IMF), World Economic Outlook projection). However, as Figure 2.6 shows, with the exception of 1995, actual real GDP

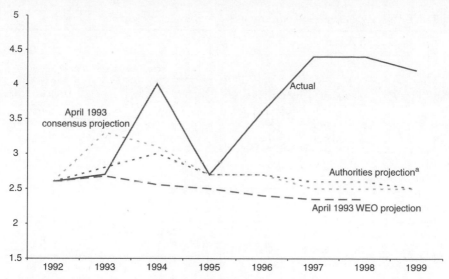

FIGURE 2.6 Projected and Actual Real GDP Growth (in percent)
[a]"Economic Report of the President," 1994.

growth significantly exceeded the projection. Through the operation of the automatic stabilizers, higher GDP growth would reduce cyclically sensitive spending (mainly unemployment support) and increase revenues. As automatic stabilizers are more potent on the revenue side, the expectation would be that stronger growth would increase revenues more than reduce spending, as confirmed by the data.

Another important variable is the cost of borrowing for the government. As shown in Figure 2.7, both long-term and short-term nominal interest rates turned out higher than projected during 1993–98, by 1–2 percentage points on average. Only in 1998 did long-term bond yields fall below projection. Arguably, stronger than projected (demand-driven) economic growth was one of the reasons why interest rates turned out higher than projected.

On the other hand, higher inflation (and inflation expectations) does not seem to have contributed to higher interest rates: GDP deflator inflation turned out at 2 percent during 1994–1998, about 1 percentage point below initial projections. If anything, lower than projected inflation contributed negatively to deficit reduction. In all, higher real GDP growth and lower GDP deflator roughly canceled each other out, so that the nominal GDP growth rates turned out fairly close to projections.

Thus, while stronger than projected real GDP growth contributed to stronger revenue performance and lower spending, this is only part of the story. Indeed, as shown in Figure 2.2, the cyclically adjusted budget balance

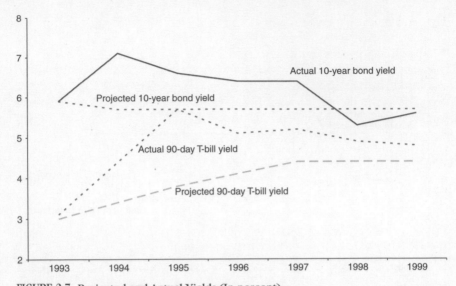

FIGURE 2.7 Projected and Actual Yields (In percent)

Sources: "Economic Report of the President," February 2004; *World Economic Outlook,* IMF.

also improved significantly during the 1990s—though somewhat less than the overall balance.

There seems to be agreement in the literature on the important role of noncyclical factors in reducing the deficits. M. Leidy (1998) argues that less than half of the deficit reduction between 1992 and 1997 was cyclical, and that almost half of the improvement in the structural (cyclically adjusted) deficit was the result of tax increases.[18] Leidy estimates that these tax increases raised the structural revenue-to-GDP ratio by 2 percentage points (with measures adopted under OBRA-93 having been the main driver of the tax revenue increase). The remainder of the structural improvement resulted mainly from defense spending cuts of 1.5 percentage points of GDP and nondefense discretionary cuts of 0.5 percentage point of GDP.

Similarly, Auerbach (1999) concludes that a large part of the fiscal balance improvement during the 1990s was due to noncyclical factors. Until 1996, much of the deficit reduction could be explained by the OBRA-93 legislation and other policy changes during that period. This is also obvious when looking at Figure 2.4: the lines showing CBO/Administration projected deficit move in parallel with the actual deficit during 1993–96. However, starting in 1997, the improvement in deficits was more than fully explained by other factors. Like Leidy, Auerbach emphasizes the role of higher tax revenue, specifically individual income tax revenues: the increase in federal tax collection from 17.5 percent of GDP in 1992 to 19.5 percent of

GDP in 1999 was almost fully driven by an increase in individual income tax collection from 7.6 to 9.4 percent of GDP.[19]

Auerbach argues that the increase in individual federal tax collection was partly due to its progressivity, through the following mechanisms. First, the rapid rise in real incomes during the 1990s pushed *more taxpayers* to brackets facing higher marginal income tax rates. Second, and more important, a widening in the income distribution led to a *rising share of income* accruing to high-income individuals, who face higher tax rates. In addition, the stock market boom brought about increased capital gains realization, which also boosted individual income tax revenues.[20]

On the spending side, the main driving force underlying deficit reduction was cuts in defense spending, the "peace dividend." Income security outlays (mainly unemployment support) also declined, because of the economic boom and lower unemployment. Moreover, following the spike in the mid-1990s, interest payments fell noticeably, reflecting falling public debt and long-term bond yields. Medicare outlays were the only major spending category displaying a gradual but steady growth during the 1990s. The reduction in defense spending, which contributed for about two-thirds of the decline in total outlays, reflected mainly international political and security developments. However, according to Leidy (1998), the statutory spending caps established under OBRA-93 allowed the reversal of mandatory spending (including unemployment support), which had been growing sharply before 1992.

A further perspective on fiscal outcomes during the 1990s, compared with the budget plans/expectations, is provided by the budgetary "surprises" estimated by the CBO, which analyzed the annual difference between the budget resolution targets for revenues, outlays, and budget balance, and actual outcomes during the period 1980–2002.[21] The CBO defined three sources of such differences, as follows: (i) policy differences—cases where unanticipated legislation was enacted, or anticipated legislation was not enacted; (ii) economic differences—differences between actual and assumed GDP, taxable income, unemployment, inflation, and interest rates; and (iii) technical differences—such as changes in administrative tax rules, changes in the number of entitlement beneficiaries, and so on.

Figure 2.8 shows the difference between fiscal balances according to the annual budgetary resolutions (there was no resolution in 1999) and actual fiscal balances. There is a clear change in the pattern during the 1990s: actual balances were stronger than budget resolution targets—a pattern that was reversed only in 2001. Figure 2.9 provides further details on the factors driving the differences in outlays: again, the period 1991–1998 stands out because actual outlays ended up lower than targeted under the budget resolution. Although policy factors pushed actual outlays higher, this was broadly offset by economic factors, whereas technical factors dominated

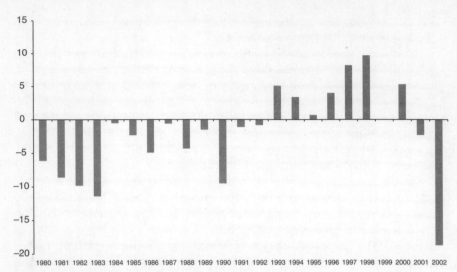

FIGURE 2.8 Budget Balance: Difference between Actual Outcome and Budgetary Resolution (in percent of actual outlays)

Source: CBO.

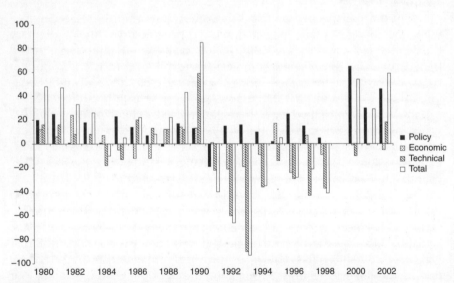

FIGURE 2.9 Federal Outlays: Difference between Actual Outcome and Budget Resolution (in billions of dollars)

Source: CBO.

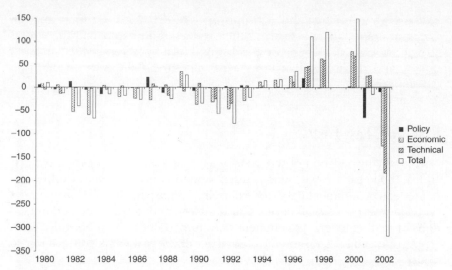

FIGURE 2.10 Federal Revenues: Difference between Actual Outcome and Budget Resolution (in billions of dollars)

Source: CBO.

(lower than projected spending for deposit insurance played the main role). Similarly, on the revenue side of the budget (see Figure 2.10), the 1990s also stand out, with revenues higher than budget resolutions, and with both economic and technical factors contributing to the overperformance. The dramatic reversal of that trend in 2002 is noteworthy, with technical factors playing again an important role in that regard.

To summarize, for most of the 1990s, revenues turned out higher, and outlays lower, than projected in the budget resolutions. Annual "surprises" were consistent with the five-year "surprise" (see Table 2.8, last column). The surprises were repeated for several years. Economic and technical factors were the main driving force of revenue overperformance, whereas technical factors were the main contributor to lower outlays. Policy factors played a negligible role on the revenue side, but contributed to larger than projected outlays.

Finally, what about the expected benefits of the deficit reduction? The Clinton Administration had argued that reducing fiscal deficits would lower interest rates and boost investment and economic growth. Did these benefits materialize, and can they be linked to the deficit reduction?

As a matter of empirical observation, both investment and growth strengthened during the Clinton years. The United States experienced the fastest acceleration in investment growth among the G-7 during 1993–2000 compared with 1983–1992. However, whether the reduction in fiscal deficits *caused* high investment and growth is open to debate. While some authors assign an important role to the deficit reduction in explaining the strong growth, others see strong growth as being driven by factors other than fiscal policy, and declining deficits as a result rather than a cause of these developments.[22]

Easy Won, Easy Lost?

The fiscal consolidation of the 1990s was clearly a success beyond expectations. In the early 2000s, serious discussion took place about a world without federal government debt (for example, Greenspan, 2001). However, the budgetary surpluses of 1998–2001 did not last, and debates on the implications of retiring federal government debt turned out to be premature. Deficits reappeared in 2002, and the federal government debt ratio began to rise again.

In the early 1990s, no one had projected the sharp improvement in the fiscal balance and the budget surpluses by the end of the decade. Likewise, at the beginning of the 2000s, with policymakers debating what to do with fiscal surpluses and the implications of disappearing public debt, no one expected that by the end of the decade, the fiscal deficit-and-debt ratio would be at a new postwar high. Figures 2.11 and 2.12 show the huge discrepancy between the CBO projection of fiscal deficit and public debt at the

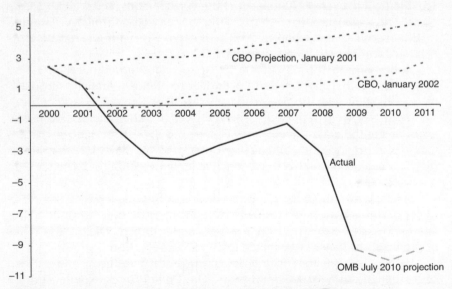

FIGURE 2.11 Federal Government Balance, Projected and Actual, 2001–2011 (in percent of GDP)

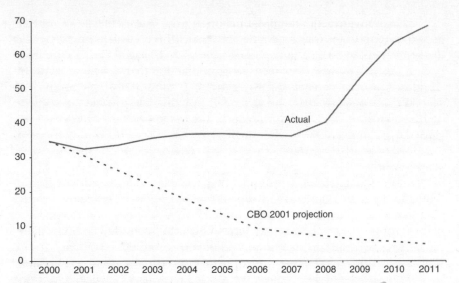

FIGURE 2.12 Federal Debt Held by Public, Projected and Actual, 2000–2011 (in percent of GDP)

Source: The Budget and Economic Outlook: Fiscal Years 2002–2011.

beginning of the decade and the actual outcome. It is almost a mirror image of the 1990s (see Figure 2.4).

What were the driving forces of the deteriorating budgetary position in the 2000s? During the first phase, from 2000 to 2003, the deficit widened gradually but steadily. Both lower revenues and higher outlays contributed to the widening, but the decline in revenues by more than 4 percent of GDP was the main factor.[23] Looking at the composition of federal budget receipts, the dominant role of declining individual income tax revenues is apparent: it explained about three-fourths of the decline in total receipts. As for spending, almost all categories, measured as a percent of GDP, recorded a moderate increase in 2000–2003.

The second phase, from 2003 to 2007, was characterized by gradually diminishing deficits, as federal outlays stabilized and receipts began to increase again as percent of GDP, thanks to the strong performance of individual and corporate income tax, reflecting strong economic growth and a buoyant stock market. The third phase began in 2008, when the crisis pushed the deficit sharply up.

To what extent were these shifts in revenues and expenditures during the 2000s driven by economic developments and technical factors, and to what extent by policy changes?[24]

The improvement in the fiscal balance at the end of the 1990s created pressures to return to taxpayers "their" money. This consideration motivated the first tax cut in 2001. Auerbach and others (2008) argue that the foremost part of the discrepancy between projected and actual deficits during the 2000s results from policy actions—spending increases and tax cuts in 2001 and 2003. As noted earlier, the sharp fall in individual income tax contributed significantly to deficit widening in the early 2000s. CBO (2008) concluded that during 2000–04, about half of the decline in this item was due to the effect of legislation, and half was due to other effects—notably the weak stock market.[25]

Finally, the spending constraints that had played an important role in reducing the deficit during the early and mid-1990s were gradually eroded beginning in the late 1990s. Even though the BEA rules remained formally in place through 2002, the spending limits began to be eroded as budget surpluses appeared and limits became politically unpalatable (Orszag, 2007). While discretionary spending was supposed to remain at about $550 billion, by 2002, it exceeded $700 billion. BEA rules were simply ignored by Congress, and eventually were allowed to expire in 2002.

Conclusion

The U.S. fiscal performance during the past few decades underwent significant swings, reflecting both policy efforts to rein in deficits and budgetary impacts of economic developments. Deficits were large between the late 1970s and the early 1990s, and the federal government debt ratio doubled during that period. This was followed by an unprecedented improvement in fiscal balance during the mid- to late 1990s that culminated in fiscal surpluses and a rapidly falling debt ratio. However, the surpluses did not last long, and the impressive improvement in the fiscal balance during the 1990s was soon reversed. A longer-term perspective on the past century reveals that after large increases—excluding the Second World War—the debt/GDP ratio did not return to its initial level, suggesting an upward trend (see Figure 2.13).

Nevertheless, each time the fiscal deficit widened and the debt ratio began to grow, policymakers eventually responded with corrective measures. We have analyzed three such efforts to put in place rules and mechanisms seeking to bring the fiscal deficit under control: (i) the 1985 Balanced Budget and Emergency Deficit Control Act (Gramm-Rudman-Hollings Act, GRH); (ii) the Omnibus Budget Reconciliation Act of 1990 (OBRA-90); and (iii) the Omnibus Budget Reconciliation Act of 1993 (OBRA-93). These efforts had mixed results: either they failed to reach the objectives or the improvement in fiscal balance was not sustained.

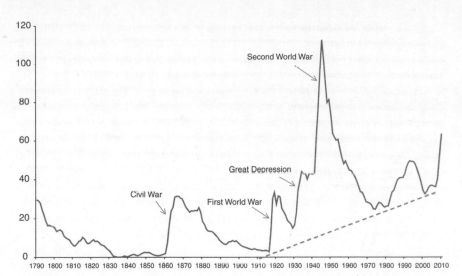

FIGURE 2.13 **Federal Debt Held by Public, 1790–2000 (in percent of GDP)**
Source: CBO.

The first attempt, the 1985 GRH Act, committed the president to submit budgets in line with declining deficit targets and introduced sequestration to correct for any deviations. Although GRH may have prevented a worse outcome, it failed to eliminate the fiscal deficit. There was insufficient political support for maintaining the tight spending constraints required by the GRH deficit targets, and creative ways were used to circumvent spending sequestration. GRH was too inflexible with respect to economic conditions. This flaw became evident during the recession of 1990–91, when meeting the GRH target would have required excessive fiscal tightening.

The second approach to deficit reduction, adopted in 1990 under the OBRA-90 Act and the BEA, was supposed to correct for GRH weaknesses. The BEA replaced GRH deficit limits with caps on discretionary spending. In addition, it introduced the PAYGO mechanism to ensure that new tax and spending legislations do not increase the deficit. OBRA-90 also included tax increases. However, like its predecessor, OBRA-90 did not achieve the targeted deficit reduction, both for exogenous reasons (the recession and budgetary costs of the savings-and-loan crisis) and because of failure to control the rising costs of programs already legislated that were not covered by the PAYGO system.

The third effort began in 1993, with the adoption of OBRA-93, which built on the mechanisms of OBRA-90/BEA. The BEA 1990 discretionary spending caps were extended, with a five-year nominal spending freeze. Mandatory expenditures were to be tightly controlled, and revenue measures—including corporate and income tax rate hikes—were introduced.

This time, deficit reduction proceeded faster than projected and, by the end of the 1990s, the federal budget was in surplus, though partly for reasons unrelated to the OBRA-93 measures. The improvement turned out to be temporary, and in 2003 the deficit again approached 4 percent of GDP.

As Auerbach and others (2008) observe, history shows that U.S. federal budget rules do not operate well when they deviate too far from consensus policy. Or, as Reischauer (1990) put it, "no budget process can force those engaged in it to commit what they regard to be political suicide. The nation, therefore, will probably have larger than desired deficits until the political costs of continued large deficits are perceived to exceed those of spending cuts and tax increases." The silver lining of these gloomy prognostications is that, in the aftermath of the recent financial crisis, the economic and political costs of continued large deficits seem to be increasingly recognized by broad sections of the public.

Acknowledgments

The author is grateful to Alan Auerbach, Yang-Hyun Jin, Martin Sommer, and the editor for comments.

Notes

1. For a review of factors driving the deficit widening, see Masson and Mussa (1995). Throughout this chapter, tables and figures use the CBO definition of *automatic stabilizers*, which is narrower than the definition used in the remainder of this book.

2. There were earlier attempts to improve budgetary process and deficit control. The Legislative Reorganization Act of 1946 attempted to introduce appropriation ceilings, but the ceiling was broken the first year it was introduced. In 1974, The Congressional Budget and Impoundment Control Act was approved, which created a Budget Committee for each house and charged them with setting overall revenues, expenditures, and deficit, or surplus targets, rather than having total spending emerge as a sum of individual appropriation decisions. Even though it was hailed as revolutionary at that time, the 1974 Act did nothing to curb spending and deficits, only made them explicit. As Buchanan and Wagner (1977) noted, "expenditure ceilings, like pie crust, are meant to be broken."

3. Although President Reagan was reelected in 1984 with a large majority and Republicans kept control of the Senate, Democrats kept control of the House.

4. "Economic Report of the President," 1986, p.7. See also Summers (1986), who argued that although increasing government debt did not pose the risk of default, it had potentially serious consequences for economic growth through crowding out and could exacerbate debt problems in the private sector through higher interest rates.

5. President Reagan welcomed GRH and committed to submit budgets each year to satisfy the GRH's budget targets. He even spoke in favor of constitutional amendment to provide permanently balanced budgets ("Economic Report of the President," 1986, p. 7).

6. Responsibility for making this determination and ordering across-the-board cuts was initially given to the Comptroller General, the head of the General Accounting Office. However, this law was challenged and the Supreme Court ruled that the Comptroller General could not exercise this authority. Congress amended the law and gave the responsibility to the Office of Management and Budget.

7. "Sequestration" involved automatic, mainly across-the-board spending cuts (see Keith, 2004).

8. To some extent, higher interest payments reflected a higher debt stock stemming from the failure to observe the GRH targets. More significant, however, the yield on Treasuries did not fall as expected: in February 1986, the CBO projected a gradual decline in the three-month T-bill rate from 6.8 percent in 1986 to 5.4 percent in 1991. The projection for 1991 was on the mark (as a result of the recession) but in the preceding two years the rates were in the 7.5–8 percent range.

9. Reischauer (1990) offered this summary: "GRH may not have brought the deficit cows back into the barn, but at least it has kept them from stampeding over the cliff."

10. Senate Budget Committee: Committee History.

11. The breach of the campaign promise, "Read my lips: no new taxes," made by President G.H.W. Bush in 1988 at the Republican National Convention became a major issue in the 1992 presidential election.

12. "Economic Report of the President," 1991, pages 64–65.

13. Beside the weak economy, an important contributor to the 1991–92 deficits was the spending by the Resolution Trust Corporation to deal with the aftermath of the savings-and-loan crisis.

14. The vote was very close: all Republicans and some Democrats voted against the bill: the House passed the bill by a vote of 218 to 216, and Senate by a vote of 51 to 50, with Vice President Gore casting his vote to break the tie. Republicans submitted an alternative proposal cutting $355 billion in spending with $129 billion of the cuts coming from entitlement programs (the actual bill cut entitlement spending by only $42 billion). The amendment would also have eliminated any tax increases.

15. For an account of the debates that led to this decision, see Rubin and Weisberg, 2008.

16. "Economic Report of the President," 1994, pages 34–36, notes that in response to the announcement of the measures to cut deficits, long-term interest rates fell, which should have minimized the adverse impact of fiscal consolidation on growth: "deficit reduction accompanied by sufficient decline in long-term interest rates need not be contractionary. It is . . . what we experienced in 1993."

17. Interestingly, the 1998 deficit was projected to reach $240 billion, about $50 billion more than projected in the "Economic Report of the President" released in February 1993 (Table 2.4).

18. Leidy appropriately acknowledges the uncertainties in the measurement of output gaps and revenue and outlays elasticities to the output gap. The Administration and the CBO estimated that 35–40 percent of the deficit reduction during 1992 and 1997 was due to cyclical factors.

19. Other studies found that cyclical factors contributed by more than half to fiscal improvement—but for a somewhat longer period, 1992–2000. See Mühleisen (2004).

20. The CBO's *Economic and Budget Outlook, Fiscal Years 2004–2013*, January 2003, page 57, provides a detailed breakdown of factors underlying faster growth of individual income tax liability during 1994–2000.

21. CBO, *Economic Budget Outlook*, January 2003. The budget resolution is the concurrent resolution adopted by both Houses of Congress that sets forth the Congressional budget plan with targets for revenues, spending, budgetary balance, and debt held by the public, and is implemented through the subsequent legislation.

22. For example, Frankel and Orszag (2002) note that the improvements in government balance explained all the improvements in net national savings during 1993–2000, which restrained long-term interest rates and boosted private sector investment and growth. In contrast, Berglund and Vernengo (2004) argue that deficit reduction was largely the consequence of the economic boom, which in turn was fueled by the bubble in the stock market and unrealistic expectations about future earnings that pushed up both investment and consumption.

23. Particularly noteworthy was the decline in revenues in nominal terms in three subsequent years—the first time this happened in postwar history.

24. We focus on the first episode of deficit widening, which is more relevant from the perspective of assessing the fiscal consolidation of the 1990s. For the discussion of factors driving the deficit widening after 2008, see IMF (2010b).

25. Mühleisen (2004) estimates that over 1 percent of GDP of the fiscal balance improvement in the late 1990s was due to a temporary boost to income tax from realized capital gains. With the burst of the stock market bubble in the early 2000s, this factor began to work in reverse, contributing to the decline in income tax revenues.

CHAPTER 3

France: Virtue and Fortune

Edouard Martin, Irina Tytell, and Irina Yakadina

Introduction: Factors Underlying the Need for Fiscal Consolidation

Fiscal consolidation attempts have been motivated by continuous fiscal deficits and sustained increases in public indebtedness over the last 35 years (see Figure 3.1). The 30 years following World War II ("The Glorious Thirty" in the parlance of French economic history) were characterized by strong economic growth, broadly balanced budgets or small surpluses, and declining debt-to–Gross Domestic Product (GDP) ratios. However, deficits averaged 2 percent of GDP during the late 1970s and 1980s, and exceeded 3 percent of GDP on average in both the 1990s and 2000s. These continued deficits have contributed to an almost uninterrupted increase in debt ratios, from a postwar low of 20 percent of GDP in 1980 (when France had the lowest gross debt–to–GDP ratio among G7 countries) to more than 80 percent of GDP today.

France's deficits and rising debt reflected a steep increase in general government expenditures not matched by higher revenues (see Figure 3.2). From the early 1960s to the mid-1990s, the spending-to-GDP ratio increased from 35 to 55 percent. While similar trends were at play in other G7 countries,[1] France had both the highest starting point in 1960 and largest increase in primary spending through the mid-1990s. As a result, in 1993 its primary spending–to–potential GDP ratio was, at 51 percent, 11 percentage points higher than the average of G7 countries. After more or less keeping pace with spending until the late 1970s—essentially through continued increases in social contributions—revenues then slowed down, before stabilizing at around 50 percent of GDP in the mid-1990s.

The rapid growth in general government spending reflected, in large part, rising expenditures by the social security administrations and by

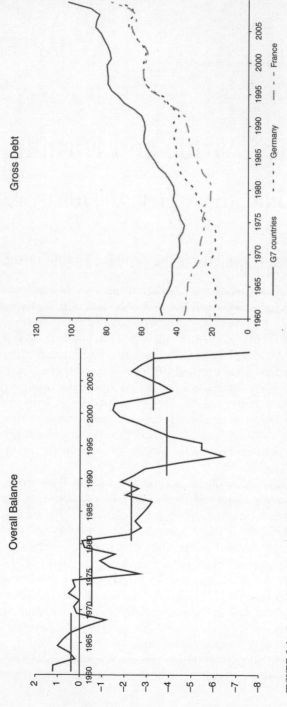

FIGURE 3.1 General Government Balance and Gross Debt, 1960–2009 (in percent of GDP)

Sources: National Institute of Statistics and Economic Studies (INSEE) and IMF staff estimates.

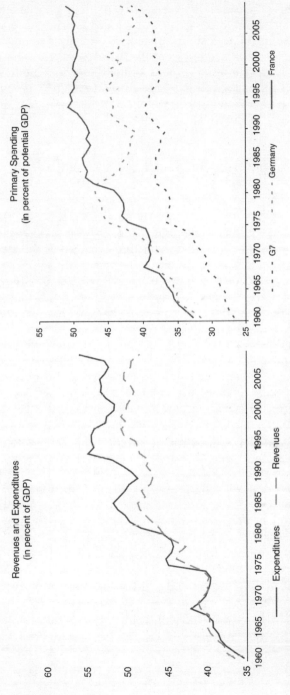

FIGURE 3.2 General Government Revenues and Expenditures, 1960–2009

Sources: INSEE and IMF staff estimates.

59

local governments. The social transfers–to-GDP ratio doubled between the early 1960s and the mid-1990s, from 11 to 23 percent, as a result of significant extensions of the social insurance system and a sustained increase in unemployment. Starting from the early 1980s, France embarked on a massive fiscal decentralization that shifted an increasing amount of responsibilities to the subnational levels of government (see Box 3.1). Partly as a result, both the social security administrations and local

Box 3.1: Central Government, Social Security, and Local Governments

France is often perceived as having a highly centralized government; yet, from a budgetary perspective, the social security administrations and the four layers of local governments are quite independent from the central government. Indeed, by the Constitution, the social security administration and local governments are given financial autonomy over their revenues and expenditures. These entities also follow budgetary processes separate from those of the central government, with annual budget laws for the social security administration voted by parliament during separate sessions (until Fiscal Year (FY) 2011) and an independent budgetary process for local governments with a different timeline.

Since the early 1980s, France has implemented an important fiscal decentralization, shifting many responsibilities from prefects representing the central state to the 22 regions, 96 departments, and over 36,000 communes and inter-communal cooperation establishments. As a result, local authorities have become responsible for an important share of public service provision, including three-fourths of public investment. New responsibilities boosted the number of civil servants employed at the local level without any significant reduction of the central government size. (Only recently has the policy of nonreplacing every other retiring central government civil servant started to bear fruit, but the estimated elimination of about 30 thousand posts a year will take more than a decade to offset the additional 340,000 by local governments between 1995 and 2005.) Local governments are subject to a golden rule that requires funding all their operating expenditures out of their own revenue, about half of which comes from the central government in the form of financial transfers and various grants. The golden rule has effectively limited local governments' indebtedness, but has not been sufficient to constrain the overall growth of public spending.

governments have been operating under soft budget constraints and have relied on growing transfers from the central government. Consequently, their spending grew even as their deficits remained relatively contained (see Figure 3.3).

Several fiscal consolidation attempts over the past three decades sought to stem the increase of public spending and help ensure macroeconomic sustainability (see Figure 3.4). The most prominent plans, which usually followed sharp deteriorations of the fiscal balance, included the *"Plan Barre"* of 1976, the *"Virage de la Rigueur"* of 1983, the first five-year budgetary plan of 1993–97 prepared for European Monetary Union (EMU) accession, and the Excessive Deficit Procedure (EDP) of 2003–07 under the Stability and Growth Pact (SGP). This chapter will discuss briefly the first two episodes, and will focus on the two most recent ones, as they were cast in a multiyear budgetary framework.[2]

Early Attempts at Fiscal Adjustment

The first two prominent attempts at fiscal consolidation—*Plan Barre* of 1976 and *Virage de la Rigueur* of 1983—followed increases in fiscal deficits triggered by countercyclical policies in response to an economic slowdown. While partly reflecting fiscal sustainability considerations, these early adjustment plans were primarily motivated by demand management concerns in view of high inflation and deteriorating external current account balances. The duration of these early fiscal consolidation attempts, however, was limited. Formalized medium-term fiscal consolidation attempts would begin only a decade later, in the first instance as part of the Maastricht process.

The Plan Barre

Countercyclical fiscal policies implemented to help the French economy recover from the 1974–75 recession led to a significant deterioration of the fiscal balance. In 1974–75, the French economy, along with most Organization for Economic Cooperation and Development (OECD) countries, experienced its first serious recession since the end of World War II. After giving priority to the fight against inflation during the first months of 1975, the authorities gradually geared the policy mix toward a more expansionary stance. This translated into successive rounds of fiscal stimulus; including transfers to the least privileged social groups and to companies, subsidized loans to Small and Medium Enterprises (SMEs) and exporters, incentives for investment (e.g., Value Added Tax (VAT) deductions) and job creation, as well as increases in public

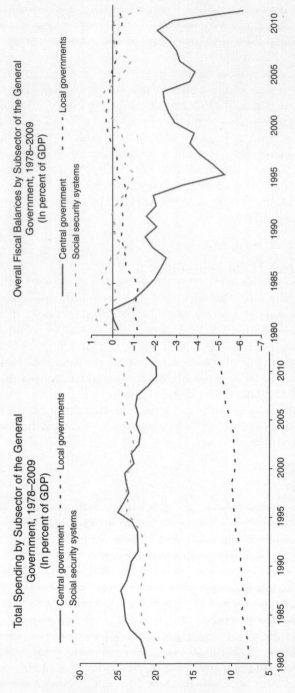

FIGURE 3.3 Spending and Balances by Subsector of the General Government, 1960–2009

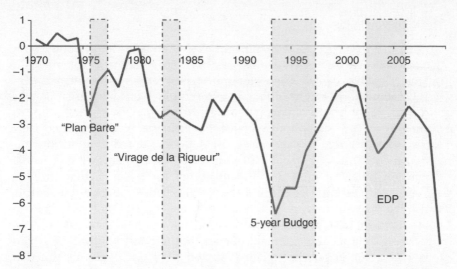

FIGURE 3.4　Attempts at Fiscal Consolidation, 1970–2010 (overall balance in percent of GDP)

investment and employment. These measures, combined with a cyclically induced decline in revenue, led to a worsening of the fiscal balance in 1975 and the first half of 1976.

Faced with higher inflation and a deterioration in the external current account balance, in September 1976 the government adopted an austerity package, the *Plan Barre*. This package aimed at ensuring that the initial 1976 budget objective of reducing the fiscal deficit would be met while providing for drought-related outlays. The plan included a temporary surcharge on personal and corporate income taxes as well as increases in registration and fuel taxes. The budget for 1977 sought to bring the central government balance back to equilibrium, through further current and capital spending cuts partly offset by a cut in the VAT rate.

While not bringing the budget fully back to equilibrium, these efforts reduced the deficit. The general government deficit declined from 2.7 percent of GDP in 1975 to 0.9 percent in 1977, as the rise in taxes and social security contributions as a share of GDP more than offset the increase in spending. Consolidation efforts were suspended in 1978 but renewed temporarily in 1979, when increases in fuel taxes and social security contributions contributed to a further reduction of the general government deficit in 1979, to near-balance.

The Virage de la Rigueur

Strongly expansionary domestic policies implemented in 1981 coupled with consolidation efforts carried out by partner countries led to a rapid increase in France's public debt, a large deterioration of its current account, and continued inflationary pressures. France entered the 1980s with fiscal deficits and public debt levels significantly lower than in the rest of the European Community. The Mitterrand Socialist government elected in mid-1981 carried out a strong expansionary fiscal policy aimed at reducing unemployment. This policy combined countercyclical elements with a sizeable expansion of social programs and tax relief for lower income groups. The external current account and the fiscal balance deteriorated sharply and inflationary pressures continued, but the sought-after reduction in unemployment failed to materialize.

Facing internal and external imbalances, the French authorities opted for a major shift in policies in late 1982 and early 1983. Reforms aimed at bringing the social security and unemployment insurance back into balance and doing so in the 1983 budget. Further measures were announced in March 1983 as part of a broader adjustment program remembered as "Virage de la Rigueur"; the fiscal policy stance was tightened, which aimed at eliminating the trade deficit within two years and avoiding a further deterioration of the fiscal balance.[3] These measures included increases in taxes on households and oil products, the introduction of a new levy on personal incomes to finance the social security system, increases in public service charges, a compulsory savings scheme, and expenditure cuts. These efforts were pursued also in 1984, through the extension of revenue-raising measures and further spending restraint.

As a result, inflationary pressures declined and the current account was brought back to balance but the impact on the fiscal deficit was more limited. In fact, the structural improvement of the fiscal accounts was largely offset by the adverse impact of the economic slowdown on revenues. Also, higher interest payments on the rapidly growing public debt more than offset modest consolidation efforts made by the local governments and social security administration.

A First Attempt at Medium-Term Fiscal Consolidation, 1994–97

In the early 1990s, it became clear that fiscal consolidation was necessary and that, to that end, a medium-term approach was required. This was also consistent with the gradual process that would ultimately lead to entry into the EMU.

The 1994 Guidance Law for the Public Finances

In response to a deterioration of the fiscal situation in the early 1990s, the authorities adopted, in 1994, a five-year Guidance Law on Public Finance Control. This law constituted an implementing tool of the convergence program presented jointly by France and Germany to the European Council (EC) in November 1993. In the case of France, this envisaged a reduction of the general government deficit from a projected 5.5 percent of GDP in 1993 to 2 percent of GDP by 1997. The adoption of this law was triggered by: (i) a significant increase in the central government deficit from 1.4 percent of GDP in 1990 to 3.2 percent of GDP in 1992;[4] and (ii) an increase in the public debt to 30 percent of GDP in 1992 and in the debt service burden to 16 percent of government revenue in 1992 (compared to 12 percent in 1990).

The 1994 Guidance Law placed, for the first time, the central government budget in a multiyear framework and set the stabilization and then reduction of the public debt as the main objective of fiscal policy. Meeting this objective was expected to deliver several benefits by:

- Creating fiscal space through debt service reduction
- Avoiding crowding-out effects on private investment
- Allowing further declines in interest rates and eliminating the interest rate differential vis-à-vis Germany (setting fiscal policy in a medium-term framework was expected to increase investor confidence)
- Smoothing out the necessary accommodation of the projected increase in age-related spending from 2005 onward
- Putting France on a path toward meeting the fiscal criteria set forth under the Maastricht treaty for becoming a member of the EMU (overall general government deficit of less than 3 percent of GDP and public debt below 60 percent of GDP in 1997)

To help meet its overarching goal, the 1994 Guidance Law set a number of quantitative medium-term objectives. The central government deficit was to be brought back to 2.5 percent of GDP by 1997. In turn, to help meet this objective, overall spending was to remain unchanged in real terms (given the projected increase in interest payments, this was consistent with a 0.4 percent annual decline in real primary spending). Revenues were projected to grow in line with real GDP.[5] Any additional revenues from better than expected economic developments were to be saved or used for a reduction of the tax burden. To ensure that the Maastricht fiscal deficit criteria, which related to the general government, would be met, the law also provided for a gradual reduction in local government and social security deficits, to be balanced by 1997. Finally, the law called for future central government budgets to be set in a multiyear framework, with annual draft budget laws to be accompanied by five-year budgetary projections.

A Mixed Start: 1994–95

The 1994 budget law was consistent with the objectives set forth in the 1994 Guidance Law. The budget called for a 0.5 percent of GDP decline in the central government deficit. Spending was projected to decline in real terms on account of a reduction in the number of civil servants, wage moderation, a substantial decline in investment spending, and a reduction in the growth of transfers to local governments. A slight decline of the tax burden was also envisaged, primarily through a reform of personal income taxation. Sizable projected privatization receipts, which were at that time accounted for as revenues, would also play a role in the adjustment.

The 1994 deficit turned out to be in line with budgetary objectives, but underlying spending was significantly higher than planned. Contrary to what was stipulated under the 1994 Guidance Law and in line with a supplementary budget adopted subsequently, additional revenues resulting from higher than projected growth were used for additional expenditures, including increases in school allowances, social spending, labor market measures, and peace-keeping operations.

Ex-post spending overruns continued in 1995. The 1995 budget provided for a further decline in the deficit to 3.5 percent of GDP (including privatization receipts), based on expenditure restraint and increases in excises. Spending was expected to stay flat in real terms on account of real declines in transfers to local governments, unemployment benefits (owing to a recovering labor market), and capital spending. However, the Alain Juppé government formed after the May 1995 presidential elections adopted a supplementary budget with additional spending in support of employment, the social housing sector, and SMEs. These outlays, along with spending overruns observed during the first half of the year, were to be offset by temporary increases in taxes (mainly VAT, corporate income tax, and wealth tax) and savings on non-priority spending. But an economic slowdown in the second half of 1995 further weakened revenue collections. The original fiscal deficit target was met only through new measures—including expenditure cuts and the mobilization of additional nontax revenue—undertaken as part of another supplementary budget adopted in November.

Expenditure Restraint, at Last: 1996–97

The 1996 budget was accompanied by an updated medium-term plan, which reiterated the commitment to deficit reduction through expenditure restraint. The updated plan covered 1996–99 and, in line with the original plan, aimed at a gradual reduction of the deficit, from 4.1 percent of GDP (excluding privatization receipts) in 1995 to 3 percent in 1997 and 2 percent in 1999.[6] Again, the adjustment was to be achieved by keeping spending constant in real terms and maintaining the tax-to-GDP ratio unchanged.

Expenditures were successfully restrained in 1996. Expenditure growth was contained through a mix of further cuts in capital spending, defense spending, and social transfers; a stability pact with local governments aimed at moderating central government transfers; and a freeze of the pay scale of public sector employees.

However, to meet the Maastricht fiscal deficit criterion, the authorities had to take ad-hoc corrective measures in 1997. Faced with a cyclical short-fall in revenue and difficulties in meeting the annual budget law objective of keeping spending unchanged in nominal terms, the Lionel Jospin government formed after the May 1997 parliamentary elections commissioned a public finance audit. This audit projected the general government deficit at 3.5–3.75 percent of GDP based on unchanged policies. Consistent with its commitment to meeting the Maastricht fiscal deficit criterion, the government adopted a corrective plan providing for an exceptional increase in the corporate income tax, the abolition of the preferential rate on long-term corporate capital gains, and additional expenditure cuts.

Overall Performance

Although significant fiscal consolidation was accomplished, the central government deficit was not reduced as much as envisaged (see Table 3.1 and Figure 3.5). Including privatization receipts, the fiscal deficit declined by 1.2 percent of GDP between 1993 and 1997, some 0.8 percent of GDP less than initially planned.[7] This underperformance resulted from higher than planned increases in spending, both interest payments (0.4 percent of GDP) and primary spending (0.7 percent of GDP)—the latter from compensation of employees, pensions, and economic transfers, whereas capital spending declined significantly—lower nontax revenue (0.2 percent of GDP), and lower than expected economic growth (which contributed to an increase in the deficit-to-GDP ratio of 0.2 percent). These factors were partly offset by an increase in central government tax revenue (0.5 percent of GDP), which reflected both an increase in taxes collected by the central government and a decline in the share of tax revenues redistributed to other levels of government.

The general government deficit was under 3 percent of GDP and the Maastricht fiscal deficit criterion was met in 1997. Four main factors contributed to this success. First, the initial plan aimed at a reduction of the general government deficit to 2 percent of GDP, thus leaving significant margin for meeting the Maastricht target. Second, the improvement of local government

TABLE 3.1 1994 Guidance Law Targets and Outcomes for the Central Government (in percent of GDP)

	Plan (p)			Actual (a)			Overperformance (actual relative to plan)		
								Of which:	
							$1997a-1997p$ = 1997 actual minus 1997 planned	$\Delta a - \Delta p$ = Actual improvement minus planned improvement	$1993a-1993p$ = 1993 actual minus 1993 preliminary estimate from plan ("base effect")
	1993p	1997p	Δp	1993a	1997a	Δa			
Revenues	15.7	15.7	−0.1	15.7	16.0	0.3	0.4	0.4	0.0
Cyclical	−0.7	−0.5	0.2	−0.6	−0.5	0.1	0.0	−0.1	0.1
Structural	16.5	16.2	−0.3	16.4	16.6	0.2	0.4	0.5	−0.1
Expenditures	20.2	18.2	−2.0	20.2	19.3	−0.9	−1.1	−1.2	0.0
Primary	17.7	15.6	−2.1	17.9	16.6	−1.4	−0.9	−0.7	−0.2
Interest	2.5	2.5	0.0	2.3	2.7	0.5	−0.2	−0.4	0.2
Overall balance	−4.5	−2.5	2.0	−4.5	−3.3	1.2	−0.8	−0.8	0.0
Primary balance	−2.0	0.0	2.0	−2.2	−0.5	1.7	−0.6	−0.4	−0.2
Structural primary balance	−1.3	0.5	1.8	−1.6	0.0	1.6	−0.5	−0.2	−0.3

Sources: 1994 Guidance Law for the Public Finances; French Ministry of Finance; and IMF staff estimates.

Note: The "1996 preliminary out-turn" reported in the 1997 plan is not to be confused with the "1996 final actual" sourced from a database such as the World Economic Outlook (IMF).

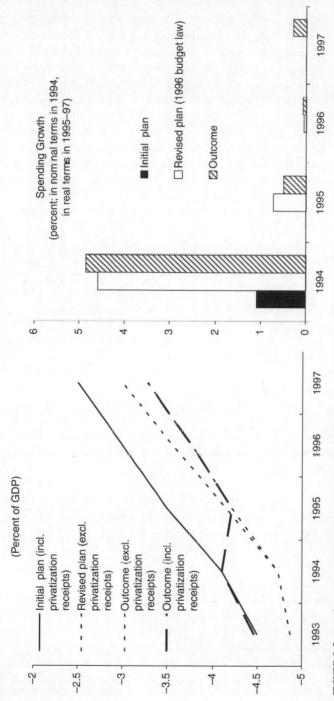

FIGURE 3.5 1994 Guidance Law Targets and Outcomes for the Central Government

Sources: French government; and IMF staff estimates.

accounts was larger than expected, and they registered a surplus of 0.2 percent of GDP in 1997. Third, last-minute mobilization of one-off payments from France Telecom contributed additional revenue of 0.5 percent of GDP. Fourth, some statistical changes, introduced primarily to bring the French accounting system in line with European standards, contributed to a further reduction of the estimated deficit. At the same time, the far-reaching reform of the social security system adopted in 1996 contributed to a 0.6 percent of GDP reduction of its deficit, but this improvement was insufficient to bring the social security accounts to balance as initially envisaged.

The previous comparison of plan targets with outcomes illustrates both the usefulness of, and institutional limits to, France's first attempt at medium-term budgeting (see Box 3.2). As the quantitative objectives of the 1994 Guidance Law were not legally binding, there was considerable discretion

Box 3.2: From Economic Planning to MultiYear Budgeting

During the postwar period, five-year economic plans provided a framework for setting medium-term policies. These plans, required under the Constitution, set a number of economic and social objectives, as well as an overall strategy ensuring the consistency of the policies of different economic actors. Although these plans were indicative and had no binding legal status, the main actors of the private and public sectors were involved in their preparation, as part of the national planning commission ensuring broad ownership of their objectives.

The connection between five-year plans and annual budgets was, however, somewhat loose. In budgetary terms, the five-year plans primarily focused on setting priorities for public investment and fiscal incentives—a small share of government spending. Also, as these plans were only indicative, short-term considerations often took precedence over longer-term objectives, as evident during the economic slowdown of the mid-1970s. A 1982 law on economic planning tried to strengthen the linkage between five-year plans and annual budgets through better monitoring and reporting of the plans' implementation and the budgetary resources allocated to the attainment of their objectives, but limited progress was made.

In the context of the SGP and the 2001 Organic Budget Law, the introduction of a medium-term budget framework (MTBF) provided a credible link between medium-term planning and short-term fiscal policy making. In line with SGP guidelines, since 1998 the government has prepared annual MTBFs comprising:

(continued)

(*continued*)

- A medium-term target for the general government balance
- An annual path toward this objective, which has to be consistent with a one-half percent of GDP annual improvement in the structural balance (for as long as the medium-term target has not been met)
- Key economic assumptions
- A description of fiscal and structural measures envisaged
- A sensitivity analysis

The 2001 Organic Budget Law also calls for the inclusion of MTBFs in the Economic, Social, and Financial Reports annexed to annual budget laws.

Yet, the existence of medium-term targets did not prove to be a binding constraint. A 2007 report by the *Inspection Générale des Finances* concluded that multiyear programming had not been respected, because of slippages on the spending side, and identified two major contributing factors: (i) MTBFs were prepared mainly to satisfy the SGP requirements and had no direct link with annual budget preparation procedures; and (ii) MTBFs were not supported by operational targets that would allow the achievement of public finance objectives. The report also noted that spending norms only applied to the state budget, representing 40 percent of the general government spending.

To tackle these weaknesses, the government introduced multiyear budgeting in 2008. This new model of budgeting, which started being implemented with the 2009 budget, drew heavily upon the UK Spending Review. It was characterized by:

- A "2+1" approach, according to which expenditure ceilings are set for three years but reviewed every two years
- Coverage of central government spending only
- Breakdown of overall three-year ceilings into 32 sub-ceilings along with an indicative ceiling on tax expenditures
- Contingency reserves amounting to 1 percent of central government spending by the third year of programming

In addition, the legal status of medium-term budgeting was strengthened: multiyear budgets are presented to parliament for discussion and approval, along with the annual budget laws.

in the conduct of fiscal policy (at least as long as the overall deficit stayed on a declining path). Moreover, in the absence of binding limits on spending growth, the government did not fully embrace expenditure restraint, especially when revenues were higher than envisaged. At the same time, the French government spared no efforts to comply with Maastricht prerequisites for Euro entry.

A More Systematic Approach to Medium-Term Budgeting: Consolidation Experiences under the Stability and Growth Pact

France issued a total of 12 annual stability programs (SPs) over 1998–2009, of which six envisaged reductions in the overall fiscal deficit of more than 0.5 percent of GDP per year in the context of excessive deficit procedures (EDPs). The first episode of significant planned fiscal consolidation included the five SPs submitted from 2003 to 2007 that aimed to reduce the general government deficit to below 3 percent of GDP, thus terminating EDPs. The second episode is ongoing and includes the recent SP submitted in January 2010 that targets a large reduction in the overall fiscal deficit under EDPs opened in February 2009. Both planned consolidation episodes followed economic downturns and significant deteriorations in the public finances. As the second episode is still unfolding, the focus of the following section will be on the 2003–07 episode.

The Fiscal Consolidation Experience of 2003–07

SP targets were occasionally missed during this period, but France ultimately succeeded in reducing the fiscal deficit below 3 percent of GDP.[8] The 2003 SP was submitted on December 11, 2003, following the excessive deficit statement from the Council on June 3. It constituted the key fiscal adjustment plan during this period. The general government fiscal deficit dipped slightly below 3 percent of GDP by 2005 thanks, in part, to one-off receipts. It then remained just below the SGP ceiling during the global economic boom of 2005–07, before the recent global financial crisis put France's public finances under severe pressure again (see Figure 3.6 and Table 3.2).

Fiscal adjustment focused on expenditure control, with revenue-to-GDP ratios targeted to remain broadly stable, so as not to constrain GDP growth. Key adjustment measures included a legally binding zero real growth rule for central government spending (see Box 3.3), as well as significant health and pension reforms. To bring the deficit below 3 percent of GDP in 2005, the 2003 SP set more ambitious spending targets than its predecessors. Yet, the program envisaged reducing the deficit marginally below the 3 percent

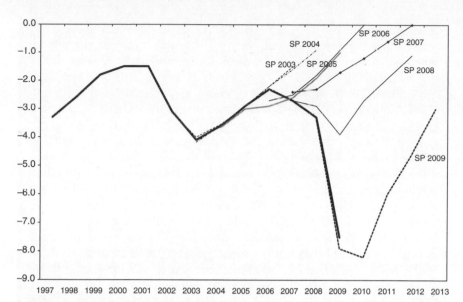

FIGURE 3.6 Central Government Balance—Stability Program Targets and Outcomes (in percent of GDP)

Sources: Stability Programs, World Economic Outlook (International Monetary Fund (IMF)), and IMF staff estimates.

TABLE 3.2 General Government Balance: Targets and Outcomes

(in percent of GDP)

	2004	2005	2006	2007	2008	2009
Actual	3.6	2.9	2.3	2.7	3.3	7.5
SP 2003	−3.6	−2.9	−2.2	−1.5		
SP 2004		−2.9	−2.2	−1.6	−0.9	
SP 2005			−2.9	−2.6	−1.9	−1.0
SP 2006				−2.5	−1.8	−0.9
SP 2007					−2.3	−1.7
SP 2008						−3.9

Box 3.3: The Evolution of Fiscal Rules in France

Until the early 1990s, the French authorities relied mainly on a simple budgetary rule, defining a nominal deficit target on a year-ahead basis, independently of the subsequent performance of the economy. This

(continued)

(*continued*)

rule required, in effect, expenditures to be reduced in line with falling revenues in a downswing, and increased expenditure (or tax cuts) during an upswing of the economy. From 1998 onward, medium-term expenditure targets were set at the general government level as part of the stability programs. These initial targets were missed due both to the lack of consistency between the annual budget laws and these medium-term objectives and to spending slippages in the implementation of the budget laws (Moulin, 2004).

In 2003, the authorities adopted a "zero volume growth" spending rule in annual budget laws. This rule essentially states that central government expenditures (until 2008, excluding transfers to other government subsectors and the European Union (EU)) should remain constant in real terms. This rule restrained central government spending, but it did not prevent slippages at the local government and social security levels. Some argue that this may have contributed to a loosening of the local government budgetary constraint (Champsaur, 2010).

To address this issue, the government recently broadened the scope of the zero volume growth spending rule to encompass revenue transfers to local governments and the EU, as well as earmarked revenue for quasi-fiscal activities by nongovernmental entities. Implementation of this rule in 2009 was mixed, even abstracting from stimulus measures (*Commission des Finances du Sénat*, 2010).

The focus of the fiscal rules on spending rather than revenues has contributed to the proliferation of tax exemptions leading to an erosion of the tax base. The government recently committed to a sizable reduction in excessive tax deductions and strictly limited the introduction of new tax exemptions.

target and, therefore, was vulnerable to adverse macroeconomic and budgetary developments.

Spending overruns were partly offset by favorable economic developments and one-off receipts. To assess the relative contributions of economic developments and fiscal effort to the overall fiscal adjustment performance, implementation relative to SP targets is decomposed into: (i) cyclically adjusted revenues and primary expenditures; (ii) interest spending; and (iii) cyclical balances (see Box 3.4). This decomposition shows that underperformance in the 2003 SP was associated entirely with structural shortfalls (see Table 3.3, and Figure 3.7). Indeed, the 2007 structural primary balance fell short of target by 2.5 percent of GDP (1.8 percent excluding base effects), while the overall balance underperformed by

Box 3.4: A Method of Decomposing Program Implementation

Implementation relative to SP targets can be decomposed into components corresponding to cyclically adjusted revenues and primary expenditures, interest spending, and cyclical balances, as follows:

$$\left(b_t^A - b_t^T\right) = \left(r_t^A - r_t^T\right) - \left(g_t^A - g_t^T\right) - \left(i_t^A - i_t^T\right)$$
$$= \left[\left(r_t^{A,S} - r_t^{T,S}\right) - \left(g_t^{A,S} - g_t^{T,S}\right)\right]$$
$$+ \left[\left(r_t^{A,C} - r_t^{T,C}\right) - \left(g_t^{A,C} - g_t^{T,C}\right)\right] - \left(i_t^A - i_t^T\right)$$

where b, r, g, and i stand, respectively, for the overall balance, revenues, primary expenditures, and interest spending (all relative to GDP), superscripts refer to actual (A), target (T), cyclical (C), and cyclically adjusted (S), and subscripts denote years. Cyclically adjusted revenues and primary expenditures are expressed as:[a]

$$\left(r_t^{A,S} - r_t^{T,S}\right) = \left[r_t^A\left(1 - gap^A\right)^{\varepsilon_r} - r_t^T\left(1 - gap^T\right)^{\varepsilon_r}\right]$$
$$\cong \left[r_t^A\left(1 - \varepsilon_r gap^A\right) - r_t^T\left(1 - \varepsilon_r gap^T\right)\right]$$

$$\left(g_t^{A,S} - g_t^{T,S}\right) = \left[g_t^A\left(1 - gap^A\right)^{\varepsilon_g} - g_t^T\left(1 - gap^T\right)^{\varepsilon_g}\right]$$
$$\cong \left[g_t^A\left(1 - \varepsilon_g gap^A\right) - g_t^T\left(1 - \varepsilon_g gap^T\right)\right]$$

where $gap^A = \frac{Y^A - Y^*}{Y^A}$ and $gap^T = \frac{Y^T - Y^*}{Y^T}$ refer to, respectively, actual and target output gaps relative to GDP, while ε_r and ε_g denote elasticities of revenue and primary expenditure, respectively. For France, the standard revenue elasticity of 1 and the primary expenditure elasticity of 0 are appropriate, in line with recent estimates by the OECD and the European Commission.[b]

[a]See Fedelino, Ivanova, and Horton (2009) for a description of the cyclical adjustment methodology.
[b]See European Commission (2005) and Girouard and André (2005).

1.2 percent of GDP, with the difference reflecting overperformance of cyclical revenues and interest expenditures owing, respectively, to strong growth and low interest rates during the program period (see Box 3.5).

Although the deficit fell substantially short of target only in the last year of the program, spending overran targets also in the preceding years. Prior to 2007, spending overruns were offset by buoyant cyclical revenues and low debt service costs, as well as temporarily higher cyclically adjusted revenues in 2005 and 2006, partly thanks to sizable one-off receipts (see Figure 3.7). Notably, to meet the Council requirement of reducing the deficit under

TABLE 3.3 General Government Targets and Outcomes—Stability Program 2003 (in percent of GDP)

	Plan (p)			Actual (a)			Overperformance (actual relative to plan)	Of which:	
	2003p	2007p	Δp	2003a	2007a	Δa	2007a–2007p = 2007 actual minus 2007 planned	$\Delta a - \Delta p$ = Actual improvement minus planned improvement	2003a–2003p = 2003 actual minus 2003 preliminary estimate from plan ("base effect")
Revenues	50.3	50.3	0.0	49.2	49.6	0.4	−0.7	0.4	−1.1
Cyclical	−0.3	−0.3	−0.1	0.1	0.5	0.5	0.8	0.5	0.3
Structural	50.6	50.6	0.1	49.1	49.0	0.0	−1.6	−0.1	−1.5
Expenditures	54.3	51.8	−2.5	53.3	52.3	−1.0	−0.5	−1.5	1.0
Primary	51.2	48.7	−2.5	50.4	49.6	−0.8	−0.9	−1.7	0.8
Interest	3.1	3.1	0.0	2.8	2.7	−0.1	0.4	0.1	0.3
Overall balance	−4.0	−1.5	2.5	−4.1	−2.7	1.4	−1.2	−1.1	−0.1
Primary balance	−0.9	1.6	2.5	−1.3	0.0	1.2	−1.6	−1.3	−0.4
Structural primary balance	−0.6	1.9	2.6	−1.4	−0.6	0.8	−2.5	−1.8	−0.7

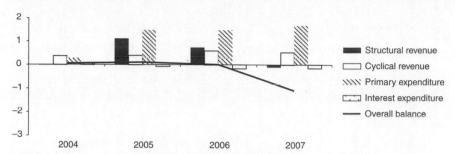

FIGURE 3.7 General Government Program Implementation: Actual minus Target, Stability Program 2003 (in percent of GDP, net of base effects)

Sources: Stability Programs, World Economic Outlook (IMF), and IMF staff estimates.

Box 3.5: Macroeconomic Assumptions

French SPs have typically included two scenarios: a cautious, or low, reference scenario with real GDP growth of 2.25–2.5 percent per year, and a favorable, or high, scenario with real GDP growth of 3 percent per year. In most of the past SPs, even the reference scenario was somewhat optimistic in comparison to the consensus forecast (CF) published ahead of SPs and covering similar time horizons.[a] That said, reference growth assumptions in the 2003 SP were close to the CF and those in the SPs of 2004 and 2005 were only marginally higher. In practice, growth was somewhat underestimated in 2004 and over-estimated in 2005, while over 2006–07 projections turned out close to actual growth rates.

REAL GDP GROWTH: SP TARGETS, CF FORECASTS, AND OUTCOMES IN PERCENT

	2004	2005	2006	2007	2008	2009
Actual	2.3	1.9	2.4	2.3	0.1	−2.5
CF 2003	1.6	2.4	2.6	2.5		
SP 2003	1.7	2.5	2.5	2.5		
CF 2004		2.2	2.2	2.3	2.3	
SP 2004		2.5	2.5	2.5	2.5	
CF 2005			1.8	2.1	2.1	2.1
SP 2005			2.3	2.3	2.3	2.3

(continued)

(*continued*)

Although consolidation efforts under the 2003–07 EDP did not rely on very conservative growth assumptions, they benefited from the favorable economic environment at the time. Notably, while the SPs of 2003–05 assumed negative output gaps throughout the program periods, actual output gaps were positive over 2004–07.

[a]Optimistic biases in growth assumptions that underlie fiscal projections have been identified in a number of countries under the SGP (Jonung and Larch, 2004, and Strauch, Hallerberg, and von Hagen, 2004).

3 percent of GDP in 2005, the government utilized one-off receipts from the electricity and gas industries in the amount of .5 percent of GDP. At the same time, tax cuts were implemented in 2006 and 2007, within the framework of the income tax reform of 2007. The primary expenditure ratio was close to target (net of base effects) only in 2004, the first program year also covered by the concurrent budget law.

A Closer Look at Spending by Level of Government

Spending overruns at the general government level were the main obstacle to successful consolidation under the 2003–07 EDP. The rate of growth of general government spending showed few signs of diminishing during this consolidation attempt (see Figure 3.8). As noted, spending overruns as a share of GDP would have been even larger, if not for strong GDP growth. Indeed, although real spending growth of the general government exceeded SP targets, it remained close to or even dipped below real GDP growth from 2004 to 2007.[9]

Spending overruns mostly reflected slippages by local governments and social security (see Table 3.4). SPs targeted annual real spending growth at all government levels.[10] During the 2003–07 EDP consolidation episode, central government spending and social security spending each accounted for close to 40 percent of general government expenditure, with local government spending taking up 20 percent. Both local governments and social security administrations spent in excess of their respective targets during this episode, with overruns by local governments being especially large. However, since the share of local governments in general government expenditure was lower than that of social security administrations, their overruns accounted for broadly similar shares of the total general government overspending over the SPs of 2003, 2004, and 2005, on average. In contrast, spending restraint by the central government helped compensate a portion

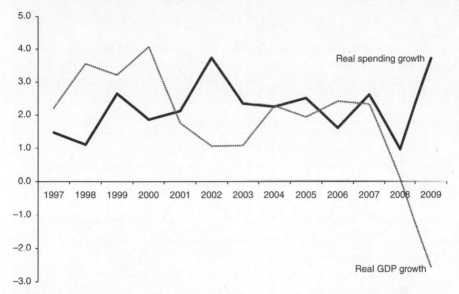

FIGURE 3.8 General Government Real Spending Growth: Stability Program Targets and Outcomes (in percent)

Sources: Stability Programs, World Economic Outlook (IMF), and IMF staff estimates.

TABLE 3.4 Real Spending Growth by Levels of Government: Targets and Outcomes

(averaging, in percent)

	General Government	Central Government	Local Government	Social Security
SP2003 Targets for 2005-07	1.1	0.3	2.0	1.7
SP2003 Outcomes for 2005-07	*2.2*	*− 1.5*	*4.3*	*2.6*
SP2004 Targets for 2006-08	1.2	0.2	1.8	1.7
SP2004 Outcomes for 2006-08	*1.7*	*− 1.9*	*3.6*	*1.8*
SP2005 Targets for 2007-09	0.6	0.0	0.5	0.9
SP2005 Outcomes for 2007-09	*2.4*	*0.7*	*3.3*	*2.8*

of these overruns, although these comparisons are complicated by inter-governmental transfers.

The central government was bound by a zero real spending growth rule and managed to slow down and eventually reduce its spending in real terms (see Figure 3.9). That said, the rule is set in budgetary

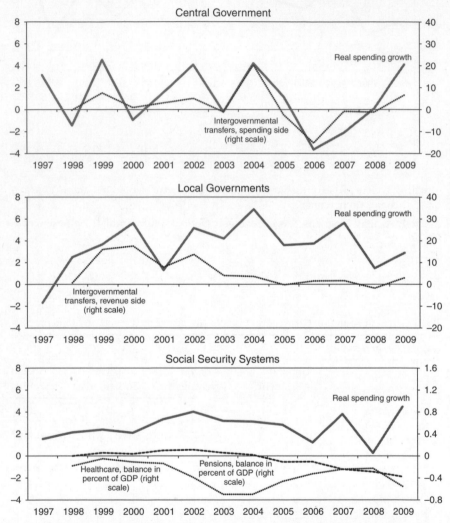

FIGURE 3.9 Real Spending Growth by Government Levels: Stability Program Targets and Outcomes (in percent of GDP)

Sources: Stability Programs, INSEE, Direction de la Sécurité Sociale, and IMF staff estimates.

accounting terms, which exclude the bulk of transfers to local governments that are part of central government spending in national accounting terms. Overall, transfers to other levels of government account for over 20 percent of central government spending and reflect, in part, transfers of responsibility from the central government to other administrations.

Local government spending grew rapidly and always exceeded SP targets over the course of the 2003–07 EDP. Approximately half of the total local government spending was taken up by operating expenditures, a quarter went into various transfers, and another quarter consisted of investment—a key responsibility of local administrations. According to the golden rule imposed on local governments, they must fund operating expenditures out of their own revenue, about half of which comes from the central government in the form of financial transfers and various grants.[11]

Social security spending also frequently overshot SP targets. About half of social security spending goes into pensions, a third is allocated to healthcare, and the rest is split up among unemployment, family, and housing support. The healthcare branch was in chronic deficits during the past decade, and the retirement branch moved into deficit over the last five years (see Figure 3.9). That said, social security spending overruns were associated also with other branches of the system, notably unemployment support.[12]

Conclusion

This chapter assessed past fiscal consolidation plans and their outcomes in France. First, it discussed the early attempts at fiscal consolidation in the 1970s and the 1980s (*Plan Barre* and *Virage de la Rigueur*) that were primarily motivated by demand management needs and suffered from the lack of medium-term budgetary planning. Second, we analyzed the first episode of medium-term fiscal consolidation in 1994–97 that allowed France to meet the fiscal criteria of the Maastricht treaty and to join the European Economic and Monetary Union. Although significant consolidation was accomplished during this episode, institutional limits—the absence of binding quantitative objectives and limits on spending growth—hindered the implementation of the plan. Third, we assessed the fiscal consolidation under the corrective arm of the European SGP in 2003–07. Although, as a result of this consolidation, France succeeded in terminating the excessive deficit procedure, the absence of binding constraints on spending of local governments and social security administrations was a key obstacle along the way.

The analyses of past fiscal consolidations in France suggest the following lessons:

- Binding constraints help focus policymakers' attention and justify
  their actions vis-à-vis the public at large. In successful fiscal consolidation episodes, the authorities were ready to do what it took in
  order to meet Maastricht fiscal criteria or exit from excessive deficit
  procedures. In this vein, the recent introduction of multiyear budgeting bodes well for the future.
- Fiscal consolidation is facilitated when spending restraint is shared and
  consolidation efforts are coordinated across all levels of government. In
  the fiscal adjustment episodes studied in this paper, the inability of the
  government to fully meet its objectives resulted primarily from higher
  than planned increases in spending, often by local governments and
  social security administrations even when progress was made at the
  central government level.
- Appropriate binding deficit targets could help in enforcing budgetary discipline in good times. Under the SGP, the 3 percent of GDP
  requirement for the fiscal deficit was viewed as a target when it
  should have been seen as a ceiling. In light of this misplaced
  emphasis, France missed a very good opportunity to consolidate the
  fiscal accounts further in the boom years of 2005–07 which in turn
  would have given the authorities more fiscal room to deal with the
  recent global financial crisis.

Acknowledgments

The authors thank Benoit Coeuré, Anne-Marie Gulde-Wolf, Erik de Vrijer,
Paolo Mauro, Ricardo Velloso, conference participants at the IMF's Fiscal
Affairs Department and seminar participants at the *Ministère de l'Économie,
de l'Industrie, et de l'Emploi* and the IMF's Fiscal Affairs Department for valu-
able comments and Pierre Ecochard and Samuel De Lemos Peixoto of the
European Commission's DG ECFIN for help with some of the data. Anastasia
Guscina provided excellent research assistance.

Notes

1. For a recent reference, see Cottarelli and Schaechter (2010).
2. Between 1986 and 1991, successive governments aimed at reducing the fiscal deficit but by smaller amounts (aiming on average at a structural adjustment of 0.2-
   0.3 percent of GDP a year).

3. The program also included a devaluation of the French franc, restrictions on spending abroad by French tourists, and the elimination of existing exchange control loopholes.

4. In this section, "central government" refers solely to the portion of the central government that is covered by the budget laws and does not include other, off-budget central government units, whose spending amounts to 3.5 percent of GDP.

5. Real GDP growth projections, at 2.8 percent over 1995–97, were somewhat more optimistic than the Consensus Forecast (2.5 percent as of the Fall of 1993).

6. Unlike the original plan, which recorded privatization receipts as above-the-line revenues, the updated plan recorded privatization receipts as part of financing, in line with the Maastricht definition.

7. Excluding privatization receipts, the deficit declined by 1.6 percent of GDP.

8. SP targets were frequently missed in many countries (Moulin and Wierts, 2006 and European Commission, 2007).

9. Real spending growth is obtained from nominal expenditures using Consumer Price Index (CPI) minus tobacco as deflator.

10. The average annual real spending growth targets were set for three years. For example, in the 2003 SP, targets were set for 2005–07. Outcomes are computed for the corresponding years. The central government targets are reported in national accounting terms, as different from real spending growth rules set in budgetary accounting terms (*Commission des Finances du Sénat*, 2010).

11. Transfers to local governments shown in Figure 3.9 are a subset of total transfers.

12. See, for example, *Commission des Finances du Sénat* (2010).

CHAPTER 4

Germany: Fiscal Adjustment Attempts With and Without Reforms

Christian Breuer, Jan Gottschalk, and Anna Ivanova

Introduction

Fiscal consolidation has been a key concern for policymakers in Germany over the past four decades, owing to the rising trend in debt ratios throughout this period (see Figure 4.1, panel 1). The drive for fiscal consolidation has been stoked by memories of hyperinflation in the early 1920s caused by World War I debt, which left the German public especially attuned to the risks of public debt accumulation. This chapter reviews the experience with federal plans for fiscal consolidation. The focus on the federal government level reflects that the rise in the federal public debt ratio was particularly pronounced, in particular in the first half of the 1990s when the federal government absorbed most of the debt incurred as part of German unification. Moreover, federal consolidation plans were embedded in, and can be assessed against, medium-term fiscal frameworks (MTFFs), which have been prepared at the federal level since the late 1960s. Specifically, these frameworks provide a discussion of policy intentions as well as key fiscal indicators for the upcoming budget year (legally binding fiscal targets) and for the following three years (indicative targets).[1]

This chapter looks closely at four distinct consolidation attempts (see Figure 4.1, panel 2, shaded rectangles), which were identified as large in comparison to other consolidation attempts embedded in MTFFs.[2] To pin down the timing of large consolidation attempts, the change in the cyclically adjusted overall balance (in percent of potential Gross Domestic Product (GDP)) was computed for all MTFFs between 1969 and 2005.[3] The MTFFs

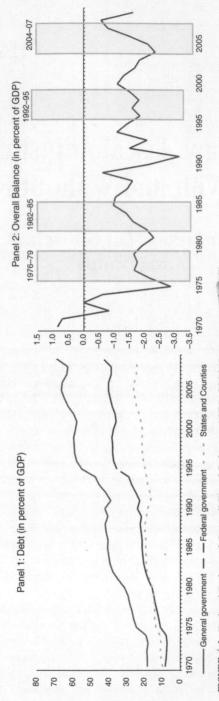

FIGURE 4.1 Federal Debt and Overall Fiscal Balance, 1970–2009 (in percent of GDP)

Sources: Council of Economic Advisers Reports; and IMF staff estimates.

Note: Before 1991, data for West Germany only.

that showed the largest *planned* improvement were chosen for further detailed assessment. The identified consolidation attempts were cross-checked with assessments of policy intentions in contemporary documents such as the International Monetary Fund (IMF) staff reports and the Organization for Economic Cooperation and Development (OECD) Economic Surveys as well as quotes from politicians of the time. As a result, we focus on the following four MTFFs, identified as containing the largest consolidation plans over the period considered:

1. *1975 MTFF, covering 1976–79.* This first attempt was motivated by a substantial pickup in debt as a result of high deficits during the 1974–75 recession. Policymakers thus saw the need for fiscal consolidation to reduce unsustainably high deficits, although initially they also viewed the economic slowdown as a sign of weak demand. This created tension between fiscal adjustment in order to stem the growth of debt, and fiscal stimulus in order to support the economy. Eventually, as shown in this chapter, fiscal stimulus won out. In hindsight, we also know that the 1974–1975 recession marked the beginning of a secular downward shift in economic growth.

2. *1981 MTFF, covering 1982–85.* The second attempt followed the recession in 1980–81 and marked an effort to reverse the high deficits of the 1970s as well as to limit the impact of the recession on the budget. During this episode, consolidation was the overriding fiscal policy objective, which ultimately was attained.

3. *1991 MTFF, covering 1992–95.* The third attempt was triggered by the high costs of German unification in the early 1990s. The fiscal costs of unification effectively reversed the consolidation successes of the preceding decade. Almost immediately, the government tried to bring deficits back down again, but had only mixed success. The main obstacles were that (i) unification aggravated existing labor market problems, thereby causing low growth, high unemployment, and large fiscal outlays; and (ii) unification costs exceeded expectations.

4. *2003 MTFF, covering 2004–07.* The final attempt in the mid-2000s consisted of an effort to reduce persistently high structural deficits, recognizing that demographic developments will put further pressures on the long-term fiscal outlook. This episode entailed substantial structural reforms, especially of the labor market and the pension system.

The next four sections of this chapter review each consolidation attempt in turn, highlighting:

- The challenges motivating the adjustment plan
- The plan's design

■ The extent to which the plan was implemented, and the sources of deviations of outcomes from plans

■ Responses to unanticipated challenges, and broader general observations

The final section distills these observations into lessons that are supported by all four episodes.

1975–79 Consolidation Attempt

The Challenge

By fall 1975, the German economy was mired in a deep recession. Growth in the preceding years had been brisk—averaging 5 percent in 1968–73, with an unemployment rate just above 1 percent in 1973. However, monetary policy was tightened significantly to curb inflation against the background of the first oil price shock of October 1973. With tighter monetary policy and rising oil prices, 1974 thus marked the beginning of a significant downturn. In 1975, the economy contracted and unemployment shot up to almost 5 percent. Fiscal and monetary policies were loosened substantially, with the general government deficit exceeding 6 percent of GDP. At that point, concern about excessively high fiscal deficits implied that an even larger fiscal stimulus to remedy the unemployment surge was seen as out of the question. Indeed, the Council of Economic Advisers' report published in fall 1975 argued that high public deficits had already led to private sector concerns over indebtedness, thereby reducing the effectiveness of fiscal policy in pulling the economy out of the recession.[4] Even though the general government's debt ratio of about 25 percent of GDP in 1975 seems moderate by today's standards, it had increased by almost a third relative to the beginning of the decade.[5]

Another contemporary concern was that the tax and social contribution burden would soon reach the limit of what the private sector could support, both from the perspective of what would be perceived as politically acceptable, fair burden-sharing, and in view of its likely adverse impact on employment. The previously mentioned Council of Economic Advisers' report, for example, calculates that taxes and social contributions would soon claim 45 percent of average household gross income.[6] In short, with public expenditures representing almost 50 percent of GDP in 1975, fiscal policy had reached its limits.

This situation created a dilemma for policymakers. On the one hand, general government deficits over 6 percent of GDP could clearly not be sustained over time, so fiscal consolidation was inevitable. Arguably there was also a need to halt or to reverse the trend increase in expenditures experienced during the previous decade. Thus, it would be desirable for fiscal consolidation to go beyond just reversing stimulus measures that had been taken in response to the recession. Moreover, shrinking the size of the public sector would have to be considered. On the other hand, high unemployment called for expansionary demand policies, for which fiscal policy was the primary instrument, consistent with the Keynesian policy assignment of the time. Hence, the need for fiscal consolidation to ensure sustainability clashed with the objective of reducing cyclical unemployment. Further complicating matters, the trend increase in expenditures over the past decade had resulted in large part from an expanded social safety net, which the government meant to preserve, thereby limiting the scope of consolidation.

Another challenge, less apparent at the time but clear with the benefit of hindsight, was that the mid-1970s marked the beginning of a secular slowdown in growth that would impose a sizeable toll on the German economy. This would lead to a reduced ability to generate a sufficient number of jobs and less scope for containing the rise in debt ratios through rapid output growth. While often associated with the oil price shocks, the secular growth slowdown in Germany owed much to a structural change in the composition of Germany's economy, especially the decline in relative importance of the manufacturing sector. High growth in the preceding decades had stemmed from a shift in employment from low-productivity agriculture to high-productivity manufacturing. By the early 1970s, however, the share of employment in manufacturing had peaked. Manufacturing employment was now being absorbed by the service sector, which displayed lower productivity growth resulting in slower economic growth. Germany's labor market institutions, including its social safety net, struggled with this structural change, and would take decades to fully adjust to it. But barely any of this was apparent in 1975.

The 1975 Fiscal Adjustment Plan

The MTFF drafted in the fall of 1975 addressed some but not all of the challenges outlined above. From the government's viewpoint, returning to full employment—which the MTFF defined as an unemployment rate below 3 percent—was the overriding macroeconomic objective. High unemployment in 1975 was seen as cyclical, and economic recovery in 1976 was expected to lead to job creation. Thus, to preserve the recovery, fiscal consolidation was "back-loaded" and set to begin in earnest only in 1977. While the MTFF relied largely on expenditure reduction, it eschewed cuts to priority areas such as social transfers and defense. It also included some measures (detailed ahead) aimed at increasing revenues.

TABLE 4.1 The 1975 Fiscal Consolidation Plan for 1976–79 (federal government, in percent of potential GDP)

	1974 Outturn	1975 Estimate	1976 Budget	1977 Plan	1978 Plan	1979 Plan
Revenues	12.3	11.4	11.0	11.8	12.1	12.2
Cyclical	−0.1	−0.1	0.0	0.0	0.0	0.0
Structural	12.4	11.4	11.0	11.8	12.1	12.2
Expenditures	13.4	14.8	14.3	13.5	13.3	12.9
Primary	12.9	14.3	13.5	12.6	12.4	11.9
Interest	0.4	0.6	0.8	0.9	1.0	1.0
Cyclically adjusted balance	−0.9	−3.4	−3.2	−1.7	−1.3	−0.7
Cyclically adjusted primary balance	−0.5	−2.8	−2.5	−0.8	−0.3	0.2
Output gap (real-time estimate/projection)	−0.9	−0.6	−0.3	−0.1	0.0	0.0

Sources: Federal government MTFFs, Council of Economic Advisers reports; and IMF staff estimates.

At the aggregate level, the consolidation plan envisioned an improvement in the federal government deficit by almost 3 percent of potential GDP between 1975 and 1979 (see Table 4.1). The planned primary improvement was somewhat larger because of the expected increase in the interest burden. Given the underlying growth assumption of the MTFF, the planned federal overall deficit of $^3/_4$ percent of GDP in 1979 would have been sufficient to stabilize the federal debt ratio in the long run at 10 percent of GDP (approximately the 1975 ratio).

Three-fourths of the planned improvement in the deficit were to come from the expenditure side. Here, the MTFF had to account for the fact that pensions and payments to war victims were projected to grow rapidly, and trimming them back would have run counter to political priorities of the Social Democratic Party—the senior partner in the ruling coalition at the time. Excluding pensions and war victim payments, meeting the aggregate target meant that average annual growth for all other primary expenditures could not exceed 2 percent per annum, compared to a projected annual nominal GDP growth rate of 9 percent. The necessary expenditure restraint was front-loaded into 1976 and 1977, with primary spending (excluding pensions and war-related obligations) projected to decline in nominal terms. Nevertheless, projected rapid growth of pension payments in 1976 meant that the overall expenditure-to-GDP ratio would decline moderately.

Besides global expenditure constraint, the 1975 MTFF focused on two areas:

1. Savings related to labor market support, through an increase in the unemployment insurance contribution rate by 1 percentage point and a reduction in federal support for qualification and retraining measures.
2. Public administration savings, through changes to retirement and promotion rules and fringe benefits, as well as public sector wage restraint.

The bulk of the remaining consolidation measures fell on the revenue side—in particular, an increase in the Value Added Tax (VAT) rate by 2 percentage points and a 20 percent increase in tobacco and alcohol excise rates amounting to over 0.75 percentage points of potential GDP. These tax rate increases were to take effect in 1977, after the economic recovery was expected to have taken hold.

Implementation

The consolidation effort remained on track until 1977 (see Table 4.2). In 1976, the cyclically adjusted deficit turned out significantly better than planned on account of better than anticipated revenue performance.[7] In 1977 this revenue overperformance subsided but was still sufficient to compensate for higher than planned expenditures, so that the deficit target was met. In the following years, however, expenditure and deficit targets were missed.

The year 1977 turned out to be an inflection point in the consolidation effort, as the government's priorities and actions switched again to renewed stimulus. The primary reason for this switch was a stubbornly high unemployment rate that had barely come down from its 1975 high. Moreover,

TABLE 4.2 Fiscal Outcomes (differences with respect to 1975 MTFF, in percent of potential GDP)

	1974	1975	1976	1977	1978	1979
Revenues	−0.1	−0.1	0.8	0.4	0.4	0.6
Cyclical	−0.1	−0.5	−0.2	−0.1	0.0	0.3
Structural	0.0	0.4	1.0	0.5	0.4	0.4
Expenditures	−0.1	−0.4	0.0	0.5	1.2	1.8
Primary	−0.1	−0.3	0.2	0.7	1.4	1.9
Interest	0.0	−0.1	−0.2	−0.2	−0.2	−0.2
Cyclically adjusted balance	0.1	0.8	1.0	0.0	−0.8	−1.4
Cyclically adjusted primary balance	0.1	0.7	0.8	−0.3	−1.0	−1.6
Output gap (real-time estimate/ projection)	0.5	−4.1	−1.3	−0.8	0.1	2.0

Sources: Federal government MTFFs, Council of Economic Advisers reports; and IMF staff estimates.

given weak global international growth, there was pressure on Germany to implement a stimulus package as part of an internationally coordinated effort to strengthen the recovery worldwide. In hindsight, however, it is clear that high unemployment reflected not demand deficiencies but structural changes in the economy. Indeed, using the full time series of GDP data through today, we reestimate potential growth for the 1970s, and find it to be a full percentage point lower than projected by the 1975 MTFF.

Overall, this consolidation attempt largely failed. The expenditure targets were missed; revenue targets were met due to reasons unrelated to the consolidation measures. The fiscal consolidation effort, however, did break the upward trend in expenditures; in particular, it halted the continuous increase in transfers and wage expenditures both at the general and federal government level, which had marked the prior decade. The wage bill remained broadly in line with 1975 MTFF targets beyond 1977. A hiring freeze implemented in 1974 and low public employment growth in 1976 and 1977 also contributed to the consolidation. Nonetheless, total spending exceeded targets, owing to the investment stimulus measures.

Overall tax revenues overperformed, especially in 1975 and 1976, but the overperformance largely reflected underestimation of revenue dynamics. Although the legislative passage of tax rate hikes proceeded as planned (with the exception of the VAT rate increase, which was initially rejected by the Bundesrat—the second legislative chamber at the federal level, representing states), excise increases yielded little revenue. Additional stimulus measures, which focused on increasing tax-free income thresholds and improving depreciation allowances, put additional pressure on income taxes.[8]

Observations on the 1975–79 Consolidation Episode

RESPONDING TO UNANTICIPATED CHALLENGES   The weaker than expected recovery and high unemployment upended the consolidation effort. Although the original plan back-loaded the consolidation profile in an attempt to foster the recovery, growth turned out weaker than anticipated and by 1977 the objective of stimulating the economy trumped the consolidation objective. One could speculate an even more back-loaded consolidation profile would have allowed for a stronger recovery in 1976–77, but this seems unlikely, in hindsight, given the clear downward shift in potential growth.

GENERAL OBSERVATIONS   Expenditure-based consolidation was relatively successful. The effort yielded some success on the expenditure side: (i) at an aggregate level, current expenditures in 1979 were only marginally higher than planned (in nominal terms); (ii) the upward trend in the wage bill as a share of GDP was stopped, with a peak 1975; and (iii) labor market-related spending was broadly consistent with the 1975 MTFF. These successes were achieved through specific legislative measures as well as general expenditure discipline. Revenue measures were less successful because they were implemented partially and late (the VAT rate increase) or yielded little revenue (excises).

Deeper expenditure cuts would have required structural reforms. The 1975 MTFF projected a large increase in pension and war-related obligations (which broadly materialized as anticipated). The 1975 consolidation eschewed structural reforms in these areas; instead, it imposed expenditure discipline (including nominal expenditure cuts) in other areas. Given the size of pension and war-related obligations, this strategy had its limits.

The consolidation effort was hindered by lack of political support and insufficient coordination between different government levels. This was evident for the most important revenue measure, the VAT rate increase, which was implemented late (in 1978), because the Bundesrat (representing states) did not go along with the federal government's proposals regarding this measure.

1981–85 Consolidation Attempt

The Challenge

In 1979, the second oil price shock led to a sizeable increase in inflation (which picked up from less than 3 percent in 1978 to over 6 percent in 1981) as well as to the emergence of current account deficits for the first time since 1965. The combination of current account deficits and U.S. interest rate hikes beginning in late 1979, which led to German capital outflows, caused the German mark to depreciate in real terms. In response, the Bundesbank tightened policy. The oil price increases combined with monetary tightening led to a contraction in output between spring 1980 and early 1981, followed by economic stagnation. Thus, in summer/fall 1981, when the 1981 MTFF was drafted, the economic outlook was unfavorable:

- The short-term outlook was marred by: stagnating economic activity, following a yearlong decline; rising unemployment, from already high levels; high inflation; and weak external balances.
- The medium-term outlook was not much better: the upward ratcheting unemployment rate pointed to deeper structural problems; the oil shock introduced another structural challenge by requiring the economy to adjust to higher energy prices and restore competitiveness (i.e., to reduce current account deficits), hence, shifting focus to the supply side.

■ The fiscal position in summer/fall 1981 was weak as well. The rather unsuccessful fiscal consolidation in the 1970s meant that deficits and public debt were at historical highs in 1979, despite the small macroeconomic upswing that followed mid-1970s recession. Fiscal policy for the following two years did aim for a modest consolidation, but the onset of the 1980–81 recession thwarted this effort. As a result, the general government deficit deteriorated to close to 5 percent of GDP in 1981, in part because the federal deficit had widened to about 2.5 percent of GDP, its highest level since 1976. Meanwhile, both general and federal debt ratios had continued to climb steadily upwards.

In sum, the situation in 1981 was similar to that in 1975: both fiscal deficits and unemployment were high, forcing a tradeoff between, on one hand, fiscal consolidation to stabilize debt ratios that had been on the rise for close to a decade; and an expansionary fiscal policy stance, on the other hand, to help reduce unemployment. In a sense, this tradeoff was even starker in 1981, because monetary policy was constrained by high inflation and the weakness of the currency, placing most of the burden for providing demand stimulus on fiscal policy. Another fiscal challenge was the need for structural reforms to match structural changes in the economy. Such need had been less apparent to policymakers in 1975 but was abundantly clear to them in 1981.

The 1981 Fiscal Consolidation Plan

Policymakers' response to the challenges above in 1981 was thus different from their predecessors' reaction in 1975: whereas the 1975 consolidation plan attempted to reconcile the fiscal consolidation/unemployment tradeoff by back-loading the former, the consolidation plan outlined in the 1981 MTFF disavowed any role of demand management for lowering unemployment and focused solely on the consolidation objective. It argued that Germany's unsatisfactory output and employment growth stemmed mostly from the oil price shock and broader structural changes, which could not be addressed through fiscal stimulus. In other words, the economic challenges resided mostly on the supply side and could not be resolved through a demand expansion. Moreover, interest rates were internationally high. Against this background—the German government argued, in its consolidation plan—the best fiscal policy could hope to accomplish was to support private investment. The latter was indispensable for structural change to proceed, by taking pressure off interest rates.

The demotion of aggregate demand management to a secondary objective of fiscal policy marked a significant break with the Keynesian policy assignment. Interestingly, this was not due to a change in government: the governing coalition of Social Democrats and Liberals in the summer/fall of 1981 was the same as in 1977. Rather, it reflected a widespread perception that demand management policies had failed in the second half of the 1970s, as unemployment had remained stubbornly high despite significant fiscal and monetary expansions; instead, the main effect of expansionary policies in many countries seemed to have been an increase in inflation. The experience of advanced economies in the 1970s changed economic thinking not just in Germany but worldwide. In the early 1980s, economic theories such as Monetarism, new classical economics, or real business cycle economics that depict demand management as ineffective or even harmful began to permeate the new mainstream.

A supply-side-oriented economic policy paradigm was also adopted by the majority of members of the Council of Economic Advisers, the preeminent body of outside experts advising the German government in economic affairs. They began to view discretionary demand measures as a source of uncertainty. A consensus emerged that fiscal and monetary policies should be rule-based.[9]

Consistent with the new thinking, the 1981 MTFF aimed for an improvement in the cyclically adjusted balance relative to 1981 by 1.25 percent of potential GDP by 1985 (see Table 4.3). Almost all of the savings would come from expenditure cuts (a reduction in primary expenditures by 1.75 percent of potential GDP in view of the projected rise in the interest burden). The largest savings were to come from reductions in both unemployment benefits and employment creation programs, as well as tighter eligibility rules for benefits and labor market-related subsidies. Other

TABLE 4.3 The 1981 Fiscal Consolidation Plan (in percent of potential GDP)

	1980 Outturn	1981 Prel. Est.	1982 Budget	1983 Plan	1984 Plan	1985 Plan
Revenues	12.6	12.4	12.7	12.5	12.4	12.5
Cyclical	0.1	0.0	0.0	0.0	0.0	0.0
Structural	12.6	12.4	12.7	12.5	12.4	12.5
Expenditures	14.5	14.6	14.3	14.0	13.7	13.4
Primary	13.5	13.5	12.9	12.5	12.1	11.8
Interest	0.9	1.1	1.4	1.5	1.5	1.5
Cyclically adjusted balance	−1.9	−2.1	−1.6	−1.4	−1.3	−0.9
Cyclically adjusted primary balance	−1.0	−1.1	−0.2	0.0	0.2	0.6
Output gap (real-time estimate/projection)	0.4	0.1	0.0	−0.1	0.0	0.0

Sources: Federal government MTFFs, Council of Economic Advisers reports, and IMF staff estimates.

measures focused on cuts to family benefits and the wage bill was to be reined in through a reduction in public employment and basic wages. The overall focus on expenditures, and especially social transfers, stemmed from the intention to improve supply conditions by reducing the size of the state while simultaneously improving expenditure composition. The decrease in unemployment benefits and labor market support also helped to shield the budget from the adverse impact of higher unemployment while reducing labor disincentives. In addition, just as in the 1970s consolidation episode, the government planned to raise the unemployment contribution rate (a reduction in the pension contribution rate was intended to neutralize the impact on taxpayers). The consolidation plan was frontloaded, with most measures taking effect in 1982.

Implementation

In popular perception, the 1981 consolidation plan already failed its first test in 1982 when the headline (cyclically unadjusted) deficit failed to come down from its 1981 level. In cyclically adjusted terms, however, the underperformance was marginal (see Table 4.4), because the poor revenue performance reflected mostly a cyclical deterioration as the economy slipped back into recession and the unemployment rate rose by another 2 percentage points from an already post war historic high in 1981. At the time, it was recognized that the deficit had improved in cyclically adjusted terms—the report of the Council of Economic Advisers, for example, presented the corresponding calculations. Nevertheless, the public focused on the large headline deficit and judged the consolidation effort largely as a failure. This in

TABLE 4.4 Fiscal Outcome (differences vis-à-vis 1981 MTFF, in percent of potential GDP)

	1980	1981	1982	1983	1984	1985
Revenues	0.1	0.0	−0.4	−0.4	−0.3	−0.3
Cyclical	0.1	−0.1	−0.4	−0.4	−0.4	−0.4
Structural	0.0	0.0	0.0	0.1	0.1	0.1
Expenditures	0.1	0.3	0.3	0.0	0.0	0.0
Primary	0.1	0.2	0.3	−0.1	0.0	0.0
Interest	0.0	0.1	−0.1	0.0	0.0	0.0
Overall balance	0.0	−0.3	−0.7	−0.4	−0.3	−0.3
Cyclically adjusted balance	−0.1	−0.2	−0.3	0.1	0.1	0.1
Cyclically adjusted primary balance	−0.1	−0.1	−0.3	0.1	0.1	0.1
Output gap	0.9	−0.6	−3.1	−3.6	−3.0	−3.3

Sources: Federal government MTFFs, Council of Economic Advisers reports, and IMF staff estimates.

turn spurred another consolidation package in the summer of 1982 that redoubled the earlier effort to cut back social transfers.

These successive cuts to social transfers, however, led to fissures within the Social Democratic Party, traditionally the champion of the social welfare state: at a party convention following the 1982 budget, the party confirmed the need for fiscal consolidation, but called for a change in course that would place a greater share of the burden of adjustment on businesses and the wealthy, through tax increases. This created a rift with the Liberals, the junior coalition partner, who wanted instead to ease the tax burden on businesses in order to support investment; given the consolidation goals, this implied even deeper cuts to social benefits. Otto Graf Lambsdorff, a senior Liberal politician and Minister of Economics at the time, defended this approach by arguing that those who called fiscal consolidation "antisocial" failed to realize that this policy was necessary for the renewal of the economic foundation of the German social welfare system.[10] This rift was one of the key factors leading to the breakup of the coalition, with the Liberals defecting to form a coalition government with the Conservatives in the fall of 1982. This new government, led by Chancellor Helmut Kohl, moderately reinforced the consolidation plan of its predecessor with new cuts in social transfers, an increase in the VAT rate, and a broadening of the income tax base. Consistent with previous policy, the burden on businesses was not increased, in order to safeguard supply conditions. In his policy statement upon taking office, Chancellor Kohl noted that the economic situation was critical, and required a balancing act to undertake a convincing fiscal consolidation while preserving an adequate level of aggregate demand.[11] But in stark contrast to the 1970s, fiscal stimulus was not even considered.

The economic recovery finally began to take hold in 1983, even though the unemployment rate climbed further to almost 9 percent in the same year and remained at that level until 1985, followed by modest declines in the following years. In cyclically adjusted terms, fiscal performance turned out in line with the 1981 MTFF from 1983 onwards. On the whole, therefore, the consolidation plan, bolstered by further measures in 1982, successfully met its targets. The improvement in the federal overall deficit was matched by states and municipalities. The trend increase in the debt-to-GDP ratio underway since the early 1970s continued through 1985, but the slope became substantially flatter.

The bulk of the savings eventually came from social transfers, which by 1985 turned out significantly lower than projected by the 1981 MTFF: deeper than planned cuts in family benefits more than offset an overrun in labor market-related expenditures stemming from worse than anticipated unemployment and social transfers were contained by the increase in the pension contribution rate and a postponement of the regular pension increase.

Legislative approval of measures taken during this consolidation episode was smooth, perhaps because social benefit cuts were initiated by a government led by the Social Democratic Party, which had previously championed the expansion of social programs and protected them during the 1970s consolidation episode.

Observations on the 1981–85 Consolidation Episode

RESPONDING TO UNANTICIPATED CHALLENGES   The consolidation effort was off to a poor start in 1982 when the economy slipped unexpectedly back into recession. This presented a similar challenge as in 1977 when the pace of economic recovery fell short of expectations. But the reaction in 1982 was different: instead of resorting to demand stimulus, policymakers reinforced the consolidation effort. In part this reflected a reevaluation of the relative effectiveness of demand and supply policies stemming from a realization that Germany's slower growth and higher unemployment were largely due to structural factors and could not be cured through demand expansion. Moreover, high interest rates in the United States spilled over to Germany, with an adverse impact on investment. In this environment, the 1981 MTFF argued that the best fiscal policy could accomplish was to contribute to lower interest rates by reducing fiscal borrowing requirements. Hence, even when the recession struck unexpectedly, consolidation remained the primary objective.

GENERAL OBSERVATIONS   A wide consensus supported the consolidation, despite the recession/weak recovery. Both the more left-leaning Social Democratic government and its more right-leaning Conservative successor pursued fiscal consolidation vigorously, ensuring swift legislative passage of the necessary measures.

Cuts in the social transfer system helped to make it more sustainable in the long-term. The structural changes in Germany's economy, with the relative decline of industry and simultaneous increase in unemployment, imposed a large burden on the social welfare system, which had not been designed for high and persistent unemployment. Rather, generous unemployment benefits had been intended for an environment of full employment occasionally punctured by sharp recessions. Likewise, the parameters of the pay-as-you-go pension system had been set during times of rapid employment and wage growth. The fiscal measures taken, especially the reduction in unemployment, family, and pension benefits, coupled with contribution rate increases and a broadening of the base, stabilized the financing of the social welfare system during the remainder of the 1980s. Hence, these measures were well targeted to remedy one of the most significant long-term weaknesses in the new low-growth environment.

The tight demand stance was not costless, though the increase in unemployment stemmed largely from structural factors. The unemployment rate in 1985 was almost 5 percentage points higher than in 1980, with a major increase in long-term unemployment during the consolidation period. While there is now a consensus that this increase resulted mainly from structural changes, relatively tight fiscal and monetary conditions may have prolonged the recession somewhat and caused cyclical unemployment to become structural—an interpretation of the facts that was prominent in the mid- and late 1980s. Specifically, it was argued that workers laid off during the recession remained unemployed for a long time and, as a result, trade unions took these unemployed workers' interests less and less into account, eventually setting wages too high to allow for their reemployment even after the recession ended.

1991–95 Consolidation Attempt

The Challenge

The successful fiscal consolidation of the early 1980s stabilized the federal debt ratio at 40 percent of GDP by the end of that decade. German unification, however, would pose major new challenges along several dimensions. It was clear from the outset that unification would be expensive for the public purse: the federal budget for 1991, the first budget year for unified Germany, authorized expenditures by more than 40 percent higher than in 1988, the year prior to the collapse of the Berlin wall. The key question was how to finance this expenditure increase, a critical and hotly debated issue for the federal elections in December 1990, just a few months after unification. Oskar Lafontaine, Social Democratic candidate for Chancellor, argued for income tax increases, especially on middle and upper incomes, while ruling out higher VAT rates in order to prevent a higher tax burden on low-income recipients in East Germany.[12] His opponent, Chancellor Helmut Kohl of the incumbent Conservative/Liberal coalition, ruled out any tax increases for financing German unification. During the campaign, Chancellor Kohl famously suggested that East Germany would be transformed into blooming landscapes ("bluehende Landschaften"), which suggested an economic strength in East Germany that would make tax increases unnecessary.

A subtler but similarly thorny question related to the difficulties in gauging the economic implications of unification and its fiscal costs. This was realized early on: Finance Minister Theo Waigel noted in his policy statement following the electoral victory of the ruling Conservative/Liberal coalition in December 1990 that the situation in the coming years would be exceptional, because of the unprecedented financing needs of unification, the difficulties in planning for this task, and its inevitability in the sense that the pace of unification was not governed by fiscal policy considerations but by the international political situation. Looking beyond fiscal policy, unification affected also macroeconomic developments and created a need for an overhaul of structural policies and institutions.[13]

This section is going to focus on the fiscal consolidation plan contained in the 1991 MTFF, published in the summer of 1991 together with the budget for 1992. At the time of the drafting of the MTFF, unification was still shaping macroeconomic and fiscal developments.

Macroeconomic conditions in 1990 and 1991 were startlingly different in East and West Germany. The East German economy collapsed in the first years after unification, as its structural weaknesses became apparent and were amplified by the adoption of the West German currency at a somewhat overvalued rate.[14] In contrast, macroeconomic conditions in West Germany were buoyant, responding to a demand surge from a newly open East German market as well as an inflow of labor from East Germany. As a result, the unemployment rate declined from 8 percentage points in West Germany in the mid-late 1980s to 6 percentage points in 1991. What was not apparent in 1991, though, was that the boom in West Germany would prove to be short-lived, and with it the fall in unemployment. Poor labor market performance in both East and West Germany would become a major challenge in the following years.

Unification-related government expenditures worsened the general government fiscal balance from a small surplus in 1989 to a deficit of almost 3 percent in 1991. A sizeable part of the expenditure increase was channeled through specially created entities such as the Unity Fund, created to finance the deficits of the new East German states and municipalities. Although these transactions were exchanged from the deficit, government debt increased nonetheless, and the federal government eventually absorbed most of it. Social transfers paid through the social security system ratcheted upwards following unification, reversing most of the consolidation gains of the previous decade. A considerable part of the social transfer burden was reflected in higher federal government transfers.

The 1991 Fiscal Consolidation Plan

Faced with the fiscal challenge of financing unification-related costs, the Conservative/Liberal coalition initially sought to eschew tax increases and to try trimming back the rising deficit through expenditure restraint, as seen in the 1990 MTFF (November 1990). However, despite having campaigned on financing unification without higher taxes, following its electoral victory in December 1990 the Conservative/Liberal coalition agreed to a large revenue package in response to the dire financial situation of the newly created East German states and the need to finance a substantial reconstruction program. This package consisted of a temporary (one-year) income tax surcharge ("solidarity surcharge") and increases in excises and fuel taxes. In addition, the unemployment insurance contribution rate was raised significantly.

The 1991 MTFF built on this revenue package and was premised on a continuation of strong labor market performance in West Germany. Despite these measures (and positive macroeconomic outlook), the projected federal deficit for 1991 still exceeded 2.25 percent of potential GDP in cyclically adjusted terms (see Table 4.5). To close the remaining gap, the 1991 MTFF relied almost entirely on expenditure restraint (excluding unification-related areas). Specifically, it aimed for returning the federal deficit (in cyclically adjusted terms) to less than 1 percent of potential GDP by 1995 (an improvement of 1.5 percent of potential GDP). To accomplish this, the expenditure share in GDP was to be reduced by 2 percent of potential GDP, whereas the revenue share would decline somewhat, with the unwinding of the temporary tax measures taken in 1991 partly compensated by a planned increase in the VAT rate.[15] In sum, the fiscal consolidation strategy was consistent with that used by the Conservative-Liberal coalition during the early 1980s and what it advocated during the 1990 campaign: it avoided increasing the tax burden, especially on businesses, with revenue measures being either temporary or focused on consumption taxes.

TABLE 4.5 The 1991 Fiscal Consolidation Plan (in percent of potential GDP)

	1990 Outturn	1991 Prel. Est.	1992 Budget	1993 Plan	1994 Plan	1995 Plan
Revenues	13.9	11.5	11.7	11.3	11.4	11.1
Cyclical	0.2	0.1	0.0	0.0	0.0	0.0
Structural	13.7	11.5	11.7	11.3	11.4	11.1
Expenditures	12.9	13.8	13.3	12.7	12.2	11.8
Primary	11.4	12.3	11.8	11.1	10.7	10.2
Interest	1.4	1.4	1.4	1.5	1.5	1.6
Cyclically adjusted balance	0.8	−2.3	−1.6	−1.3	−0.8	−0.7
Cyclically adjusted primary balance	2.2	−0.9	−0.1	0.2	0.7	0.9
Output gap (real-time estimate/projection)	1.3	0.6	0.2	0.0	0.1	0.2

Sources: Federal government MTFFs, Council of Economic Advisers reports; and IMF staff estimates.

Notes: Data for 1991 and beyond are for the united Germany, whereas 1990 represents West Germany only (comparable data for East Germany is unavailable). It should be noted that the 1990 revenue share overstates the revenue potential, because the 1991 MTFF underestimated West German GDP for this year and West German revenue collection benefited substantially from the unification boom.

The 1991 MTFF envisioned reducing federal expenditures in GDP terms in most budget areas. From a functional perspective, the two single-largest expenditure savings were in defense and social spending (together accounting for half of the total consolidation):

- Defense spending was to be lowered by 0.5 percent of GDP through the reduction in the armed forces of the unified Germany to 370,000 troops and lower costs of accommodating foreign armed forces.
- Social spending, which accounted for one-third of total federal government outlays in 1990, was expected to decline by 0.5 percent of GDP by 1995, despite the fact that unification itself would raise social spending. For example, pension benefits in East Germany would have to be harmonized with those in West Germany, creating sizeable deficits in the pension insurance system that would require higher federal transfers. Savings were expected from a planned nominal reduction in transfers to the unemployment insurance system (accomplished through the previously mentioned increase in the contribution rate and premised on strong labor market performance in West Germany). Constrained growth in war victim payments was another source of savings.

Implementation

The federal balance turned out to be better than expected in 1991 and 1992 but worse than the 1991 MTFF objective in 1993, with higher than planned deficits persisting in 1994 and 1995 (see Table 4.6).

TABLE 4.6 Fiscal Outcome (differences vis-à-vis 1991 MTFF, in percent of potential GDP)

	1990	1991	1992	1993	1994	1995
Revenues	−0.9	0.3	0.5	0.3	0.7	0.3
Cyclical	−0.2	0.1	0.1	−0.2	0.0	0.0
Structural	−0.7	0.2	0.3	0.5	0.7	0.3
Expenditures	−0.8	−0.2	0.2	0.9	1.3	1.1
Primary	−0.7	−0.2	0.2	0.9	1.2	1.0
Interest	−0.1	0.0	0.0	0.0	0.0	0.1
Cyclically adjusted balance	0.1	0.3	0.2	−0.5	−0.6	−0.7
Cyclically adjusted primary balance	0.0	0.3	0.2	−0.5	−0.5	−0.6
Output gap (real-time estimate/projection)	−1.1	0.8	1.2	−1.6	−0.3	−0.1

Sources: Federal government MTFFs, Council of Economic Advisers reports; and IMF staff estimates.

The main culprit for the overrun in 1993 was the onset of a deep recession, which put an end to the premise of strong labor market performance in West Germany: in 1993 federal labor market related expenditures substantially exceeded projections, accounting for most of the expenditure overrun.[16] In essence, the government allowed the automatic stabilizers to work during the recession and the overall deficit widened in GDP terms. If the increase in unemployment had been purely cyclical, this would not have been a fundamental setback to the consolidation effort, but it was not: unemployment remained high in the following years.

The other factor hampering the consolidation effort was unexpectedly high unification costs. Social transfer spending increased markedly but remained broadly within the parameters of the 1991 MTFF. Spending by entities outside the federal government such as the Unity Fund, however, exceeded expectations widely. This affected the federal budget in two ways. First, its direct contributions, especially to the Unity Fund, rose to a level almost twice as high as planned. Second, the federal government eventually became responsible for servicing the debt of these entities, which in 1995 totaled more than 9 percent of GDP and implied debt servicing costs of 0.75 percent of GDP annually. The largest part of this debt stemmed from the restructuring and privatization of East German public enterprises; while originally expected to yield a profit, the organization responsible for this task, the Treuhandanstalt, left a debt stock of 7 percent of GDP when it ceased operations in 1994. The federal government taking over the resulting debt service was part of a broader agreement, the Solidarity Pact, among different levels of government on sharing the costs of unification. It also entailed a change in the VAT revenue sharing formula, in which the federal government ceded part of its share to the states in order to help them pay for their portion of unification costs. To compensate the federal government partially, the income tax surcharge ("solidarity surcharge") that was temporarily in effect in 1991–92 was permanently reintroduced.

Observations on the 1991–95 Consolidation Episode

RESPONDING TO UNANTICIPATED CHALLENGES The 1991 MTFF was based on the premise that unification would usher in strong growth, initially in West Germany, but eventually also in East Germany. This did not happen. Growth in West Germany was strong initially, but mostly demand driven and therefore not sustainable. In fact, the demand boom led to a real appreciation, which weakened competitiveness and growth in the medium-term. The misjudgment of growth spilled over to the labor market assessment: the 1991 MTFF mistook the decline in West German unemployment in 1990 and 1991 as a structural improvement whereas it was only cyclical. Rigidities in the labor market kept West German structural unemployment high and hindered adjustment in the East. Even as the structural weakness of the German labor market became apparent in 1993, the response was limited to providing more generous tax incentives to businesses in order to support growth. At the same time, further expenditure measures were taken, especially as part of the 1994 budget (e.g., wage freeze and staff reductions), to keep the deficit under control. On the revenue side, social contribution rates rose, while the Solidarity Pact led to the reintroduction of the income tax surcharge, among other measures. The increase in the revenue burden arguably aggravated the problems in the labor market.

GENERAL OBSERVATIONS   There was insufficient public or political support for a realignment of the role of the state. A structural labor market reform would have required a fundamental reevaluation of the role of the German social safety net. In the early 1990s, there was little appetite for such reform. This reflected in part the loss of a majority by the governing coalition in the Bundesrat in 1991, because the Social Democratic opposition, which exerted influence on the Bundesrat during the 1990s, was traditionally the champion of the German welfare state. In fact, modest structural reforms undertaken by the Conservative government in the 1990s were initially rolled back when the opposition took power in 1998.

Revenue-based consolidation would ultimately prove less sustained. The increase in social contribution rates and direct taxes reduced work incentives. This interpretation is supported by noting that the most dynamic parts of the labor market in the 1990s were those not (or only in part) subject to mandatory social contributions (i.e., part-time and self-employment). Corporate and personal income tax rates related to business income were lowered in 1994 to bolster growth. However, these measures were intended to provide additional incentives for business investment, thereby aiming for capital-intensive growth whereas Germany would have needed more labor-intensive growth.

Fiscal consolidation proved not to be the overriding policy objective. The need for large unification-related expenditures clashed with the consolidation objective. At the federal government level, this was temporarily addressed by assigning expenditure responsibilities to entities operating outside the federal government, but the debt burden created by these entities eventually had to be serviced by the federal government. At a more fundamental level, unification was an exceedingly complex undertaking that went beyond economic policy. In this light, it is actually impressive how successful the consolidation effort was and how tenaciously the government pursued this objective with a string of measures implemented in 1991–95.

2003–07 Consolidation Attempt

The Challenge

Poor economic performance, already a major factor underlying the failure of the early 1990s consolidation episode to reach its objectives, continued for the remainder of the decade: real GDP growth averaged less than 2 percent in the second half of the 1990s, and the average unemployment rate exceeded 10 percent over the same period. A Social Democratic/Green Coalition gained power in 1998. Oskar Lafontaine, the newly installed Finance Minister, saw insufficient aggregate demand as the root cause for low growth and high unemployment and consequently championed a demand expansion while reversing some of the structural reforms initiated by the previous Conservative/Liberal coalition. After failing to find support for his policies, he resigned in early 1999. This gave Chancellor Gerhard Schroeder an opening to pursue supply-side-oriented reforms, including a wide-ranging overhaul of Germany's income tax system to boost potential growth. The last was planned to take effect in stages between 1999 and 2005 and centered on statutory rate cuts, especially for business income.[17] Despite these reforms, growth slowed down markedly in the early 2000s. By 2003, the year in which the consolidation plan was drafted that is at the center of this section, the economy had effectively stagnated for three years.

An important factor underlying the poor growth and labor market performance was the rigidity of the labor market stemming from features such as generous long-term unemployment benefits. Structural changes in the economy—resulting from the transition of East Germany's economy and the decline in manufacturing employment—required an adjustment of relative wages to allow other sectors to absorb released labor. This was a task German labor market institutions struggled with. The key obstacle was that absorbing relatively low skilled labor or labor with skills that are not easily transferred to non-manufacturing sectors meant that their relative wage had to decline, but this was hindered by generous unemployment benefits. However, lowering these benefits ran counter to a social consensus that preferred income equality; it also posed a question of fairness, because many unemployed had paid taxes and made contributions to unemployment insurance for decades.

Low growth and high unemployment also had an adverse impact on the budget: the general government deficit breached the fiscal deficit limit of 3 percent of GDP under the Stability and Growth Pact in 2002. Part of this was cyclical, as the German economy had entered into an outright recession in the second half of 2001. But even considering a longer time period when the average output gap was close to zero, such as the years 1996 to 2002, general government deficits were high, averaging 2.5 percent of GDP. In sum, the set of challenges in the fall of 2003 was similar to that of fall 1981: the economy, especially the labor market, was beset by structural problems and fiscal deficits were high, necessitating fiscal consolidation.

The 2003 Fiscal Consolidation Plan

The 2003 MTFF combined fiscal consolidation with a short-term stimulus as well as a far-reaching structural reform agenda, commonly referred to as Agenda 2010:

- With respect to the planned fiscal consolidation, the overall objective was to reach a balanced budget over the medium-term (see Table 4.7). This objective had already guided the previous two MTFFs, but for the 2003 MTFF the task had become more difficult—and the consolidation need larger—because of weak growth and its impact on the budget. In cyclically adjusted terms, the federal deficit was expected to increase in 2004 on account of the short-term stimulus, but afterwards the MTFF planned to reduce the deficit to below 0.5 percent of GDP by 2007, an improvement of 1 percent of GDP from the 2004 peak. Almost all of this improvement would come from the expenditure side. Although the MTFF focused on the federal government level, the German government had the obligation to bring the general government deficit below 3 percent of GDP as part of the Stability and Growth Pact. The stability

TABLE 4.7 The 2003 Fiscal Consolidation Plan (in percent of potential GDP)

	2002 Outturn	2003 Prel. Est.	2004 Budget	2005 Plan	2006 Plan	2007 Plan
Revenues	10.2	10.5	9.8	10.0	9.9	10.0
Cyclical	-0.1	0.0	0.0	0.0	0.0	0.0
Structural	10.3	10.6	9.8	10.0	9.9	10.0
Expenditures	11.7	11.4	11.2	10.9	10.6	10.4
Primary	10.0	9.6	9.5	9.1	8.8	8.6
Interest	1.7	1.7	1.7	1.8	1.8	1.8
Cyclically adjusted balance	−1.4	−0.8	−1.4	−0.9	−0.6	−0.4
Cyclically adjusted primary balance	0.3	0.9	0.3	0.9	1.1	1.4
Output gap (real-time estimate/projection)	−0.8	−0.4	−0.1	0.0	0.0	0.0

Sources: Federal government MTFFs, Council of Economic Advisers reports, and IMF staff estimates.

and convergence program submitted by the German government in December 2003 aimed for the deficit to fall below 3 percent of GDP in 2005, declining further to 1.5 percent of GDP in 2007, the endpoint of the projection.

- The MTFF planned to support the economic recovery by providing stimulus in 2004 through a reduction in income tax rates. Such stimulus was in contrast with the approach taken during the successful consolidation in the early 1980s. Without this stimulus—planned at 0.75 percent of GDP—the general government deficit could have declined below 3 percent of GDP already in 2004.[18] In a policy statement on the Agenda 2010, Chancellor Gerhard Schroeder presented the stimulus and structural reforms as mutually complementary. Without structural reforms, the demand impulse would dissipate quickly, whereas structural reforms would be ineffectual without support for the recovery from the demand side.[19] The fiscal cost of the stimulus was limited to 2004, as the reduction in income tax rates represented the final stage of the previously mentioned larger tax reform package that otherwise would have taken effect a year later, in 2005.

- The Agenda 2010 structural reforms tackled rigidities in the labor market as well as demographic pressures on the pension system. These two issues were linked, as a possible policy response to an aging society would involve increases in the pension contribution rate, which in turn would hinder employment creation. The MTFF aimed at maintaining the pension contribution rate at its current level while reducing federal transfers. The labor market reforms were based on recommendations of the Hartz Commission. The most significant of these was Hartz IV, the final reform stage scheduled to take effect in 2005. Prior to the reform, the newly unemployed received a generous replacement ratio for a limited time followed by somewhat less generous but open-ended assistance. The Hartz IV reforms shortened the maximum duration of unemployment benefits for the newly unemployed and merged the open-ended assistance with welfare benefits. For the long-term unemployed with formerly high-paying jobs, this reform led to a deep cut in benefits. The pension reform aimed at reducing pressure on the social security system through the introduction of a "sustainability" factor whereby the annual increase in pensions would be lowered if the relative number of pensioners to contributors were to increase.[20] Other measures included an increase in the statutory retirement age, elimination of early retirement clauses, and tighter rules for calculating imputed pension contributions.

- Finally, expenditure cuts tackled both fringe benefits (such as Christmas-related extra payments) in public administration and subsidies for residential construction, coal mining, and agriculture.

Implementation

In cyclically adjusted terms, the overall balance in 2007 missed the 2003 MTFF target by only 0.25 percent of potential GDP (see Table 4.8). Structural revenues exceeded their MTFF target in 2007 by a considerable margin, mostly as a result of a large increase in the VAT rate that took effect in January 2007, a tax policy measure not envisaged under the 2003 MTFF. This VAT rate increase was instrumental in compensating for expenditure overruns between 2005 and 2007. These stemmed from higher than expected costs of labor market reform to the federal budget.

The Agenda 2010 structural reforms aimed to bolster growth and improve labor market performance. Initially, growth disappointed, picking up only toward the end of the projection period. Nevertheless, labor market performance was impressive after the final round of labor market reforms took effect in 2005. One effect was a boost to labor supply, as former welfare recipients returned to the labor force, which led to an initial jump in the unemployment rate in 2005 (IMF Country Report No. 06/16). Labor demand responded eventually, and unemployment had dropped by 2007 to its lowest level since the unification boom. The resilience of the labor market during the 2008–10 recession also points to the effectiveness of these reforms.

The reforms paid off also in terms of improved general government finances, especially those of the social security system, whose expenditures declined by 3 percent of GDP between 2003 and 2007. Together with the consolidation effort at both the federal and state levels, this was the key factor for the substantial improvement in the overall general government

TABLE 4.8 Fiscal Outcome (differences vis-à-vis 2003 MTFF, in percent of potential GDP)

	2002 Outturn	2003 Prel. Est.	2004 Budget	2005 Plan	2006 Plan	2007 Plan
Revenues	0.1	−0.6	−0.4	0.0	0.0	0.6
Cyclical	0.1	−0.1	−0.2	−0.2	0.0	0.1
Structural	0.0	−0.5	−0.3	0.2	0.1	0.5
Expenditures	0.1	0.3	0.0	0.4	0.6	0.8
Primary	0.1	0.3	0.0	0.6	0.8	1.0
Interest	0.0	−0.1	−0.1	−0.2	−0.2	−0.2
Cyclically adjusted balance	−0.1	−0.7	−0.2	−0.2	−0.5	−0.3
Cyclically adjusted primary balance	−0.1	−0.8	−0.3	−0.4	−0.7	−0.5
Output gap (real-time estimate/projection)	0.6	−1.3	−1.7	−2.3	−0.4	1.0

Sources: Federal government MTFFs, Council of Economic Advisers reports, and IMF staff estimates.

balance, which was close to zero in 2007. As a result, the general government debt ratio stabilized in 2006 and began to decline slightly in 2007.

Considering individual expenditure measures, the 2003 MTFF envisioned significant expenditure savings from labor market reforms, but in reality these turned out to be somewhat costly for the federal budget.[21] The reduction in transfers to the pension insurance system was achieved, though the pension contribution rate had to be raised slightly. On the whole, far-reaching pension reforms undertaken in 2003–07 were considered to be effective in addressing most of the demographic pressures. Other cost-cutting objectives were attained, as the public administration wage bill in 2007 turned out smaller than planned, and subsidies were reduced as intended.

Observations on the 2003–07 Consolidation Episode

RESPONDING TO UNANTICIPATED CHALLENGES The unexpected high cost of labor market reforms to the federal budget was the most significant challenge to this last consolidation effort. The government compensated for the overrun by raising the VAT rate substantially. One could argue that such a substantial revenue measure ran against the spirit of an expenditure-based consolidation. However, after 15 years of more or less continuous expenditure restraint, the scope for additional expenditure measures was probably limited, especially on the consumption side. By 2007, federal spending on wages and goods and services in GDP terms had declined by almost 30 percent since unification to its lowest level since at least 1970. Also, since part of the additional VAT revenue was used to finance a reduction in unemployment contribution rates, this meant that this revenue measure did lower the tax burden on labor and therefore was consistent with the overall thrust of the reforms.

GENERAL OBSERVATIONS The observations for the 2003–07 consolidation episode bear similarities to those of the 1980s episode:

- As in the 1980s, the consolidation objective was not perceived as clashing with other fiscal objectives. The 2003 MTFF provided for some fiscal stimulus in 2004 in response to weak economic conditions, but the corresponding fiscal costs were small. Moreover, as in the 1980s, fiscal consolidation was seen as conducive to bolstering potential growth.
- The large structural reform component, especially labor market reform, was critical to meeting the plan's objectives. While labor market reforms turned out costly for the federal budget, they lowered expenditures at the general government level.

- Political fortune was indispensable to the outcome. The Hartz reforms were politically controversial, because the reduction in long-term unemployment benefits undercut the decades-old German social welfare model. For these reforms to become politically viable, and to attract the necessary legislative majorities, it was helpful that a Social Democratic-led government initiated them, because as the traditional defender of the German welfare state, its leadership of these reforms removed the most likely source of opposition. This in itself was possible only due to unusual intra-party circumstances involving the resignation of Oskar Lafontaine as Finance Minister, which tilted the balance in favor of the reform.

The distinctive feature of this episode, however, was a conscious effort to contain the tax burden on labor, so as to boost employment and potential growth. In particular, policymakers eschewed significant increases in social contribution rates, in contrast to all previous episodes. Moreover, the consolidation effort took place in the wake of a comprehensive tax reform initiated in 2000, and reduced both personal and corporate income tax rates while broadening the base.

Lessons

Our analysis of past attempts at large fiscal adjustment points to significant lessons. These seem relevant for future consolidation attempts not only in Germany, but in other countries as well. Key lessons include the following.

Shocks to economic growth have major implications for consolidation attempts and their outcomes. One example is the 1970s episode, which began while the economy was still mired by recession, and ultimately failed because policymakers perceived that further consolidation would hamper the recovery. Another example is the impact of the unexpected 1993 recession on the 1990s consolidation effort: sticking to the consolidation target would have meant the government had to counteract the automatic stabilizers. The government chose, probably wisely, to allow the automatic stabilizers to work and the overall deficit to widen. In the 1980s episode, the government took a different approach and continued fiscal consolidation even as the economy slipped unexpectedly into recession in 1982, with the structural improvement in the balance broadly offsetting the impact of the automatic stabilizers. Arguably, the resulting prolonged economic weakness contributed via hysteresis effects to the permanent upward ratcheting of unemployment during this period.

Eliminating a large fiscal deficit involves a realignment of the role of government. This is illustrated by comparing the relatively successful episodes of the 1980s and 2000s with the largely unsuccessful attempts of the 1970s and 1990s. In the 1980s episode, the role of fiscal policy as a tool for active demand management was abandoned; in contrast to the 1970s, this made it possible to implement consolidation despite weak economic conditions. In the 2000s episode, the government significantly downgraded the scope of social protection provided by the state, especially for the long-term unemployed, whose benefits were cut down to the level of social welfare benefits. This tackled persistently high unemployment especially for low-skilled workers and yielded sizeable fiscal benefits at the general government level. The 1990s episode, in contrast, did not address the issue whether West German norms such as generous provisions for social protection were workable for East Germany. Even though the 1990s consolidation effort succeeded in keeping the fiscal burden from unification manageable, the failure to implement more fundamental reforms came with a sizeable fiscal cost.

Unexpected challenges were overcome when the necessary policy adjustment was consistent with other fiscal policy objectives and was politically feasible:

- A comparison of the consolidation attempts in the 1970s and 1980s demonstrates the importance of consolidation being consistent with other policy objectives. Both attempts had to confront weaker than expected economic conditions. In the 1970s, this led to the abandonment of the consolidation effort, whereas in the 1980s the consolidation effort was redoubled. The difference between these two episodes was that in the 1970s episode the consolidation objective was seen as clashing with a need to respond to weak demand with a stimulus, whereas perception of the appropriate role of fiscal policy had changed by the 1980s.
- The importance of political feasibility is illustrated by a comparison between the 1990s and 2000s episodes. In the 1990s, labor market performance turned out weaker than expected, but structural labor market reform was not attempted. The government, after having lost control of the Bundesrat, did not have the necessary legislative and political support for such reforms. It would take until the 2000s for these reforms to become politically feasible, and even then it took some good political fortune.

More generally, the experience of past consolidations illustrates that risks are substantial: economic conditions may weaken and conflicting objectives may appear. This suggests that, in designing adjustment plans, important elements to consider include a reasonable buffer in the event such risks materialize and an explanation of the extent to which economic downturns would be temporarily accommodated; moreover, the plans' successful implementation importantly depends on political commitment to persevere with and to reinforce economic reforms and consolidation into the medium-term.

Acknowledgments

The authors are grateful to Alfred Boss, Kai Carstensen, Ashoka Mody, Mauricio Villafuerte, and the editor for their support and helpful comments.

Notes .

1. For example, the 1975 MTFF was prepared in the fall of 1975 and covered the period of 1976–1979 with the budget plan for year 1976 being legally binding and the plan for 1977–1979 being indicative. A detailed explanation of the Federal Budget System in Germany can be found at http://www.bundesfinanzmi nisterium.de/nn_4516/DE/BMF__Startseite/Service/Downloads/Abt__II/001, templateId=raw,property=publicationFile.pdf.

2. A background paper providing more detailed discussion of each of these attempts is available from the authors upon request.

3. The cyclically adjusted balance is computed based on a real-time output gap esti- mate for each MTFF, using the standard 0-1 elasticity approach (i.e., expenditures are assumed to be unrelated to the economic cycle, whereas revenues are as- sumed to respond proportionately to percent changes in output). See, for exam- ple, Fedelino and others (2009). The output gap estimate is derived using a standard Hodrick-Prescott filter with data available to policymakers at that time: in other words, the real GDP series used for the filter is based on real-time data: considering the 1975 MTFF as an example, historic real GDP for the period 1950– 74 is taken from the Council of Economic Advisers Report published in fall 1975, the same year the 1975 MTFF was formulated; real GDP for the years 1975–79 is based on assumptions published in the MTFF itself; the projected average real GDP growth rate in the MTFF is used to create a long-term forecast for the next ten years. Taken together, this procedure creates a real-time estimate of real GDP for the years 1950 to 1989. The Hodrick-Prescott filter is then applied to this series. The procedure is then repeated for the next MTFF.

4. See IMF Staff Report 1975–76, p. 94 and p. 106.

5. Moreover, the public debt discussion in contemporary documents was framed in nominal terms, which implied a doubling of public debt in the same period. See, for example, IMF Staff Report 1975–76, p. 106.

6. See IMF Staff Report 1975–76, p. 137.

7. This did not stem from revenue measures but an underestimation of the revenue dynamism in the MTFF (see IMF Staff Report 1977–78, p. 88).

8. On stimulus measures, see IMF Staff Report 1977–78, p. 88 and p. 91.

9. In the context of 1981 this meant that (i) the expansion of money supply should be kept in line with potential growth and refrain from expansionary impulses; (ii) fiscal policy should abstain from trying to stimulate demand beyond the stimulus already in place; and (iii) wage negotiations between employers and unions should aim at reducing wage pressures in order to support employment creation.

10. Following the Social Democratic Party convention in spring 1982, Lambsdorff published a position paper outlining detailed proposals for tax cuts benefitting mostly businesses while reducing social benefits. The full quote in German reads: "Wir stehen vor einer wichtigen Wegkreuzung. Wer einer auf die Bekaempfung der Arbeitslosigkeit gerichtete Sparpolitik als 'soziale Demontage' oder gar als 'unsozial' diffamiert, verkennt, dass sie in Wirklichkeit der Gesundung und Erneuerung des wirtschaftlichen Fundaments fuer unser Sozialsystem dient." Lambsdorff position paper, 1982, p. 9.

11. Protocol (Deutscher Bundestag, 9. Wahlperiode, 121. Sitzung, 7218).

12. Speech by Oskar Lafontaine, September 20, 1990, p. 12.

13. IMF Occasional Paper No. 75, edited by Leslie Lipschitz and Donogh McDonald, "German unification: economic issues," 1990.

14. The conversion rate was 1:2 (i.e., 2 units of the East German currency were exchanged against 1 DM), compared to a rate of 1:3 prevailing prior to currency union.

15. The plan included a 1 percentage point increase in the standard VAT rate from January 1993 to compensate for the revenue loss from the expiration of the solidarity levy.

16. See IMF Staff Report 1993/94, p. 159. In principle, the computation of cyclically adjusted balances could correct for the effect of unemployment benefits on the budget. However, the tables in this chapter use the standard simplifying assumption that expenditures are unrelated to the cycle. Adjusting unemployment benefits for the cycle would be complicated in view of difficulties to distinguish between cyclical and structural unemployment and the uncertain correlation between unemployment and the output gap.

17. See IMF Staff Country Report No. 99/129 and IMF Staff Country Report No. 00/141 for a discussion of policies in the first phase of the Social Democratic–led government.

18. See 2003-04 stability and convergence program (http://ec.europa.eu/economy_finance/sgp/convergence/programmes/2003-04_en.htm), p. 29.

19. Policy statement delivered by Chancellor Schroeder to parliament, transcript, March 14, 2003, p. 9.

20. The operation of the "sustainability" factor had to be suspended already in 2005, because applying the factor would have led to a reduction in nominal pensions, which was not foreseen by the legislation. In 2005, a new government agreed to strengthen pension reform further. In 2007, additional legislation was passed that raised the statutory retirement age and mandated catching up with the suspended operation of the "sustainability" factor beginning in 2011.

21. The 2003 MTFF projected labor market–related expenditures to decline from 1 percent of GDP in 2004 (the cyclical high of spending) to 0.5 percent of GDP by 2007, whereas actual 2007 expenditures stood at 1.25 percent. The main culprit was the Hartz IV reform, which led to a jump in federal spending in 2005 by more than 0.75 percent of GDP. In part, the underestimation of the cost of the Hartz IV reform likely reflects that during the summer of 2003, when the 2003 MTFF was developed, not all details of the reform package were known. In addition, administration of the new benefit proved more difficult than expected (not least because federal and local administrations had to be merged). See IMF Country Report No. 06/16 and IMF Country Report No. 06/438.

CHAPTER 5

United Kingdom: Four Chancellors Facing Challenges

Toni Ahnert, Richard Hughes, and Keiko Takahashi

Introduction

The last three decades have seen a series of attempts to plan and deliver large fiscal adjustments in the United Kingdom. While these attempts were typically triggered by a need to stabilize macroeconomic conditions and curb the growth of public debt, they were often sustained by a commitment on the part of the Government to shrink the state, cut marginal tax rates, and stimulate private sector activity. Those Chancellors of the Exchequer who managed to deliver on their promises typically took a comprehensive and multiyear approach to consolidation planning and focused on deep reforms delivering a long-lasting impact. The implementation of these plans was supported by binding medium-term budget frameworks that included a reasonable buffer in the event of adverse shocks. A modicum of good luck with respect to macroeconomic developments was also important, particularly in the early years of the plans.

This chapter looks at four major fiscal adjustment plans presented by the U.K. government over the past 30 years—two of which met their stated objectives and two of which did not. The aim is to identify the factors that contributed to the plans' success or failure, including:

- *Macroeconomic factors*, such as developments in economic growth and inflation relative to levels forecast in the initial plan
- *Fiscal policy factors*, such as the relative contribution of revenue increases, expenditure cuts, and asset sales to the consolidation effort;

115

and the distribution of expenditure cuts across different economic categories, sectors, and levels of government
- *Institutional factors,* such as the fiscal forecasting, budget planning, and
expenditure control regimes in place at the time

The chapter concludes by identifying ten lessons from the United
Kingdom's experience with large fiscal adjustments over the past three
decades.

Selection of Consolidation Plans

The four consolidation plans examined in this chapter are:

1. *The 1980 Medium-Term Financial Strategy* or MTFS (covering Fiscal
   Year (FY)1980–FY1983[1]) presented by Chancellor Geoffrey Howe following the Conservatives' election victory in May 1979
2. *The 1984 Budget* (covering FY1984–FY1988) presented by new Chancellor Nigel Lawson following the Conservatives' reelection in June
   1983
3. *The November 1993 Budget* (covering FY1994–FY1998) presented by
   new Chancellor Kenneth Clarke following the Conservatives' reelection
   in April 1992
4. *The 2007 Pre-Budget Report and Comprehensive Spending Review*
   or PBR-CSR (covering FY2008–FY2012) presented by new Chancellor
   Alistair Darling soon after the June 2007 beginning of Gordon Brown's
   Prime Ministership

Of the four planned consolidations, two (Lawson's 1984 Budget and
Clarke's 1993 Budget) met or exceeded their stated deficit reduction objectives while two (Howe's 1980 MTFS and Darling's 2007 PBR-CSR) failed to
deliver their envisaged reduction in public borrowing.

The criteria for choosing these four fiscal adjustment plans as the basis
for analysis are:

- All four events were preceded by a period of sustained fiscal deficits (as
in 1979 and 1983) or large deterioration in the fiscal balance (as in 1993
and 2007) as shown in Figure 5.1. This made consolidation of the public
finances the overarching imperative for fiscal policymakers.
- All selected plans presented a comprehensive, detailed, multiyear
fiscal strategy aimed at returning the public finances to a sustainable
position. This allows for a detailed comparison between what was
planned and what was delivered over the period covered by these
strategies.

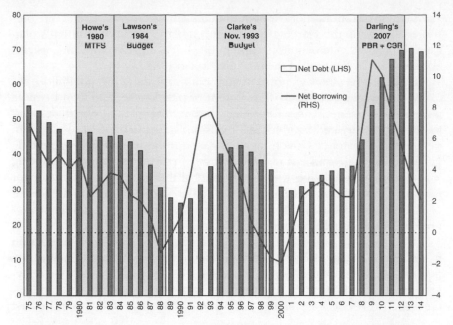

FIGURE 5.1 Public Sector New Borrowing and Debt in the United Kingdom (in percent of GDP)

■ These consolidation strategies were presented by new Chancellors of the Exchequer under newly elected or recently reelected governments. These strategies therefore stand out from other budgets, autumn statements, pre-budget reports, and spending reviews as moments when fiscal policy was (or was meant to be) substantially reoriented.

Background, Content, and Performance of the Four Adjustment Plans

This section outlines the macroeconomic background to, and motivation for, each of the plans; summarizes their content, in terms of composition of the adjustment and general strategy; and reviews their overall performance.

Geoffrey Howe's 1980 Medium-Term Financial Strategy (FY1980–83)

Geoffrey Howe's 1980 MTFS followed a decade of high inflation, rising unemployment, sluggish growth, deteriorating competitiveness, and persistent fiscal deficits. This period of economic and social turmoil saw the incumbent Labour government approach the International Monetary Fund (IMF) for a £2.3 billion loan in 1976 and culminated in a series of strikes during the 1978–79 "Winter of Discontent," which paved the way for Margaret Thatcher and the Conservatives' election victory in the spring of 1979. The MTFS, presented alongside the March 1980 Budget, was the new government's plan for returning the macroeconomy and public finances to a stable and sustainable position by the time of the next election in 1983.

Howe's 1980 plan was novel in both philosophy and format. Philosophically, it represented a decisive rejection of past Labour and Conservative governments' attempts at Keynesian fine-tuning of aggregate demand through monetary and fiscal levers. It was replaced by the strict monetarism of the early Thatcher Government, which emphasized steadily reducing government borrowing as a means of reining in the money supply, reducing inflation, and stimulating the supply side of the economy. This stronger medium-term orientation to fiscal policy-making was reflected in the format of the 1980 budget, which for the first time set out macroeconomic projections and fiscal targets for four years ahead.

The planned 5.4 percent of Gross Domestic Product (GDP) reduction in the Public Sector Borrowing Requirement (PSBR) from a deficit of 4.8 percent of GDP to a surplus of 0.6 percent over four years was to be delivered by a combination of real reductions in public expenditure and increases in revenue (see Figure 5.2). Somewhat surprisingly for the first

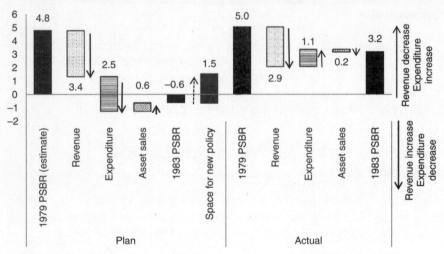

FIGURE 5.2 Geoffrey Howe's 1980 Budget Planned vs. Actual Fiscal Adjustment (in percent of GDP)

Notes: The figure shows that the government planned to bring the public sector borrowing requirement (PSBR) from 4.8 percent of GDP in 1979 to a surplus of 0.6 percent of GDP in 1983, by increasing revenues by 3.4 percent of GDP compared with 1979, cutting expenditures by 2.5 percent of GDP, and allowing a decline in revenues from asset sales by 0.6 percent of GDP. This would leave room for further spending increases or revenue cuts by 2.1 percent of GDP.

fiscal strategy produced by the Thatcher government, nearly two-thirds of the envisaged fiscal adjustment came from higher revenue, though the bulk of this was expected to come from an increase in the volumes and prices of North Sea oil.[2] The plan also foresaw real cuts in expenditure of around 1 percent per year over the four years of the plan, to be delivered by a large nominal cut in investment expenditure and a real freeze in wages, benefits, and other current expenditures. Asset sales or privatizations played little part in this early phase of the Thatcher government.[3] These revenue and expenditure measures were expected to create space for tax cuts or spending increases in future budgets, equivalent to 2.1 percent of GDP (labeled "Space for new policy" in the left-hand panel of Figure 5.2).

Howe's 1980 Budget failed to deliver much of its envisaged reduction in public borrowing. While he managed to collect most of the planned increase in revenue, real expenditure actually increased over the four-year period. Expenditure overruns occurred across the public sector from interest payments and social security, to salaries and subsidies, to public enterprises—a systematic loss of control that was later attributed to the government's brief experiment with volume-based expenditure planning and control. Despite the introduction of additional expenditure cuts and revenue increases in the November 1980 Autumn Statement and March 1981 Budget, large expenditure overruns, amounting to nearly 4 percent of GDP over the four years, could not be avoided.[4] Therefore, against the targeted improvement in the overall balance of 5.4 percent of GDP (excluding space for new policy), the net result was only a 1.8 percent improvement in the overall balance over the four years.

Nigel Lawson's 1984 Budget (FY1984–88)

Nigel Lawson's 1984 Budget came at a time when macroeconomic conditions had begun to stabilize, but the public finances lingered stubbornly in deficit. By the spring of 1982, inflation (Retail Prices Index: RPI) had fallen into the single digits and real GDP growth had turned positive. This economic recovery, together with victory in the 1982 Falklands' War, contributed to the Conservatives' reelection in June 1983. However, despite a large increase in the tax burden and a fall in interest rates, the PSBR remained above 3 percent of GDP. Howe's inability to bring down the deficit and thereby pave the way for further tax cuts was one of the factors that prompted the Prime Minister to replace him with her protégé, Nigel Lawson, following the 1983 election.

Drawing on the Conservatives' renewed electoral mandate and against a backdrop of rising economic confidence, Lawson's first Budget in March 1984 envisaged a slightly less ambitious but more expenditure-based consolidation than Howe's 1980 MTFS. The 1984 plan, which lengthened the time horizon for fiscal planning to five years, envisaged a reduction in the PSBR

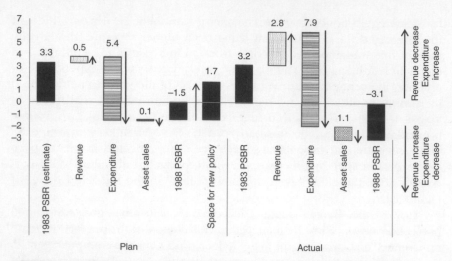

FIGURE 5.3 Nigel Lawson's 1984 Budget Planned vs. Actual Fiscal Adjustment (in percent of GDP)

Note: The "Expenditure" above takes into account the public corporations market borrowing.

from 3.3 percent of GDP in FY1983 to a surplus of 1.5 percent in FY1988 (see Figure 5.3).[5] Like Howe, Lawson made explicit provision within his plan for future discretionary tax cuts or spending increases once the planned deficit reduction was achieved.

However, Lawson's plan for cutting the deficit, unlike Howe's, relied almost entirely on a reduction in the level of public expenditure and the privatization of the country's largest public enterprises, including British Telecom, Airways, and Gas. Much of this reduction in the expenditure-to-GDP ratio came from a continuation of the reduction in the public sector workforce, which began under Howe, rather than any new specific policy measures.[6] Between FY1979 and FY1984 civil service numbers had already fallen from 732,000 to 630,000. The 1984 Budget announced the further target of reducing it to 593,000 by April 1988. Public sector wages were consequently forecast to be reduced by 2 percent of GDP over the five years. Lawson's ability to deliver reductions in public expenditure was bolstered by the decision in the 1981 budget to shift back from volume-based to cash-limited ministerial budgets, which was implemented from the 1982 Budget. The publication of a Green Paper on the long-term prospects for public spending and taxation marked a further step toward a medium-term approach to budget planning.[7]

On the revenue side, Lawson forecast a slight reduction in the tax burden over the medium-term, partly attributable to a decline in North Sea revenue, which was expected to peak in FY1984. However, the centerpiece of

Lawson's 1984 Budget was a radical but broadly revenue-neutral reduction in marginal tax rates designed to reduce distortions and stimulate private sector activity.[8] Reforms to corporation tax included the phased reduction in the main rate of corporation tax from 52 percent to 35 percent, paid for by phasing out first-year and initial investment allowances. An above-inflation increase in personal income tax allowances was paid for by raising excise duties, reflecting the government's strategy to shift the tax burden on persons from direct to indirect taxation.

Lawson overdelivered against this planned reduction in borrowing by 1.5 percent of GDP, on account of deeper expenditure cuts, stronger economic growth, and higher-than-expected receipts from asset sales. On the expenditure side, Lawson benefitted from a reduction in upward pressures on social security spending thanks to falling unemployment and inflation. The privatization of public enterprises delivered much more than the one-off revenue initially anticipated but also made possible sustained reductions in subsidies to previously state-owned enterprises. On the revenue side, a surge in corporation and other tax revenues was more than offset by a greater-than-anticipated fall in North Sea oil revenue and further discretionary reductions in marginal tax rates.

Unlike Howe, Lawson was therefore in a position to deliver on his promise of further reductions in marginal tax rates. The basic rate of personal income tax was reduced from 30 to 29 percent in the 1986 Budget, 27 percent in the 1987 Budget and 25 percent in the 1988 Budget, which also set an ultimate goal of 20 percent. Public investment, especially in transport, also made a partial recovery over this period. These expansionary measures, taken in the face of surging demand, may have contributed to a spike in inflation in the late 1980s and laid the foundation for the U.K.'s next economic and fiscal crisis discussed below. The pro-cyclicality of fiscal policy in the late 1980s can partly be attributed to an overestimation of the trend rate of economic growth and resulting overestimation of the size of the output gap at the time (HM Treasury 1997, Nelson and Nikolov 2001).

Kenneth Clarke's 1993 Budget (FY1994–98)[9]

Kenneth Clarke's November 1993 Budget was prepared in the aftermath of the financial and economic turmoil that followed the United Kingdom's ejection from the European Exchange Rate Mechanism (ERM). The origins of the ERM crisis can arguably be traced back to the tax cutting budgets of the late 1980s, which spurred a consumption-driven surge in output and inflation known as the "Lawson boom." The boom turned to bust when the Bank of England raised interest rates from 7 to 15 percent in 1988 to curb rising inflation. The Conservative Government's attempt to use ERM membership to curb domestic inflationary expectations and bring down interest rates came to an ignominious end on "Black Wednesday" in September 1992 when the government was forced to withdraw from ERM following a series of speculative attacks on sterling. The subsequent collapse in the value of the pound and spike in interest rates sparked panic in the financial and household sectors, which plunged the U.K. economy into a deep recession and the public finances into the largest deficit since World War II. Clarke succeeded Norman Lamont, whose turbulent three-year Chancellorship was marked by a series of tax raising Budgets that failed to bring down the country's yawning fiscal deficits.

Clarke's plan envisaged a more ambitious and front-loaded adjustment than either the 1980 or 1984 plan. Clarke targeted eliminating the 8 percent budget deficit by FY1998, a 1.5 percent adjustment per year, with nearly two-thirds of the adjustment coming in the first two years (see Figure 5.4). The adjustment was to be divided equally between revenue increases and expenditure reductions over the five years, with tax doing more of the work in the first two years and spending cuts picking up the slack in later years.

Like Lawson before him, Clarke benefitted from the tough decisions taken by his less fortunate predecessor. Six months prior to Clarke's

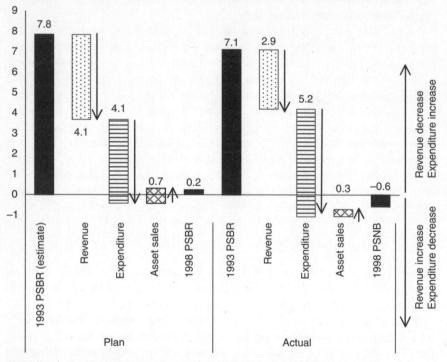

FIGURE 5.4 Kenneth Clarke's November 1993 Budget Planned vs. Actual Fiscal Adjustment (in percent of GDP)

Note: Actual 1998 borrowing is public sector net borrowing (PSNB).

November 1993 Budget, Lamont's March 1993 Budget had already announced a set of significant revenue-enhancing measures to take effect from April 1994, such as: a one percentage point rise in the national insurance contribution rate; the extension of Value Added Tax (VAT) to cover domestic fuels at a rate of 8 percent; and restrictions of personal income tax allowances. The approach of pre-announcing in 1993 revenue measures that would begin to take effect only in FY1994 had been adopted in light of the need to build credibility quickly while not stifling the nascent recovery. Clarke's November Budget announced additional measures including a tax on air travel and insurance premiums, a further increase in VAT on domestic fuels from 8 to the standard 17.5 percent, and increases in tobacco and road fuel excises in real terms in future years. These measures in the March and November Budgets were designed to boost government revenues by 2.5 percent of GDP over the three-year period to FY1996.[10]

The government's expenditure objective was to reduce public spending as a share of national income over time.[11] Clarke used a combination of a "top-down" freeze in running costs coupled with a zero-based "Fundamental Expenditure Review (FER)" of individual programs to identify those which could be better targeted or eliminated entirely.[12] The freeze on running costs in the central and local governments required any increases in public sector pay be offset by employment reductions (2 percent a year through FY1996) to hold the overall wage bill at FY1993 levels. The growth in social security spending was to be contained at 1.5 percent by tightening eligibility requirements of the disability benefit and increasing the pension retirement age for women to 65 (in line with the age for men). The increase in capital spending during the Lawson boom was also to be largely reversed over the five years.

To lock-in future expenditure reductions identified by the FER, the budgetary planning regime was further strengthened. The November 1993 budget replaced the rolling nominal expenditure ceiling on total primary spending (known as "Planning Total") which had been in place since 1982 with a fixed 3-year nominal expenditure ceiling (known as "Control Total") which excluded debt interest payments and working age benefits but still covered about 85 percent of public expenditure. Figures for Control Total presented in the November 1993 Budget indicated an average real growth over three years (through FY1996) at less than 0.25 percent a year, much lower than previously envisaged. Clarke's plan also included a major expansion of the fledgling Private Finance Initiative (public private partnerships), launched in November 1992 to fill the gap left by falling public spending and investment, but projects took longer to get off the ground than was anticipated.

Of the four plans considered in this chapter, Clarke's delivered the largest reduction in the fiscal deficit. On the revenue side, measures in the plan were all implemented except the increase in the VAT rate on domestic fuels, which was voted down in December 1994. The associated revenue loss was immediately recouped through higher excises on other goods. Although the total increase in revenues fell short of the planned increase by 1 percent of GDP, this partly reflected discretionary cuts in the personal income tax rate in the 1995 Budget as well as increased VAT avoidance by companies. On the expenditure side, spending cuts turned out bigger than planned despite continued pressures in areas such as social security and education. Major factors that contributed to this reduction included lower capital expenditure and larger than planned cuts in the wage bill brought about by an 8 percent cut in staffing compared with FY1994 levels.

Alistair Darling's 2007 Pre-Budget Report and Comprehensive Spending Review (FY2008-12)

Alistair Darling's 2007 PBR and CSR represented the first and only attempt by the Blair-Brown Labour governments to deliver a discretionary fiscal consolidation. Upon coming to power in May 1997, the government did preside over a return to budget surpluses in FY1998. However, much of this improvement was attributable to the government's decision during their first two years in office to stick to the austere spending plans set out by Kenneth Clarke in his last Budget in March 1997.

The 2007 PBR-CSR foresaw a modest reduction in the public sector deficit by 0.3 percent of GDP per year on average (see Figure 5.5). While this

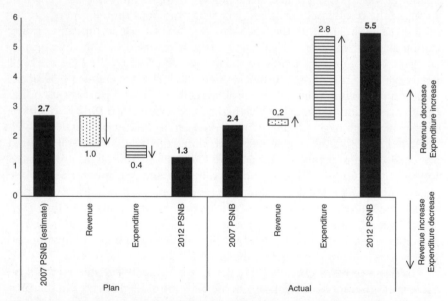

FIGURE 5.5 Alistair Darling's 2007 PBR-CSR Planned vs. Actual Fiscal Adjustment (in percent of GDP)

Note: "Actual" for 2012 are based on projections in the June 2010 Budget.

was a relatively modest consolidation by international and U.K. historical standards, it was still a challenge to reduce the real rate of growth in public spending while allocating resources between competing priorities, given the rapid increase in spending observed since the beginning of the century.[13]

The 2007 CSR was the fifth bi/tri-annual review of the government's spending priorities. Such reviews started in FY1998 and concluded by setting out fixed three-year expenditure ceilings for each ministry. The 2007 CSR envisaged halving the real rate of growth in public spending from 4 percent per year over the previous decade to 2 percent per year over the following three years—a half percent lower than the trend rate of growth of the economy. Some departments were nevertheless given higher spending growth in this CSR than in the previous (notably those responsible for overseas aid, the intelligence agencies, defense, and the environment) in recognition of their role in responding to "global challenges." Planned growth in capital spending was dramatically reduced by comparison with the preceding decade.[14] The plan also envisaged an increase in the tax burden due to fiscal drag, discretionary measures such as the introduction of an 18 percent single rate of capital gains tax, and measures to tackle tax avoidance.

However, the 2008 global financial crisis and the recession that followed led to a sharp deterioration in the public finances. The sudden downturn in economic activity and asset prices caused a drop in income and corporation taxes, VAT, and capital taxes. Rising unemployment and interest payments also pushed expenditures above levels set out in Darling's plan. Finally, a discretionary fiscal stimulus of 2 percent of GDP comprised of a temporary reduction in the VAT rate and an acceleration of planned capital expenditure further added to the deficit.[15] In the end, the crisis left the U.K. government with a forecast deficit for 2012 of 5.5 percent of GDP rather than the 1.3 percent of GDP planned in the 2007 PBR-CSR.

Determinants of Success and Failure

This section examines the factors that contributed to the success or failure of the different plans including macroeconomic factors, the timing, pace, and composition of the fiscal adjustment plans, and the supporting fiscal and budgetary frameworks.

Timing of Consolidation Announcement

The timing of their formulation and announcement was a critical determinant of the extent to which different adjustment plans met their stated objectives. Howe's 1980 MTFS and Darling's 2007 PBR-CSR simply came too early to be properly calibrated to the scale and pace of adjustment that was

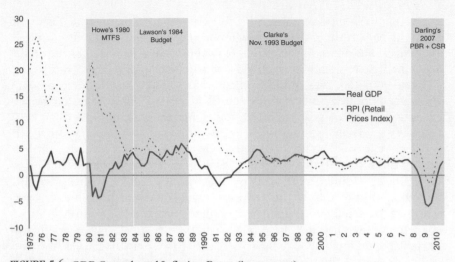

FIGURE 5.6 GDP Growth and Inflation Rates (in percent)

Sources: Office of National Statistics and World Economic Outlook (IMF).

ultimately required. Howe's 1980 MTFS was released in the eye of a macroeconomic storm of falling output and surging inflation (see Figure 5.6). It was therefore built on sands that were still shifting under the Chancellor's feet and quickly rendered his plans and targets out of date. Darling's October 2007 PBR-CSR was prepared against a backdrop of unprecedented macroeconomic stability marked by 61 consecutive quarters of positive growth, unemployment at historic lows, and inflation remaining close to its 2 percent target. However, the financial crisis and sharp recession that followed in the autumn of 2008 pushed the fiscal deficit and public debt to levels that were scarcely imaginable a year earlier. By contrast, Lawson's 1984 and Clarke's November 1993 plans were prepared and announced after output had turned the corner and inflation had stabilized and therefore enjoyed greater credibility and durability.

Macroeconomic Assumptions

None of the four Chancellors can be faulted for their forecasts of economic growth, all of which were in line with the consensus prevailing at the time (see Figure 5.7). These growth forecasts turned out to be pessimistic in all but Darling's case—a factor which played an important part in the success of the Lawson and Clarke plans. However, difficulty in estimating the underlying cyclical position of the economy may have led to more expansionary fiscal policy than intended toward the end of these successful adjustment plans. Nelson and Nikolov (2001) show that real-time output measurement

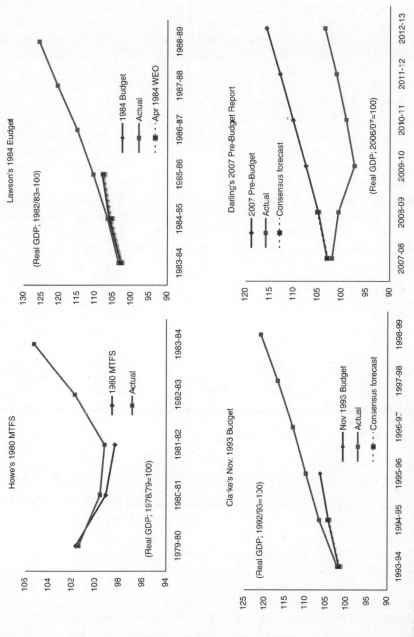

FIGURE 5.7 Forecast versus Outturn for Real GDP

errors were particularly large in the 1970s and 1980s both due to initial GDP estimate errors and optimistic views on potential output, suggesting that the government assumed large spare capacity in the economy. Large base effects appear in estimated cyclical and structural non-oil revenues, reflecting such potentially large output gap mismeasurement (see Appendix 5A).

The relationship between the forecast level of inflation and the success of the consolidation plans is complex but revealing. As in the case of growth, inflation forecasts underlying the adjustment plans were similar to those of independent observers, but significant surprises emerged (see Figure 5.8). Howe's 1980 MTFS underestimated inflation for FY1980, which, combined with the fact that departmental budgets were indexed to inflation, accounted for part of the overspending against his original plan. Clarke's November 1993 Budget initially overestimated inflation. However, with budgets now fixed in nominal terms, such lower than anticipated inflation contributed to higher real expenditure growth, especially after the move to fixed, three-year nominal spending caps. Likewise, the overestimation of inflation under Darling's 2007 plan contributed to unexpectedly large real increases in departmental expenditure, which was fixed in nominal terms out to FY2010.

Scale and Pace of Adjustment

There was no clear connection between the scale and pace of the planned adjustment and the ultimate success of the different plans. Howe's 1980 plan, Lawson's 1984 plan, and Clarke's November 1993 plan each targeted an average annual reduction in public sector net borrowing of between 1 and 1.5 percent of GDP, whereas Darling's 2007 plan was less ambitious (see Figure 5.9). While all deficit reduction plans were front-loaded, the actual pattern of adjustment under successful adjustment plans tended to be more back-loaded, with between 60 and 75 percent of the total adjustment delivered during the second half of the period.

Balance between Revenue Increases, Expenditure Reductions, and Asset Sales

Successful adjustment plans relied on expenditure reductions to deliver at least half of the planned adjustment and turned out to be even more expenditure-driven in execution. Lawson's 1984 plan relied entirely on expenditure reductions whereas Clarke's 1993 plan split the adjustment burden equally between revenue increases and expenditure reductions. Both plans ended up cutting expenditures more deeply than envisaged, which helped to compensate for some early revenue underperformance and pay for discretionary tax cuts toward the end of period. By contrast, Howe's 1980 and Darling's 2007 plans relied on revenue increases to deliver the bulk of the envisaged adjustment but were undermined by slippage on the expenditure

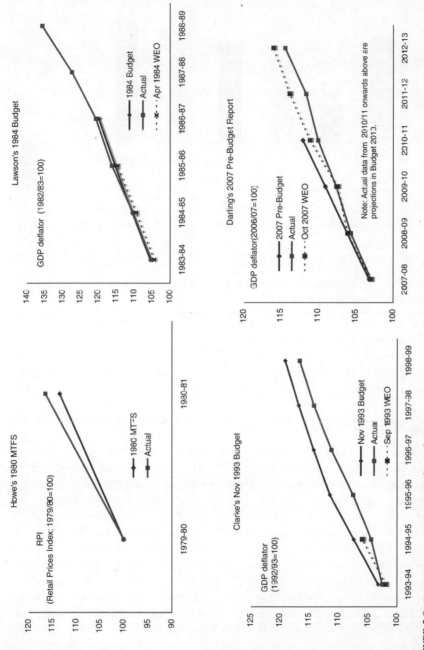

FIGURE 5.8 Forecast versus Outturn for Inflation

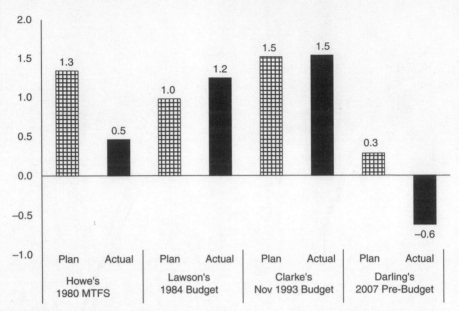

FIGURE 5.9 Average Planned versus Actual Fiscal Adjustment (average annual deficit reduction, in percent of GDP)

side. Receipts from the sale of financial or fixed assets made a modest contribution to all four consolidation plans, though the privatization of public enterprises enabled both Lawson and Clarke to deliver sustained reductions in subsidies.

Composition of Revenue Increases

All four fiscal adjustment plans overestimated the improvement in revenues over the plan period (see Figure 5.10). However, some of this underperformance can be attributed to discretionary policy decisions, especially in the run-up to elections. For example, in Howe's March 1983 budget (his last before the election), the Chancellor delivered on his promise of income tax relief for households through a modest increase in personal allowances and thresholds, despite disappointing revenue and expenditure performance in the interim.[16] Lawson took advantage of economic and fiscal recovery to reduce personal tax rates from 30 to 25 percent over his chancellorship. Clarke also took the opportunity of the improving fiscal situation to reduce the basic rate of personal income tax by one percentage point and increase personal allowances by more than inflation in his preelection budget in 1996. However, nondiscretionary factors also explained some of the revenue underperformance. During the Lawson plan, a negative surprise in North

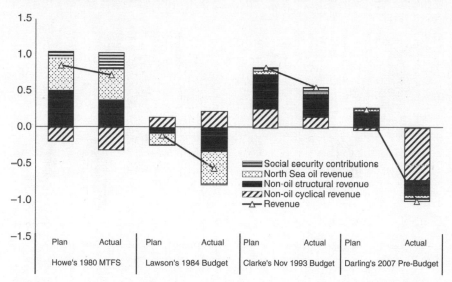

FIGURE 5.10   Planned and Actual Revenue Increases (average annual change, in percent of GDP)

Note: In the Darling's 2007 Pre-Budget above, decompositions of the planned and actual revenue are between 2007–08 and 2009–10.

Sea oil revenue accounted for around half of the unexpected revenue loss. In Darling's case, the collapse in revenue was largely associated with the financial and economic crisis, with the largest losses stemming from the financial, housing, and consumption taxes.

Composition of Expenditure Reductions

LEVELS OF GOVERNMENT   While earlier adjustment plans overestimated the contribution of local governments to the adjustment effort, later plans were more balanced across central and local governments. Despite the fact that local authorities accounted for about 30 percent of general government primary expenditure in the 1980s and 1990s, Howe's 1980 and Lawson's 1984 plans envisaged local government's delivering a real cut in spending which was much more than that planned for the central government. However, local government expenditure proved difficult to cut in practice (see Figure 5.11). Clarke's plan, which assumed a modest real expenditure increase with more balanced relative contribution of central and local governments to fiscal adjustment, did contain local government real expenditure increases within the planned level. This positive result stemmed in part from improved central government control over local government spending during the early 1990s, through broader application of expenditure "capping"

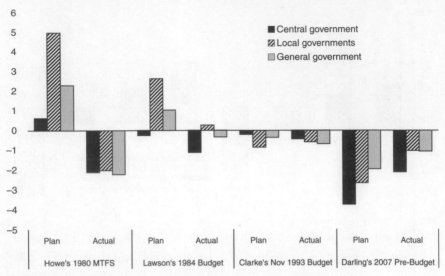

FIGURE 5.11 Distribution of Expenditure Cuts between Central and Local Governments (average annual real reductions, in percent)

through Total Standard Spending (TSS)[17] announced by the central government at an early stage of the local budgetary process (Bladen-Hovell, 1996).

ECONOMIC CATEGORIES The burden of expenditure reductions—both planned and actual—under all three Conservative Chancellors fell disproportionally on public investment (see Figure 5.12). Nearly all of the expenditure reductions planned and delivered under Howe's 1980 plan came from cuts in capital expenditure. Lawson and Clarke also planned and delivered substantial reductions in capital expenditure. As a result, between 1975 and 2000, public sector net investment fell from 5.6 percent to 0.5 percent of GDP, with the steepest reductions coinciding with periods of falling public borrowing (see Figure 5.13). Some of this reduction in capital expenditure reflected the privatization of nationalized companies and a shift toward privately funded public infrastructure investment under the Private Finance Initiative (Van den Noord, 2002). However, by the end of the 1990s, the United Kingdom had one of the lowest public investment–to-GDP ratios among advanced economies and an aging infrastructure.[18]

More lasting benefits came from permanent reductions in grants and subsidies under Lawson and in wages and salaries under Clarke. Conversely, slippage against planned expenditure reductions under the 1980 Howe and 2007 Darling plans was largely attributable to overspending on grants and subsidies to households and corporations. Finally, while all four Chancellors

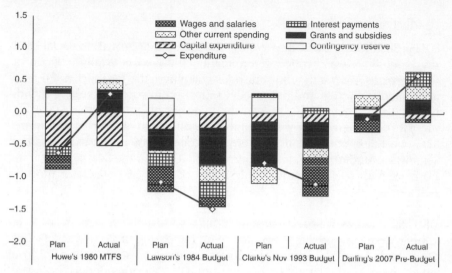

FIGURE 5.12 Planned versus Actual Change in Expenditure by Economic Classification (average annual change, in percent of GDP)

incorporated an explicit contingency reserve into their expenditure allocations, this dwindled from between 1 and 1.5 percent of GDP under the three Conservative Chancellors' plans to less than 0.5 percent under the Darling plan.

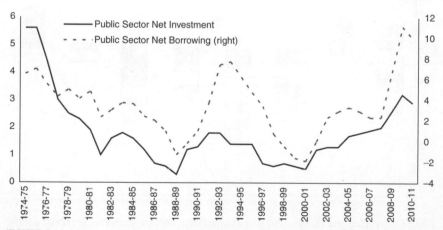

FIGURE 5.13 Public Sector Borrowing and Investment (in percent of GDP)

Distribution between Sectors

SOCIAL SECURITY The ability to slow the real rate of growth in social security expenditure was a critical determinant of the success or failure of consolidation plans. Across the four episodes examined, the two successful fiscal adjustments planned and delivered a reduction in social security expenditure of 1–2.5 percent of GDP over the five-year planning horizon (see Figure 5.14). Social security expenditure was effectively frozen in real terms. The two failed consolidations were associated with an increase in social security expenditure of at least 2 percent of GDP over the five-year planning horizon, with social security expenditure rising by 5 percent or more in real terms.

DEFENSE Successful fiscal consolidations also reaped the benefits of a decline in defense spending associated with the easing of Cold War tensions. Over the last two decades of the 20th century, defense spending fell from over 5 percent of GDP to 2.5 percent of GDP. Over this period, both successful consolidations planned and delivered sizable real-terms reductions in defense expenditures. By contrast, both unsuccessful consolidations witnessed real-term increases in defense expenditures due in part to the unanticipated costs of military operations in the Falklands and Afghanistan, respectively.

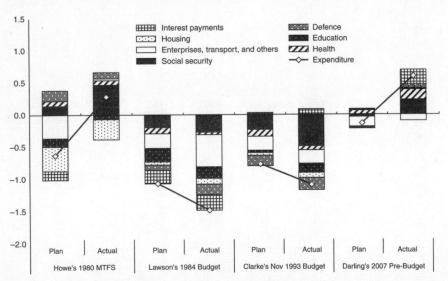

FIGURE 5.14 Planned versus Actual Change in Expenditure by Sector (average annual change, in percent of GDP)

TRANSPORT AND HOUSING A further one percent of GDP reduction in expenditure delivered under successful consolidations came from real cuts in the capital-intensive housing and transport sectors. Over the five-year planning horizons of Lawson's and Clarke's plans, real transport expenditure fell by 20 and 30 percent, respectively. In the mid-1980s this was delivered largely through steep fare rises, cuts in services, and the sale of British Airways, Rolls-Royce, British Airport Authority, and some smaller public transport companies. The privatization of British Rail in 1993 provided a further opportunity to reduce public expenditure on transport under Clarke. By contrast, transport spending continued to rise as a share of GDP over Howe's 1980 and Darling's 2007 plans. This was due in part to the costs of major investment programs which were effectively "locked-in" over the period of the two consolidation plans. There were the rollout of high-speed inter-city trains in the late 1970s and early 1980s under Howe and the construction of the transport infrastructure for the 2012 Olympic Games in London under Darling.

Housing expenditure was substantially cut under all the three Conservative Chancellors, reflecting a drive to privatize the social housing stock, liberalize rents in the remaining stock of social housing, and reduce rent and supply subsidies. Only Darling's 2007 plan was associated with a real increase in housing expenditure in an attempt to keep pace with the rising cost of living, especially in London and Southeast England.

HEALTH, EDUCATION, AND POLICING None of the four Chancellors managed to cut spending on health, education, and policing in real terms. Over the Howe and Darling plans, public expenditure on these services, as a share of GDP, rose by 0.8 and 2.4 percent, respectively. Slowing the real rate of growth in these large labor-intensive items contributed a 1 percent decline in the expenditure/GDP ratio under Lawson's and Clarke's plans. Success in reining in expenditure growth in these sectors was delivered by a combination of workforce reductions in education and policing and expansion of user charging and competition in the National Health Service.

Fiscal and Budgetary Frameworks

Medium-term fiscal and budgetary frameworks, and their evolving design features, played a critically important role in the success and failure of the different adjustment attempts.

MEDIUM-TERM FISCAL FRAMEWORKS Starting with Howe's Medium-Term Fiscal Strategy in the 1980s, successive Chancellors have made use of medium-term fiscal frameworks to lock in their adjustment plans beyond the budget year. From Howe's MTFS onward, the target for fiscal adjustments was the PSBR as a proportion of GDP, a broad fiscal aggregate which included the central government, local government, and public enterprises. This reduced the scope for Chancellors to resort to burden shifting within the public sector to deliver their fiscal objectives, though in hindsight, there may have been a certain amount of wishful thinking about how much of the burden could be borne by local authorities and public enterprises.

Budget documentation, in the form of the *Financial Statement and Budget Report (FSBR)* on budget day, provided detailed economic and fiscal projections for 4–5 years ahead, which reflected the medium-term, macro-fiscal impact of the government's announced policies. The FSBR also set the top-down aggregate expenditure envelope for the *Public Expenditure White Paper* published every autumn (replaced by the *Spending Review White Paper* every second or third summer), which set out multiyear expenditure estimates for each ministry. In 1997, the incoming Labour government replaced the rolling fiscal targets of the Conservatives with a set of permanent fiscal rules: (1) a Golden Rule that required the government to keep the public sector current budget in balance or in surplus over the economic cycle; and (2) a Sustainable Investment rule requiring the government to keep public sector net debt below 40 percent of GDP over the cycle. These fiscal rules were abandoned in 2008 in the aftermath of the crisis and replaced with a commitment to halve public sector net borrowing over five years and reverse the increase in public sector net debt.

MULTI-YEAR EXPENDITURE PLANNING AND CONTROL   In all four cases, the Chancellor's fiscal objectives were supported by some form of a medium-term budget framework (see Table 5.1). However, these frameworks proved to be either a help or hindrance depending on how they were designed. Since the 1960s, the Government had used the FSBR to fix a rolling three-year nominal ceiling on total primary general government expenditure, an aggregate known as Planning Total, which covered 87 percent of general government expenditure. High and volatile inflation in the 1970s and early 1980s prompted the Treasury to move from nominal- to real-terms expenditure planning as a means of reducing the "ratchet effect" of inflation on wages and prices. The shift from cash- to volume-based expenditure limits proved costly when inflation turned out higher than expected, and the Treasury had to provide ministries with more cash to meet their real spending plans. This brief experiment with volume-based expenditure planning was abandoned in 1982 when Planning Total was returned to a cash basis and privatization proceeds were added to the list of excluded items. The recasting of Planning Total in nominal terms helped to reestablish Treasury control over the year-on-year growth in total expenditure over the 1980s.

TABLE 5.1 Evolution of Medium-Term Budget Frameworks in the United Kingdom

| | Control Method | | | Coverage | | |
Plan	Name	Unit of Control	Basis of Planning	% of Gen. Govt.	Main Items Excluded	Frequency of Revision
Howe's 1980 MTFS	Planning Total	Total GG[a] Primary Spending	Real Cash	87%	Debt Interest	Annual
Lawson's 1984 Budget	Planning Total	Total GG Primary Spending	Nominal Cash	85%	Debt Interest	Annual
Clarke's 1993 Budget	Control Total	Total GG Structural Spending	Nominal Cash	83%	Debt Interest Working Age Benefits	Triennial
Darling's 2007 PBR/CSR	Departmental Expenditure Limits	25 Ministerial Budgets	Nominal Accrual	60%	Debt Interest LG[b] Own Exp. Social Security	Triennial

Note: All medium-term budget frameworks have a time horizon of three years.
[a]General government.
[b]Local governments.

Multiyear expenditure discipline was further strengthened in 1992, with the introduction of the Control Total: this set a three-year nominal ceiling on 85 percent of general government expenditure which, unlike Planning Total, was not revised over a three-year period. This additional degree of discipline came at the expense of coverage, as cyclically sensitive working age benefits were added to the list of items excluded from the ceiling. The shift from the rolling Planning Total to fixed Control Total was nonetheless associated with a substantial improvement in expenditure discipline beyond the budget year, and a reduction in average nominal overspending against the government's planned expenditure level. This improvement in aggregate multiyear expenditure control was critical to the success of the Clarke plan.

By the time of Darling's 2007 PBR-CSR, aggregate Control Total had been replaced by a system of fixed three-year budgets for each ministry known as Departmental Expenditure Limits (DELs), introduced in 1998 by the Labour Government alongside its fiscal rules. DELs were fixed at the conclusion of Spending Reviews, of which the 2007 CSR was the fifth. This more detailed set of multiyear spending restrictions contributed to a further improvement in multiyear expenditure discipline during the relatively benign economic conditions that prevailed between 1998 and 2007. However, it turned out to be a liability over the period of the 2007 CSR period for two reasons:

- First, DELs were fixed in nominal terms, so that when inflation turned out below expectations in 2008–09, real expenditure growth surged.
- Second, greater discipline at the level of ministries came at the expense of a further reduction in coverage, as all social security and local authority self-financed expenditure (LASFE) were added to the list of items excluded from the control aggregate. As shown in Figure 5.14, overspending on these excluded items (especially social security) accounted for a larger share of the total overruns in Darling's 2007 plan.

Lessons from Success and Failure

The foregoing account of the determinants of consolidation success and failure in the United Kingdom suggest the following lessons for future attempts at fiscal adjustment:

- Have a contingency plan for lower economic growth. Probably the biggest factor that undermined both the Howe and Darling plans was the fact that real growth plummeted shortly after their announcement. By contrast, the implementation of both the Lawson and Clarke plans was facilitated by healthy economic growth.

- The impact of surprises in inflation depends on the budgeting rules. Where budgets and tax thresholds are set in real terms (as they were in the early 1980s), a key fiscal risk comes from underestimating inflation (as happened under Howe's 1980 plan). Where budgets and tax thresholds are set in nominal terms (as they were from FY1982 onwards), the risks stem from overestimating inflation (as happened under Darling's 2007 plan).

- Sustained reductions in expenditure are a key ingredient. None of the four Chancellors delivered the revenue increase they initially planned, owing to both discretionary and nondiscretionary factors. The two Chancellors who met or exceeded their deficit targets did so by overachieving on their planned expenditure cuts, and used part of the room thus created to reduce the tax burden.

- Celebrate success, but don't overdo it. Howe, Lawson, and Clarke all used the promise of future reductions in marginal income tax rates to build and maintain Cabinet and backbench support for the painful decisions involved in their planned adjustments. However, as the economy and public finances recovered more quickly than planned, Lawson ended up cutting taxes more aggressively than originally envisaged. This procyclical reduction in tax rates arguably contributed to an unsustainable boom in consumption and investment.

- Cutting investment is tempting in the short-term but unsustainable in the long-term. The ratio of public investment to GDP was more than halved during the 1980s and again over the 1990s to one of the lowest levels among advanced economies by the year 2000. Increased use of public-private partnerships (PPPs) only made up for part of the cuts in public capital. It took more than a decade for public investment to recover. In the meantime, the United Kingdom's public infrastructure fell behind other advanced economies.

- Reductions in wages and benefits had a more durable impact on the fiscal balance. A key factor that distinguished the Lawson and Clarke plans from the less successful attempts was their determination to tackle the key drivers of cost in the public sector: social security, health, education, and defense (by function); and payroll, transfers, and subsidies to public enterprises (by economic classification).

- Strike a fair balance in expenditure reductions between central and local governments. There was a tendency in early adjustment plans to overestimate the share of the adjustment that could be imposed on local authorities. Later adjustment plans were more balanced and, in this regard, more successful. Strengthening central government control over local authority expenditure in the 1990s also helped to ensure the implementation of planned adjustment at the local level.

■ The real dividends from privatization come from lower subsidies, rather than in the form of one-off capital receipts. The sale of public corporations and other assets played an important role in both of the successful adjustment programs. However, the one-off capital receipts from these asset sales were a small share of total fiscal adjustment. The sizable and lasting fiscal benefit from the divestiture of state assets came instead from the permanent reduction in government subsidies to the entities concerned.

■ Medium-term budget frameworks can help lock in the planned reduction in expenditures, but only if they are comprehensive and binding. All the fiscal adjustment plans were supported by medium-term budget frameworks, which enhanced expenditure discipline. However, the design of these frameworks evolved over time with greater fixity and detail being achieved at the expense of lower coverage of public expenditure.

■ The five-year forecasting or electoral cycle may be too short a timeframe over which to judge the success or failure of a consolidation plan. For example, although Howe in the early 1980s and Lamont in the early 1990s failed to eliminate the deficit during their three-to-five-year tenures, their policies laid the foundation for more favored design and implementation of plans under Lawson and Clarke. Conversely, while Lawson exceeded his target for reducing government borrowing over the five-year horizon of his 1984 Budget, some have argued that his subsequent expansionary budgets laid the foundation for the U.K.'s next major economic and financial crisis. Finally, while Darling failed to deliver the deficit reduction in his 2007 plan, his decision to relax the fiscal stance over 2008 and 2009 may have prevented a more serious financial, economic, and fiscal crisis.

Appendix 5A

United Kingdom: Fiscal Adjustment Plans and Outturns

The following tables (Tables 5A.1–5A.4) provide detailed information comparing plans with outturns, with a breakdown of expenditure and revenue items, for each planned adjustment episode.

TABLE 5A.1 Howe's 1980 Medium-Term Financial Strategy: Plan versus Actuals (in percent of GDP)

| | Plan (p) | | | Actual (a) | | | Overperformance (actual relative to plan) | | |
| | t (1979p) | $t+4$ (1983p) | $t+4-t$ (Δp) | t (1979a) | $t+4$ (1983p) | $t+4-t$ (Δa) | $1983a-1983p$ = 1983 actual minus 1983 planned | Of which: | |
								$\Delta a-\Delta p$ = Actual improvement minus planned improvement	$1979a-1979p$ = 1979 actual minus 1979 preliminary estimate from plan ("base effect")
Revenues	**39.2**	**42.6**	**3.4**	**39.6**	**42.5**	**2.9**	**-0.1**	**-0.5**	**0.4**
Non-oil taxes and revenues	31.9	33.2	1.3	32.4	32.6	0.3	-0.5	-1.0	0.5
Cyclical	-1.0	-1.7	-0.8	0.8	-0.5	-1.2	1.3	-0.5	1.7
Structural	32.9	34.9	2.0	31.6	33.1	1.5	-1.8	-0.5	-1.3
North Sea oil revenue[a]	1.4	3.2	1.8	1.2	2.9	1.7	-0.3	-0.1	-0.2
Social security contributions	5.9	6.3	0.4	6.1	7.0	0.9	0.7	0.5	0.1
Expenditures[b]	**44.8**	**42.3**	**-2.5**	**45.0**	**46.2**	**1.1**	**3.8**	**-3.6**	**-0.2**
Primary	40.1	38.1	-1.9	40.2	41.3	1.1	3.2	-3.0	-0.1
Interest	4.8	4.2	-0.6	4.8	4.9	0.0	0.7	-0.6	-0.1
Asset sales	0.6	0.0	-0.6	0.2	0.4	0.2	0.3	0.7	-0.4
Expenditures on programs[c]									
by level of government	39.9	37.2	-2.7	39.9	40.3	0.4	3.1	-3.1	-0.1
Central government	28.9	28.4	-0.5	28.3	28.9	0.6	0.5	-1.1	0.6
Local governments	10.4	8.3	-2.0	11.0	11.2	0.2	2.8	-2.2	-0.6
by economic classification[c]									
Current expenditure	34.5	34.1	-0.4	34.5	36.9	2.4	2.8	-2.9	0.0
Wages and salaries	12.0	11.2	-0.8	12.7	12.8	0.2	1.7	-1.0	-0.7

(*continued*)

141

TABLE 5A.1 (Continued)

| | Plan (p) | | | Actual (a) | | | Overperformance (actual relative to plan) | | |
| | t | t+4 | t+4−t | t | t+4 | t+4−t | | Of which: | |
	1979p	1983p	Δp	1979a	1983a	Δa	1983a−1983p = 1983 actual minus 1983 planned	Δa−Δp = Actual improvement minus planned improvement	1979a−1979p = 1979 actual minus 1979 preliminary estimate from plan ("base effect")
Goods and services	6.7	6.9	0.1	7.3	8.0	0.7	1.1	−0.5	−0.6
Subsidies	2.6	2.5	−0.1	2.5	2.0	−0.5	−0.5	0.4	0.1
Grants	13.2	13.6	0.4	12.0	14.1	2.1	0.5	−1.7	1.2
Capital expenditure	5.4	3.2	−2.1	5.5	3.4	−2.1	0.2	−0.1	−0.1
by program (selected items)									
Social security	10.5	11.0	0.5	9.6	11.9	2.2	0.9	−1.7	0.9
Health	5.0	5.3	0.3	4.5	4.7	0.2	−0.6	0.0	0.6
Education	5.4	4.9	−0.5	5.5	5.4	−0.1	0.5	−0.4	−0.1
Defence	4.3	4.9	0.6	4.7	5.1	0.4	0.2	0.2	−0.4
Contingency reserve	0.0	1.1	1.1	–	–	–	–	–	–
General government overall balance	**−5.0**	**0.3**	**5.3**	**−5.3**	**−3.3**	**2.0**	**−3.6**	**−3.4**	**−0.2**
Public corporations market borrowing	−0.3	−0.3	0.0	−0.3	−0.1	0.1	0.2	0.1	0.0
Public sector overall balance	**−4.8**	**0.6**	**5.4**	**−5.0**	**−3.2**	**1.8**	**−3.8**	**−3.5**	**−0.3**
Primary balance	0.0	4.8	4.8	−0.2	1.7	1.9	−3.1	−2.9	−0.2
Structural non-oil primary balance	−1.3	3.1	4.3	−2.5	−1.2	1.3	−4.3	−3.0	−1.3

Memorandum (in percent of potential GDP)

Cyclically-adjusted primary balance	0.1	5.8	5.7	−1.2	2.0	3.2	−3.8	−2.5	−1.3
Structural non-oil revenue[d]	31.9	34.9	3.0	32.4	32.6	0.3	−2.2	−2.7	0.5
Primary expenditure	38.9	38.2	−0.7	41.0	40.3	−0.6	−2.1	0.0	−2.1

[a] As oil revenue projections are not presented in the March 1980 Financial Statement and Budget Report (FSBR), those projected in the March 1981 FSBR are used for estimates.
[b] General government total expenditure in national accounts terms, which was the definition of public expenditure lying behind the general government borrowing requirement, excluding asset sales, which was treated as negative expenditure.
[c] Expenditure on programs by central and local governments and nationalized industries' and other public corporations' borrowings. Debt interest payments and other adjustments (in national account terms) are not included. Planned figures at $t + 4$ are authors' estimates.
[d] Excluding social security contributions.

TABLE 5A.2 Lawson's 1984 Budget: Plan versus Actuals (in percent of GDP)

	Plan (p)			Actual (a)			Overperformance (actual relative to plan)		
							1988a−1988p = 1988 actual minus 1988 planned	Of which:	
								Δa−Δp = Actual improvement minus planned improvement	1983a−1983p = 1983 actual minus 1983 preliminary estimate from plan ("base effect")
	t	t+5	t+5−t	t	t+5	t+5−t			
	1983p	1988p	Δp	1983a	1988a	Δa			
Revenues	**42.3**	**41.7**	**−0.5**	**42.5**	**39.7**	**−2.8**	**−2.0**	**−2.3**	**0.2**
Non-oil taxes and revenues	32.2	32.5	0.3	32.6	32.1	−0.5	−0.4	−0.8	0.4
Cyclical	−1.7	−1.0	0.7	−0.5	0.6	1.1	1.7	0.4	1.2
Structural	33.9	33.5	−0.4	33.1	31.5	−1.6	−2.0	−1.2	−0.8
North Sea oil revenue	3.0	2.2	−0.8	2.9	0.7	−2.2	−1.5	−1.4	−0.1
Social security contributions	7.1	7.0	0.0	7.0	6.9	−0.1	−0.1	0.0	−0.1
Expenditures[a]	**46.1**	**40.8**	**−5.3**	**46.2**	**38.8**	**−7.4**	**−2.0**	**2.1**	**0.0**
Primary	41.2	36.9	−4.3	41.3	35.1	−6.2	−1.8	1.9	−0.1
Interest	4.9	3.9	−1.1	4.9	3.7	−1.2	−0.2	0.2	0.1
Asset sales	0.4	0.5	0.1	0.4	1.5	1.1	1.0	1.0	0.0
Expenditures on programs[b]	40.0	35.0	−5.0	40.3	33.4	−6.9	−1.6	1.9	0.3
by level of government[b]									
Central government	28.2	25.9	−2.3	28.9	24.3	−4.6	−1.6	2.3	−0.7
Local governments	10.7	8.1	−2.6	11.2	8.8	−2.4	0.7	−0.3	−0.4
by economic classification[b]									
Current expenditure	36.6	32.9	−3.8	36.9	31.2	−5.7	−1.6	1.9	−0.3
Wages and salaries	12.7	10.8	−1.9	12.8	11.6	−1.3	0.8	−0.6	−0.2
Goods and services	8.1	7.9	−0.2	8.0	6.7	−1.3	−1.2	1.1	0.1

Subsidies	2.0	1.0	-1.1	2.0	1.1	-0.9	0.1	-0.1	0.0
Grants	13.8	13.3	-0.6	14.1	11.9	-2.2	-1.3	1.6	-0.2
Capital expenditure	3.5	2.2	-1.3	3.4	2.2	-1.2	0.0	-0.1	0.1
by function (seleced items)[b]									
Social security	12.0	11.0	-1.0	11.9	10.5	-1.4	-0.5	0.4	0.1
Health	4.8	4.4	-0.5	4.7	4.5	-0.2	0.2	-0.3	0.1
Education	5.4	4.3	-1.1	5.4	4.8	-0.5	0.5	-0.5	0.0
Defence	5.2	4.8	-0.4	5.1	4.3	-0.8	-0.5	0.4	0.1
Contingency reserve	0.03	1.3	1.2	–	–	–	–	–	–
General government overall balance	**-3.5**	**1.5**	**4.9**	**-3.3**	**2.4**	**5.7**	**1.0**	**0.8**	**0.2**
Public corporations market borrowing	-0.2	0.0	0.2	-0.1	-0.6	-0.5	0.6	0.7	0.0
Public sector overall balance	**-3.3**	**1.5**	**4.7**	**-3.2**	**3.1**	**6.2**	**1.6**	**1.5**	**0.1**
Primary balance	1.6	5.3	3.7	1.7	6.7	5.0	1.4	1.3	0.1
Structural non-oil primary balance	-0.2	3.7	3.9	-1.2	3.3	4.5	-0.4	0.7	-1.0
Memorandum (in percent of potential GDP)									
Cyclically-adjusted primary balance	3.0	6.2	3.1	2.0	5.6	3.5	-0.6	0.4	-1.0
Structural non-oil revenue[c]	32.2	32.5	0.3	32.6	32.1	-0.5	-0.4	-0.8	0.4
Primary expenditure	38.8	35.3	-3.4	40.3	34.3	-6.0	-1.0	2.6	-1.6

[a]General government total expenditure in national accounts terms, which was the definition of public expenditure lying behind the general government borrowing requirement, excluding asset sales, which was treated as negative expenditure.
[b]Expenditure on programs by central and local governments and nationalized industries' and other public corporations' borrowings. Debt interest payments and other adjustments (in national account terms) are not included. Planned figures at $t + 5$ are authors' estimates.
[c]Excluding social security contributions.

TABLE 5A.3 Clarke's November 1993 Budget: Plan versus Actuals (in percent of GDP)

| | Plan (p) | | | Actual (a) | | | Overperformance (actual relative to plan) | | |
| | t | t+5 | t+5−t | t | t+5 | t+5−t | | Of which: | |
	1993p	1998p	Δp	1993a	1998a	Δa	1998a−1998p = 1998 actual minus 1998 planned	Δa−Δp = Actual improvement minus planned improvement	1993a−1993p = 1993 actual minus 1993 preliminary estimate from plan ("base effect")
Revenues	**36.2**	**40.3**	**4.1**	**36.1**	**38.9**	**2.8**	**−1.4**	**−1.4**	**0.0**
Non-oil taxes and revenues	29.8	33.5	3.7	29.9	32.2	2.3	−1.3	−1.4	0.1
Cyclical	−1.4	−0.2	1.3	−0.7	0.0	0.7	0.1	−0.6	0.7
Structural	31.2	33.6	2.4	30.6	32.2	1.6	−1.4	−0.8	−0.6
North Sea oil revenue	0.2	0.5	0.2	0.2	0.3	0.1	−0.2	−0.1	0.0
Social security contributions	6.1	6.4	0.3	6.1	6.4	0.4	0.0	0.1	0.0
Expenditures[a]	**45.0**	**40.9**	**−4.1**	**44.3**	**38.8**	**−5.5**	**−2.1**	**1.4**	**0.7**
Primary	41.9	37.7	−4.2	41.2	35.3	−5.9	−2.4	1.7	0.7
Interest	3.1	3.2	0.1	3.1	3.5	0.4	0.3	−0.3	0.0
Asset sales	0.8	0.1	−0.7	0.8	0.5	−0.3	0.4	0.4	0.0
Control Total[b]	38.5	34.5	−4.0	37.5	31.7	−5.8	−2.8	1.8	0.9
by level of government[c]									
Central government	32.0	28.0	−4.0	31.9	27.7	−4.2	−0.3	0.2	0.1
Local governments	11.0	10.0	−1.1	10.4	9.1	−1.3	−0.9	0.2	0.6
by economic classification[c]									
Current expenditure	38.1	33.3	−4.8	38.2	33.0	−5.2	−0.3	0.4	−0.1
Wages and salaries	10.2	10.3	0.1	10.3	7.7	−2.6	−2.6	2.7	−0.1
Goods and services	9.3	8.0	−1.3	9.4	9.2	−0.2	1.3	−1.1	−0.1

Subsidies	1.2	1.0	-0.2	0.9	0.9	0.0	-0.1	-0.1	0.2
Grants	17.4	14.0	-3.4	17.5	15.2	-2.3	1.2	-1.0	-0.1
Capital expenditure	3.7	3.1	-0.7	3.0	2.3	-0.7	-0.7	0.0	0.7
by function (selected items)[c]									
Social security	12.8	11.8	-1.0	14.9	12.4	-2.5	0.6	1.5	-2.1
Health	4.7	4.3	-0.4	4.7	4.4	-0.3	0.0	-0.1	0.0
Education	5.2	5.0	-0.2	5.2	4.5	-0.7	-0.5	0.5	0.0
Defence	3.7	3.0	-0.7	3.6	2.6	-0.9	-0.4	0.2	0.1
Contingency reserve	0.0	1.4	1.4	–	–	–	–	–	–
General government overall balance	**-7.9**	**-0.5**	**7.5**	**-7.3**	**0.6**	**7.9**	**1.1**	**0.4**	**0.6**
Public corporations market borrowing	-0.2	-0.2	-0.1	-0.2	0.0	0.2	0.2	0.3	0.0
Public sector overall balance	**-7.8**	**-0.2**	**7.5**	**-7.1**	**0.6**	**7.7**	**0.8**	**0.1**	**0.7**
Primary balance	-4.7	3.0	7.7	-4.0	4.1	8.1	1.1	0.4	0.7
Structural non-oil primary balance	-4.5	2.3	6.8	-4.5	3.3	7.8	1.0	1.0	0.0
Memorandum (in percent of potential GDP)									
Cyclically-adjusted primary balance	-4.1	2.7	6.8	-3.4	4.1	7.5	1.3	0.7	0.7
Structural non-oil revenue[d]	29.8	33.5	3.7	29.9	32.2	2.3	-1.3	-1.4	0.1
Primary expenditure	40.0	37.5	-2.4	39.4	34.8	-4.6	-2.7	2.1	0.6

[a]General government total expenditure in national accounts terms, which was the definition of public expenditure lying behind the general government borrowing requirement, excluding asset sales.

[b]Excludes cyclical social security and central government debt interest payments.

[c]Planned figures at $t + 5$ are authors' estimates.

[d]Excluding social security contributions.

TABLE 5.A.4 Darling's 2007 Pre-Budget Report and Comprehensive Spending Review: Plan vs. Actuals (in percent of GDP)

	Plan (p)			Actual (a)			Overperformance (actual relative to plan)		
								Of which:	
	t	$t+5$	$t+5-t$	t	$t+5$	$t+5-t$	$2012a-2012p =$ 2012 actual (projection) minus 2012 planned	$\Delta a - \Delta p =$ Actual improvement minus planned improvement	$2007a-2007p =$ 2007 actual minus 2007 preliminary estimate from plan ("base effect")
	2007p	2012p	Δp	2007a	2012a^c	Δa			
Revenues	**39.2**	**40.2**	**1.0**	**38.6**	**38.4**	**-0.2**	**-1.8**	**-1.2**	**-0.6**
Non-oil taxes and revenues	31.8	32.7	0.9	31.2	31.2	0.0	-1.5	-0.9	-0.7
Cyclical	0.1	0.0	-0.1	0.2	-0.6	-0.9	-0.6	-0.8	0.1
Structural	31.8	32.7	0.9	30.9	31.8	0.9	-0.9	-0.1	-0.8
North Sea oil revenue	0.5	0.5	0.0	0.5	0.7	0.1	0.2	0.1	0.0
Social security contributions	6.9	7.0	0.1	6.9	6.6	-0.3	-0.4	-0.5	0.0
Expenditures[a]	**41.9**	**41.5**	**-0.4**	**41.1**	**43.9**	**2.8**	**2.4**	**3.2**	**0.8**
Primary	39.8	39.4	-0.3	39.0	40.7	1.6	1.2	-2.0	0.7
Interest	2.1	2.1	-0.1	2.1	3.2	1.1	1.2	-1.2	0.0
by level of government[b]									
Central government	30.1	29.8	-0.4	28.9	32.4	3.5	2.7	-3.9	1.2
Local governments	11.1	10.8	-0.3	10.7	11.4	0.7	0.5	-1.0	0.4
by economic classification[b]									
Current expenditure	36.4	35.5	-0.9	35.8	37.8	2.0	2.3	-2.8	0.5
Wages and salaries	6.7	5.8	-0.9	5.6	5.5	-0.1	-0.3	-0.8	1.1
Goods and services	9.6	10.1	0.5	10.3	10.7	0.4	0.5	0.1	-0.6

Subsidies	0.5	0.4	−0.1	0.5	0.4	−0.1	0.0	0.0	0.0
Grants	19.6	19.2	−0.3	19.4	21.2	1.8	2.0	−2.1	0.2
Capital expenditure	3.4	3.6	0.1	3.2	2.9	−0.3	−0.7	0.5	0.2
by function (selected items)[b]									
Social security	9.9	9.7	−0.2	9.7	11.0	1.3	1.3	−1.5	0.2
Health	7.5	7.8	0.3	7.0	8.0	0.9	0.2	−0.6	0.4
Education	5.5	5.6	0.1	5.4	5.6	0.3	0.0	−0.1	0.2
Defence	2.7	2.7	−0.1	2.7	2.9	0.2	0.2	−0.3	0.1
Contingency reserve	0.0	0.4	0.4	–	–	–	–	–	–
Public sector overall balance	−2.7	−1.3	1.4	−2.4	−5.5	−3.1	−4.2	−4.5	0.3
Primary balance	−0.6	0.8	1.3	−0.3	−2.3	−1.9	−3.0	−3.3	0.2
Structural non-oil primary balance	−1.1	0.3	1.4	−1.2	−2.3	−1.1	−2.5	−2.5	0.0

[a] Public sector (total managed expenditure).

[b] Planned figures at $t + 5$ are authors' estimates.

[c] Actual figures at 2010 are based on the 2010 Budget.

Notes

1. The fiscal year runs from April through March. The notation of FY1994, for example, refers to the fiscal year running from April 1994 to March 1995.

2. Howe's first "emergency" budget in 1979 had already introduced a significant increase in the VAT rate from 8 to 15 percent and cut marginal income tax rates as the first step in a longer-term strategy of rebalancing the tax burden from direct to indirect taxes.

3. According to the conventions of the time, the authorities' objectives were framed in terms of the public sector borrowing requirement, with proceeds from asset sales being computed as negative expenditure.

4. Expenditure measures in the November 1980 Autumn Statement included temporary moratoria on new defense contracts and on new capital spending on housing by local authorities, while allowing more spending on industrial support and on special employment measures. Revenue measures included increases in the rate of employees' national insurance contributions and the taxation of income from North Sea oil.

5. Projections for the two final years were published only on main aggregate fiscal figures for largely "illustrative" purposes, while detailed projections by economic classification and program were presented for a three-year horizon.

6. Nigel Lawson stated in his budget speech (in March 1984) that "in contrast to previous years, I have no package of public expenditure measures to announce in this Budget. The [Public Expenditure] White Paper plans stand."

7. Presented to Parliament by the Chancellor of the Exchequer, "The Next Ten Years: Public Expenditure and Taxation into the 1990s" (March 1984).

8. Nigel Lawson stated in his March 1984 budget speech that "we have seen a massive enlargement in the role of the state, at the expense of the individual, and a corresponding increase in the dead weight of taxation holding back our economic progress as a nation. This process has to stop. But it has arisen because much public spending was directed to eminently desirable ends. This raises difficult issues which deserve the widest possible consideration and debate."

9. The November 1993 Budget was the first budget to consolidate revenue and expenditure measures, which were previously announced in spring and autumn respectively. The March 1993 Budget focused on revenue decisions, with expenditures set during the spending round of the previous autumn.

10. Financial Statement and Budget Report 1993–94 (March 1993), Financial Statement and Budget Report 1994–95 (November 1993), and IMF Background Paper: The United Kingdom (October 1994).

11. HM Treasury, Financial Statement and Budget Report 1994–95, November 1993.

12. The early results of the first four reviews—into social security, education, health, and the Home Office—had already led to concrete policy changes in the November Budget (such as the tightening of eligibility rules for invalidity benefits).

13. The overall public expenditure envelope grew steadily as a share of the economy from 37 percent in FY1999 to 42 percent by FY2007.

14. Despite the slowdown in the capital spending envelope, the government managed to finance within this envelope two of the largest infrastructure projects in U.K. history—the construction of the park, venues, and facilities for the 2012 Olympic Games, and the Crossrail project, a high-speed rail link between Heathrow Airport and the growing commercial and residential centers in the Thames estuary.

15. For a detailed treatment, see IMF Staff Report, July 2009.

16. The increase in personal allowances and thresholds reduced revenues by an estimated £1.7 billion relative to a fully indexed but unchanged tax structure (IMF Recent Economic Developments: The United Kingdom, February 1985).

17. The amount that the central government thinks local governments should spend on revenue expenditure.

18. This legacy of underinvestment was a principal motivation cited by the incoming Labour Government in the late 1990s for the adoption of a Golden Rule, which allowed it to borrow to invest in the revitalization of public assets.

Acknowledgments

The authors are grateful to David Heald, Paolo Mauro, Kevin Fletcher, colleagues in the European Department, and seminar participants at HM Treasury for valuable comments and discussions. Stephanie Eble provided helpful inputs at an early stage of the project.

CHAPTER 6

Italy: Medium-Term Fiscal Planning under Frequent Government Changes

Fabrizio Balassone,
Sandro Momigliano, and Pietro Rizza

Introduction

The story of Italy's rapidly growing public debt in the 1970s and 1980s and its subsequent experience "living with" high public debt has been told in several studies (beginning with classic contributions such as Giavazzi and Spaventa, 1988). Less well known, however, is the story of the many attempts at achieving and maintaining a high primary surplus aimed to halt and to reverse the trend increase in public debt. To tell this story, this chapter analyzes the motivation, design, and implementation of Italy's medium-term fiscal adjustment plans, from the first fully fledged plan presented in 1988 to the plan released in 2005 and covering 2006–08, the last plan whose execution was not disrupted by the recent global economic and financial crisis.

Our analysis shows that overall performance under the plans was generally poor: medium-term targets were seldom attained and when this happened it was often thanks to unexpectedly favorable macroeconomic developments. This said, implementation of the plans (even if at times only partial) was instrumental to stabilizing the debt ratio, albeit at high levels, and to meeting the criteria for Euro entry. Under pressure, Italy delivered, but the choice of policy tools was too often sub-optimal, leaving behind a challenging legacy.

A preview of the key findings is as follows:

- A large portion of the deviations of fiscal outturns from plans occurred in the first year and often reflected an underestimation of the initial fiscal deficit. These slippages were seldom offset in subsequent years, as multiyear targets seemed to fall by the wayside—a shortcoming perhaps to be expected given that the average duration of governments was 15 months.[1]
- Other main sources of ex-post deviations were errors in macroeconomic forecasts and current primary expenditure overruns.[2] Instead, revenues often overperformed as ratios to Gross Domestic Product (GDP) (therefore adjusting for errors in macroeconomic forecasts), partly reflecting the implementation of tax-based "mini-budgets" introduced to partly compensate for fiscal slippages.

Turning to policy implications, these findings point to the following areas as priorities for improvement:

- To avoid underestimating the initial deficit in fiscal planning and to strengthen the execution of annual budgets, introduce an integrated financial management information system for the general government.
- To strengthen the institutional framework buttressing budget implementation, introduce mechanisms to ensure that multiyear targets are not abandoned, such as: multiyear expenditure ceilings; mechanisms to offset fiscal slippages, particularly deviations occurring early on in the implementation of plans; and an independent fiscal monitoring authority.[3]

The remainder of this chapter is organized as follows. The first section presents a concise history of fiscal planning in Italy. Next, we analyze the performance of medium-term fiscal plans against outturns and identify the main sources of deviations. The following section focuses on the implementation of plans for the year ahead. The next section delves into the design and implementation of two especially important medium-term plans (selected on the basis of ex-ante characteristics): the 1994 plan, which covered the three years leading to the launch of the European Monetary Union (EMU) and was thus characterized by strong motivation to meet the Maastricht convergence criteria by 1997; and the 2002 plan, which was devised and ultimately executed by a single government.[4] The Conclusion summarizes the main findings and their policy implications.

A Brief History of Italy's Fiscal Planning Framework

Until the late 1970s, medium-term fiscal planning was not on Italy's institutional menu. Even the annual budget had little planning ahead of its implementation. Budget preparation was strictly bottom-up, with the overall balance representing the outcome of independently approved spending decisions rather than a constraint over those decisions. Macroeconomic planning was in the policymaker's toolkit right from the birth of the Republic,[5] but it often followed a sector-by-sector approach, with no guarantee of consistency between macroeconomic targets and the means for their attainment.

The risks involved in this approach to public financial management were largely masked by the rapid growth of the 1950s and 1960s, which helped to contain government debt below 40 percent of GDP (see Figure 6.1). Over the 1970s, however, with the economy slowing down and public expenditure rising rapidly (reflecting the lagged impact of reforms that had extended the coverage of public intervention in education, health care, and social security; see Franco, 1993), the general government deficit swelled (from less than 4 percent of GDP in 1970 to almost 10 percent in 1979; see Figure 6.2) and the debt-to-GDP ratio reached 60 percent. Against that background, the need to provide tighter links between macroeconomic and fiscal targets on the one hand, and budgetary decisions on the other, was gradually recognized.

A major reform of the budgetary process took place in 1978, when Law 468 introduced two new fiscal management tools: (a) the finance law, a bill to be approved annually to modify revenue and expenditure legislation in

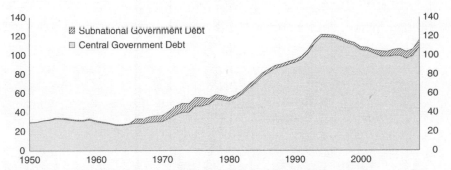

FIGURE 6.1   General Government Debt, 1950–2009 (in percent of GDP)

Sources: Francese and Pace (2008) and Banca d'Italia.

Notes: General Government Debt is the sum of Central Government Debt and Subnational Government Debt. The latter includes regions, provinces, municipalities, and other subnational government bodies.

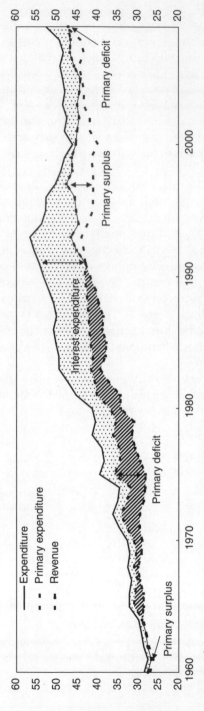

FIGURE 6.2 Revenues, Expenditures, and Fiscal Balances, 1960–2009 (in percent of GDP)

line with the policies set forth in the *Planning and Forecasting Report* (*Relazione Previsionale e Programmatica*, a document introduced in the 1960s, specifying plans for the following year); and (b) a multiyear budget to be drafted in two versions, one based on current legislation and the other on government plans.

However, the government debt ratio rose rapidly to 100 percent of GDP by the end of the 1980s. The finance laws failed to curb galloping public spending: their approval still followed a bottom-up approach, with the budget balance target being voted last, after all spending and tax decisions had been taken. The resulting deficits approved by Parliament were much higher than the original government proposals, sometimes by as much as one half (Crescenzi, 2007). Multiyear budgets were only drafted based on current legislation and figures for the outer years did not represent a constraint on the selection of targets to be embedded in the annual budgets.

In an attempt to regain control of the public finances, a second reform of the budget process was undertaken in the context of Law 362/1988, which: (a) introduced the Economic and Financial Planning Document (EFPD—*Documento di Programmazione Economico-Finanziaria*), to be transmitted to Parliament each year by May 15, showing the government's public finance forecasts and targets for the following three years as well as their underlying macroeconomic assumptions; (b) required that any legislative proposal be accompanied by a report quantifying its impact on the public finances; and (c) effectively extended to the finance law the constitutional provision prohibiting deficit financing of new legislation (article 81).[6]

Italy's medium-term fiscal framework has remained essentially unaltered since the approval of Law 362/1988, but fiscal targets have found an external anchor in European fiscal rules (the Excessive Deficit Procedure (EDP) and the Stability and Growth Pact (SGP)). In addition, the definition of *public sector* has evolved over time to fall in line with European requirements, and the structure of the State budget was streamlined several times. This said, even the recent reform (Law 196/2009), which replaces the EFPD with a Decision on the Public Finances and pays more attention to issues of coordination across government levels, does not change the basic features of Italy's public financial management.

Short-Term Origins of Medium-Term Failures

In this section, we outline our methodology, review key facts on the degree of ambition and implementation of pre- and post-EMU plans, and suggest that weak medium-term performance under the plans had short-term origins, owing to weaknesses in fiscal recording and monitoring and failure to take remedial action.

Methodology

We split our analysis into two periods, 1988–96 and 1997–2005, thus distinguishing between pre- and post-EMU plans.[7] Most plans drafted in 1988–96 referred to the State sector (an aggregate that broadly corresponds to central government). Since the mid-1990s, however, official documents have included forecasts and targets also for the general government, the reference for the European fiscal framework. Our analysis of EFPDs refers to the State sector over 1988–96 and to the general government over 1997–2005.

The EFPDs present medium-term targets for several fiscal indicators (primary balance, overall balance, gross debt, and, more recently, cyclically adjusted balance). We only consider targets up to three years ahead, even though some EFPDs planned for longer horizons. Also, we focus on the primary balance, the main aggregate directly controlled by policymakers, and on the overall balance, the main indicator in the policy debate and the European fiscal framework. We also examine the fiscal effects of differences between the macroeconomic scenarios underlying plans and outturns.

Facts

Pre-EMU plans were more ambitious. They targeted on average an improvement in the primary balance of 2.7 percent of GDP over three years, compared to 0.8 in post-EMU plans. The average planned improvement in the overall balance was, respectively, 4 and 1.5 percent of GDP.

Comparing primary balance targets and outturns for the 1988–96 plans returns a mixed picture. About half of the three-years-ahead primary balance targets were met and, on average, the difference between outturns and targets was 0.5 percent of GDP, a relatively small amount compared to the planned improvement. In terms of the overall balance, however, the score is less satisfactory. Only one-third of the targets, those set in 1994–96, were achieved. On average, actual deficits exceeded targets by 1.4 percent of GDP[8] (see Figure 6.3).

The performance of the 1997–2005 plans was far worse. Although three-years-ahead targets for the primary and overall balance were less ambitious (partly because initial deficits were lower than prior to Maastricht qualification), they were only met once and twice, respectively. On average, outturns for the primary and overall balance fell short of targets by, respectively, 2.7 percent and 2.0 percent of GDP (see Figure 6.4). The primary balance deteriorated over most of the period; the "EMU dividend" from lower interest rates was dissipated.

The timing of the emergence of discrepancies from plans is revealing. In pre-EMU plans, on average, outturns were broadly on target for the first two years, for both the primary and overall balance, with the slippage occurring

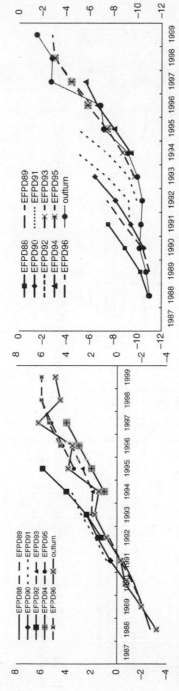

FIGURE 6.3 Pre-EMU Targets (by vintage) and Outturns (in percent of GDP; state sector; left side: primary balance; right side: overall balance)

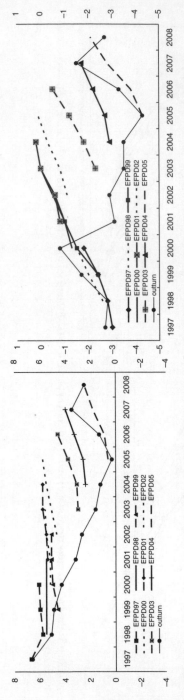

FIGURE 6.4 Within EMU Targets (by vintage) and Outturns (in percent of GDP; general government; left side: primary balance; right side: overall balance)

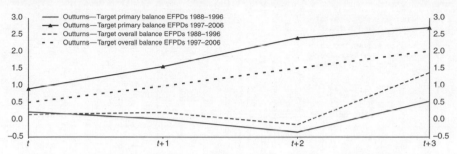

FIGURE 6.5 Gap between Outturns and Targets during the Plans (A positive value indicates that the actual balance was lower than the target; in percent of GDP)

in the third year. However, the plans with the largest gap between outturns and projections (1991 and 1992 EFPDs) showed an optimistic assessment of the initial fiscal position and suffered from poor budget implementation in the first year. These shortcomings featured also in later plans: after 1998 an optimistic appraisal of the initial fiscal position and slippages in each of the following three years contributed more or less equally to the final gap. Thus, half of the gap was already built up by the first year of the plan (see Figure 6.5).

A Closer Look at the Causes for Poor Performance

Difficulties in correctly assessing the initial fiscal position and implementing the plan's first year budget would have had a limited impact on medium-term targets if offsetting fiscal effort had been undertaken. However, this feedback mechanism was missing: the fiscal effort planned in year t for year $t + 1$ (as measured by the planned improvement in the overall balance) was not positively correlated with the gap between the overall balance in t (as assessed in the same year) and the target set for year t in year $t - 1$. In fact, when a slippage is detected (in two-thirds of the sample) this correlation has the wrong sign and is relatively high, indicating that the larger the slippage, the smaller the effort planned in the following year. In these cases, the effort planned in year t for year $t + 1$ is also on average lower than the effort planned for the same year ($t + 1$) in year $t - 1$.

Difficulties in meeting fiscal targets also stemmed from worse than assumed macroeconomic outturns. Figure 6.6 compares GDP growth forecasts and outturns for the year in which EFPDs were presented and for the subsequent 3 years. On average, EFPDs projected a substantial acceleration in economic growth, with rates expected to double between year t and $t + 3$. Actual growth, however, remained broadly constant.

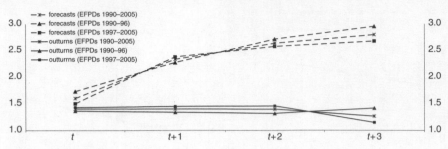

FIGURE 6.6   Growth Rates: EFPD Forecasts and Outturns (percentages)

This said, growth projection errors were only slightly larger than those made by independent forecasters. Over the period 1990–2005, cumulative growth forecast over a three-year projection horizon in EFPDs was, on average, 0.6 percentage points higher than *Consensus Forecast*, which in turn was 3.1 p.p. higher than outturns.[9]

The combined gap between GDP forecasts and outturns was even higher, 4.5 p.p., if one restricts attention to the cases (two-thirds of the sample) in which the target for the overall balance in year $t + 3$ was not achieved. Assuming a budget semi-elasticity to output of 0.5,[10] these GDP forecast errors account for an average difference at year $t + 3$ between fiscal targets and outturns of 2.25 p.p. of GDP, or 80 percent of the actual slippage.

A Narrative of Design and Performance of Pre- and Post-European Monetary Union Plans

In this section, we return to the design and performance under pre- and post-EMU plans, using a more narrative approach and delving into greater detail regarding the composition of fiscal adjustment.

Before EMU

During this period, policymakers clearly understood the need for fiscal adjustment. In the initial years, their objective was to curb the rapid growth in public debt, viewed as a danger for the stability of the economy, with the primary deficit the crucial control variable (Sartor, 1998).[11] The Treaty of Maastricht, signed in 1992, gave new impetus to fiscal consolidation: the debt-to-GDP ratio was to be put on a declining path and the overall deficit reduced below 3 percent of GDP, the requirements to join EMU.

Over 1988–96, the target set for the State sector primary balance at $t + 3$ missed five times by a sizable margin (see Figure 6.7). In three cases,

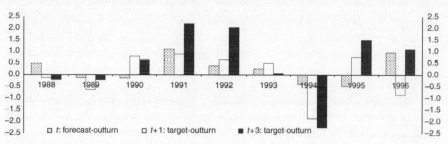

FIGURE 6.7 State Sector Primary Balance: Differences between Targets and Outturns (in percent of GDP)

outturns were slightly better than targets. In 1997, the year of Maastricht qualification, the primary surplus turned out larger than planned.

The performance in terms of the overall balance is marked by two clearly distinct phases: targets were missed by a wide margin over 1988–93, whereas outturns were better than targets over 1994–96. The slippage over 1988–93 was on average larger for the overall balance than for the primary balance as interest payments turned out larger than forecast. Over 1994–96, lower than forecast interest payments on average contributed to improved fiscal performance vis-à-vis targets.

The primary balance followed an improving trend during the period considered, but the tendency of outturns to fall short of targets in the first part of the period had a bearing on overall fiscal performance: the primary surplus in 1999 was 1.5 p.p. of GDP lower than the target set for 1995 in the 1992 EFPD. Moreover, fiscal consolidation in 1992–97, while successful in stabilizing public debt and securing EMU participation, left a difficult legacy. The consolidation relied heavily on tax increases and cuts to capital spending; recourse to temporary measures was large, especially in 1997 (Balassone et al., 2002; Degni et al., 2001; Marino, Momigliano, and Rizza, 2008). Thus, post-EMU plans aimed at alleviating the tax burden and increasing public investment, together with the achievement of targets for the budget balance.

Within EMU

Over this period, plans became gradually less ambitious. Initially, targets were consistent with the commitment, taken in March 1998 at the Economic and Financial Affairs Council (ECOFIN), to maintain a primary surplus equal to or above 5 percent of GDP.[12] The rationale for such a target was to rapidly bring down the debt ratio toward 60 percent of GDP, the threshold set by European agreements. Later EFPDs gave prominence to the objective set in the SGP of achieving a budget position close-to-balance or in surplus in the medium term (this was broadly consistent with the previous primary surplus commitment). Plans generally set achievement of these targets for the end of, or even beyond, the forecasting horizon. In reality, the main relevant priority during this period was to keep the general government deficit below 3 percent of GDP.

For the plans presented in 1997–2005, the targets set for the overall fiscal balance were met twice, thanks to stronger than expected economic growth, but on average deficits turned out larger than targeted, by 2.2 percent of GDP. Slippages were somewhat larger for the primary balance (2.8 percent of GDP on average), reflecting lower than projected interest payments. This last result genuinely reflected a welcome surprise rather than prudence in forecasting interest payments, which since the late 1990s has been largely a technical exercise, based on the future levels of interest rates expected by markets (i.e., the forward rates implicit in the yield curve).

With the exception of 1999, plans always started with an optimistic perception of fiscal developments during the year of drafting (see Figure 6.8). Discrepancies were often large: the projected primary surplus for the year in which the plan was drafted was on average 0.9 percent of GDP higher than the outturn. A pattern emerges clearly: a significant part of the deviation from plans over 1998–2004 occurred in the first year, due to bad in-year assessment and poor implementation of the subsequent budget. The next plan recognized the slippage but made no attempt to make up in subsequent years for the ground lost: the curves in Figure 6.4 slide but do not get steeper; indeed, they often flatten.

Measures with temporary effects on the fiscal balance (on average, 1 percent of GDP over 1995–2006) were often used to comply formally with EU fiscal rules without incurring the economic and political costs of more durable adjustments (Momigliano and Rizza, 2007). Such measures include various tax amnesties (most notably, the one introduced in 2003, which increased revenues by 1.3 percent of GDP) and several reduced-rate withholding taxes on one-off revaluations of corporate and personal assets.

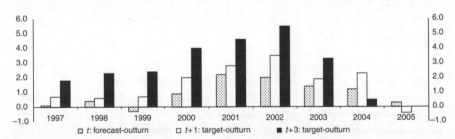

FIGURE 6.8 General Government Primary Balance: Differences between Targets and Outturns (in percent of GDP)

Implementing Plans for the Year Ahead

The previous section showed that a significant part of the slippages with respect to medium-term targets already occurred in the first year of fiscal plans. This section provides further analysis of this phenomenon for the period 1998–2008, by comparing outturns with targets for the following year, as reported in the *Planning and Forecasting Report* (PFR, November version), the last fiscal report of the year.

Basing the analysis on PFRs has two advantages compared to using EFPDs, namely:

- PFRs provide a full set of fiscal variables, taking into consideration the budget for the following year as submitted to Parliament at the end of September. This detailed information is seldom included in EFPDs, which usually only set targets for the primary and overall balances and provide information on the size of the fiscal adjustment to be implemented.
- PFRs include updated fiscal and macroeconomic projections compared to EFPDs. This is especially relevant for those relatively frequent instances in which a mid-year budget was passed during the summer, after the EFPD was presented.

Figure 6.9 plots the primary balance in year t as targeted in year $t - 1$, along with the outturn as measured both in year $t + 1$ and in the latest statistical release. The distance between the two outturn lines ($t + 1$ and final) shows the relevance of the statistical revisions that occurred after the publication of the first outturn, which was especially large in 2000–04.[13] On average, the target primary surplus, as set in year $t - 1$, was 0.8 percent of GDP

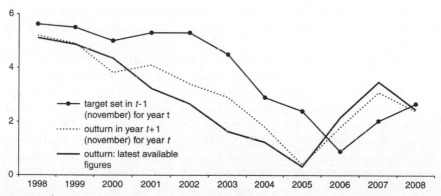

FIGURE 6.9 Primary Balance (in percent of GDP)

higher than the outturn measured at $t + 1$ and 1 percent higher than the finalized outturn.[14]

The gap between targets and outturns declines to 0.6 percent of GDP if one focuses on the changes in the primary balance, a measure that excludes the base effect arising from incorrect assessment of initial conditions: on average, governments targeted (in year $t - 1$) an *improvement* in the primary balance by 0.3 percent of GDP, whereas the latest available data point to a *worsening* by 0.3 percent. This is the net result of the expenditure-to-GDP ratio increasing by 0.8 p.p. more than planned, and the revenue-to-GDP ratio turning out 0.2 p.p. higher than planned.

Errors in forecasting nominal GDP had a small impact on the gap between target and outturn expenditure ratios. In 1998–2008, nominal growth was, on average, 0.4 p.p. lower than planned. Assuming, as an approximation, that in the short run primary expenditure is independent of price and real macroeconomic developments, if GDP had been as expected, the slippage on the expenditure ratio would have amounted to 0.6 p.p. of GDP.

Slippages in 1998–2008 were therefore largely determined by the dynamics of nominal primary expenditure. Excluding 2002 and 2008, the annual increase in primary spending turned out to be always larger than what had been planned the year before.[15] Over the whole period, the average nominal growth of primary expenditure was 4.5 percent, against a targeted growth of 3 percent. Most of the expenditure slippage came from current primary outlays.

The better than expected revenue performance partly relates to mid-year budgets (usually passed during the summer) containing measures to increase revenues, which were not included in year $t - 1$ forecasts. This factor amounts on average to 0.1 percent of GDP. Another possible explanation is that GDP is an imperfect indicator to project revenues: tax forecasts are better linked to the dynamics of more specific proxies for the main tax bases (i.e., consumption for indirect taxes and labor income for social security contributions). Usually, the forecasting error concerning these variables is smaller than for other, more volatile, GDP components (e.g., net exports).

But our results also signal prudence in forecasting revenues, or even political economy motives because, especially in the years we analyze, a high tax burden was a politically sensitive indicator and governments made its reduction a priority. Our evidence is in line with the findings of Buettner and Kauder (2010), who run a regression on a panel of 12 Organization for Economic Cooperation and Development (OECD) countries controlling for GDP forecasting errors, and find that Italy is the only country for which revenue forecasts display a statistically significant bias (at the 5 percent confidence level), with revenue forecasts being systematically lower than outturns.

Two Important Plans Analyzed in Detail

We select two EFPDs for in-depth analysis, one from each of the two sub-periods identified in the section entitled Short-Term Origins of Medium-Term Failures. The first was presented in 1994 and covered the three years leading to the launch of EMU: it is therefore the EFPD characterized by the strongest motivation to achieve targets. The second is the 2002 EFPD, which was planned and implemented by the same government (the 2001–05 Berlusconi Government). Selecting this plan thus enables us to exclude government changes, which might have weakened the implementation of fiscal plans.

The 1994 Plan: Qualifying for EMU

The foreword to the 1994 EFPD stressed how far away Italy was from meeting the fiscal criteria for participating in EMU from the outset. The document provided detailed tables concerning fiscal targets for the State Sector and the wider Public Sector.[16] It envisaged an improvement by about 3 percent of GDP in the primary balances of both sectors (almost entirely from lower expenditure), which, albeit topped up by a reduction of 1 percent of GDP in the interest bill, still left the overall balances at 6 percent of GDP in 1997, well above the Euro entry threshold (see Table 6.1). In the rest of this section, we focus on the Public Sector and refer to targets in terms of changes vis-à-vis 1994 to avoid base effects. Fiscal targets were based on a macroeconomic scenario in which real GDP growth would increase sharply in

TABLE 6.1 EFPD 1994 Main Fiscal Targets versus Outturns (public sector, in percent of GDP)

	1994		1995		1996		1997	
	Target	Outturn	Target	Outturn	Target	Outturn	Target	Outturn
Borrowing requirement	10.2	9.6	8.6	7.3	7.2	6.9	6.1	3.1
Interest expenditure	10.7	10.8	10.3	11.1	9.9	10.6	9.8	9.3
Primary borrowing requirement	−0.5	−1.2	−1.7	−3.8	−2.7	−3.7	−3.7	−6.2
Primary expenditure	45.7	44.3	44.4	41.9	43.1	44.7	42.0	44.5
Revenue	46.1	45.5	46.1	45.8	45.7	48.4	45.6	50.8
Debt	127.6	128.5	128.5	127.8	128.2	124.2	126.6	118.5

TABLE 6.2 EFPD 1994 GDP Growth Forecasts versus Outturns

	1995		1996		1997		Cumulative Growth 1995–97 Outturn Minus Forecast
	Forecast	Outturn	Forecast	Outturn	Forecast	Outturn	
Nominal	5.5	8.2	5.4	5.7	5.6	4.2	1.7
Real	2.7	3.0	2.8	0.7	3.1	1.5	−3.6

1995, and remain high (marking a slight acceleration) in 1996 and 1997 (see Table 6.2).

Figure 6.10 (panel a) compares the gap between forecast and outturn for the main fiscal aggregates over the three-year horizon of the 1994 EFPD. It shows that the overall balance improved significantly more than originally envisaged. Although a larger than expected reduction in the interest bill helped, the primary surplus improved by 5 percent of GDP against a planned improvement of 3 percent of GDP. However, contrary to the original plan, the adjustment occurred entirely on the revenue side.

This better than planned performance was not the result of a continuous effort. In 1995, both economic growth and fiscal consolidation accelerated compared to the original program (see Figure 6.10, b). This was followed by a setback in 1996, when an increase in expenditures more than offset a further rise in revenues (see Figure 6.10, c). This temporary halt, which occurred in the context of a slowdown in economic activity, still left the cumulative outturn ahead of plans. Finally, in 1997, there was a final rush to the finish line, ultimately leading to Euro entry, on the basis of stronger than planned revenues and tighter budget implementation than originally envisaged, despite lower than projected real growth (see Figure 6.10, d).[17]

It is difficult to assess the impact of the errors in macroeconomic projections on the performance of the 1994 EFPD. Although real growth over 1995–97 was some 3.6 p.p. lower than forecast, nominal growth was in fact 1.7 p.p. higher. In a multiyear context, price developments may be expected, as a first approximation, to have broadly compensating effects on revenues and expenditures. We would thus conclude that actual developments, compared to macroeconomic projections, made the achievement of the budget balance target harder, lowering taxes by 1 percent of GDP and increasing by a more limited amount, spending related to unemployment. However, the exceptionally large positive inflation surprise in 1995 may have facilitated consolidation, because it is politically less costly to delay the passthrough of higher prices onto expenditures than to outright reduce nominal expenditures.

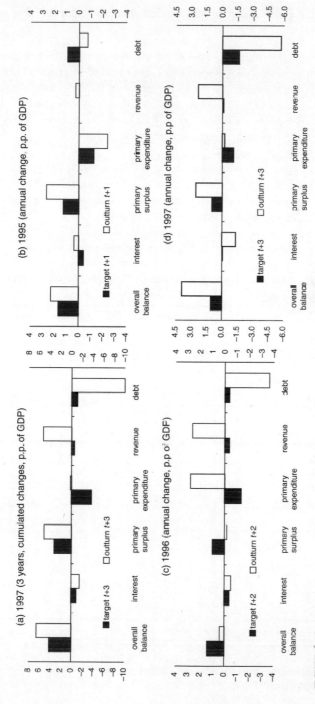

FIGURE 6.10 Public Sector: 1994 Targets and Outturns (in percentage points of GDP)

The 2002 Plan: Fiscal Planning and Implementation under a Stable Government

In view of the relatively favorable fiscal situation projected for 2002 (a general government deficit just above 1 percent of GDP), the EFPD presented in July of that year planned a limited (1 percent of GDP) improvement for the primary balance in 2003–05 (see Table 6.3). The Government, however, aimed to reduce by almost 2 percent of GDP the revenue ratio. A large adjustment in current primary expenditures would therefore have been necessary to achieve both targets.[18]

The fiscal strategy assumed rapid real GDP growth throughout the projection period; this optimistic scenario, as in most other EFPDs, did not materialize (as for several other plans, projections for the GDP deflator proved instead lower than outturns; see Table 6.4).

TABLE 6.3 EFPD 2002 Main Fiscal Targets versus Outturns (General Government, in percent of GDP)

	2002	2003	2004	2005
	t	$t+1$	$t+2$	$t+3$
I. EFPD presented in July 2002	Preliminary estimate	Proj	Proj	Proj
Revenues[a]	46.2	45.8	45.3	44.3
Expenditures	47.3	46.6	45.6	44.2
Primary	41.4	40.7	39.8	38.5
Primary (in percent of potential GDP)	40.9	40.4	39.7	38.5
Overall balance	−1.1	−0.8	−0.3	0.1
Primary balance	4.7	5.1	5.5	5.8
II. Final actual	Actual	Actual	Actual	Actual
Revenues	44.5	45.1	44.5	44.2
Expenditures	47.4	48.6	48.0	48.5
Primary	41.9	43.4	43.3	43.9
Primary (in percent of potential GDP)[b]	42.1	43.2	43.3	43.9
Overall balance	−2.9	−3.5	−3.5	−4.3
Primary balance	2.7	1.6	1.2	0.3

[a]The plan does not include targets for expenditure and revenue ratios but only for the tax burden, which represents 92 percent of the latter. We assume the residual part of revenue to remain constant as a ratio to GDP over the period 2003–05 and compute the expenditure ratio consistent with such assumption and targets for the overall balance.
[b]Computed applying the Hodrick-Prescott filter to latest available figures for real GDP.

TABLE 6.4 EFPD 2002 GDP Growth Forecasts versus Outturns (percent)

	1995		1996		1997		Cumulative Growth 1995–97 Outturn Minus Forecast
	Forecast	Outturn	Forecast	Outturn	Forecast	Outturn	
Nominal	4.8	3.1	4.8	4.2	4.8	2.7	−4.8
Real	2.9	0.0	2.9	1.5	3.0	0.7	−6.9

The EFPD targeted a surplus of 0.1 percent of GDP for 2005. The outturn was instead a deficit of 4.3 percent of GDP. More than a third of the difference can be attributed to a large base effect: the actual deficit in 2002 was 1.8 percent of GDP worse than the assessment in the 2002 EFPD.

If we focus on changes (to exclude the base effect), the outturn for the year 2005, a deficit increase of 1.4 percent of GDP, differs from plans by 2.6 percent of GDP. This gap reflects a large slippage in primary expenditure: its ratio to GDP was planned to fall by 2.9 p.p., but it actually increased by 2 p.p. (see Figure 6.11). If we exclude the "denominator effect" arising from the outturn for real GDP (lower than projected in the EFPD), the slippage more than halves, but remains sizeable. The impact of primary expenditure overruns was partially offset by interest payments falling more rapidly than projected and by the revenue ratio declining by far less than planned. The personal income tax reform outlined in the 2002 EFPD was partially implemented in 2003 and 2005, but its impact was largely compensated by the fiscal drag (income tax brackets were, and still are, not indexed to inflation) and by small increases in other revenues.

More than a third of the slippage (in terms of level of the overall balance) was already evident one year after the plan was launched, when the July 2003 EFPD reassessed the 2002 deficit to be as high as 2.3 percent of GDP and estimated it to remain constant in 2003. The new EFPD also

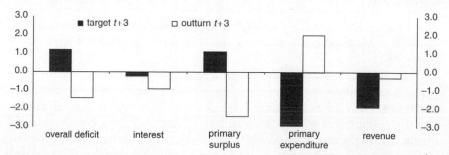

FIGURE 6.11 EFPD 2002 Targets versus Outturns (changes in percent of GDP)

pointed to significantly weaker GDP growth in 2003. In this context, the 2003 EFPD aimed at the minimum effort consistent with abiding by European fiscal rules, that is, a 0.5 percent structural improvement in the overall balance. Therefore, the new plan only partially offset the fiscal slippage.

A similar story unfolds in 2004: a larger slippage is recognized (the 2004 deficit is assessed at 2.9 percent of GDP), but the 2004 EFPD aims for limited fiscal consolidation in 2005, targeting a deficit of 2.7 percent of GDP (the structural improvement, excluding the effects of the cycle and of temporary measures, amounts to 0.4 percent of GDP).

Main Lessons from the Two Episodes

Starting on the right footing, in the sense of an accurate assessment of the starting fiscal position, is key. Success in 1997 also owes to the unusually good performance (compared to initial projections presented in the plan) in 1994. Failure in 2005 owes significantly, though not exclusively, to a large "base effect" (the actual deficit in 2002 was 2.9 percent of GDP, 1.8 percent higher than the assessment made in the 2002 EFPD).

Longer-lived governments do not necessarily outperform short-lived ones, at least when macroeconomic circumstances are less favorable (cumulative growth in 2003–05 was 2.2 percent, against 5.2 percent in 1995–2007), and worse than forecast.

Commitment is important for fiscal performance, even in the absence of a multiyear plan. The decision to make it into EMU in 1996 boosted performance vis-à-vis the 1994 plan. However, the 1996–97 episode shows that when time is tight, consolidation has to rely heavily on tax increases, especially if the capacity to control spending is poor.

Lastly, though their effects over a multiyear horizon are difficult to assess, large positive surprises in prices (such as the one in 1995) may at least temporarily help a government committed to fiscal consolidation.

Conclusion

This chapter has identified several factors underlying the frequent, large deviations of fiscal outturns from medium-term fiscal plans in Italy in 1988–2008.

Typically, a large part of the slippage occurred in the first year of the plan, usually reflecting an overly optimistic assessment of the initial fiscal conditions. This raises two issues: the quality of in-year fiscal information, and the institutional mechanisms aimed at buttressing implementation of medium-term fiscal plans. The first issue recently prompted policymakers to launch the harmonization of accounting standards across the general government and to plan the implementation of an integrated financial management information system—key objectives of the recent reform of Italy's fiscal framework (Law 196/2009). Although it will take some time for tangible improvements to occur, this seems to be primarily a technical factor where better data and information systems can be of great help.

The second issue (i.e., the absence of institutional mechanisms to enforce that slippages incurred in the first year be compensated for in subsequent years) seems to reflect broader political factors. Frequent government changes likely played a role here, but as shown in the chapter, the issue was relevant even under the one stable government included in our sample. Indeed, it may partly reflect a more general lack of ownership of European fiscal rules and targets, which is not unique to Italy and which the 2005 reform of the SGP attempted to address. To ensure that past slippages are not forgotten, an appropriate national institutional setup could be considered, for instance involving an automatic mechanism to compensate in subsequent years any slippage occurring early on during the execution of medium-term plans.[19]

As most slippages came from spending overruns, introducing expenditure ceilings and accompanying them to similar adjustment mechanisms as those mentioned previously with reference to the overall balance could help to shrink the gap between fiscal plans and outturns.[20] In this respect, introducing an independent authority with the task of assessing the consistency of annual budget plans with medium-term targets could help to raise public awareness of policy choices and to keep governments accountable.[21]

Macroeconomic forecasts were somewhat optimistic in the sample analyzed.[22] The independent fiscal authority mentioned previously could play a role also in this respect, although many independent observers already provide alternative macroeconomic forecasts, and the evidence shown in the chapter reveals that negative growth surprises were, for the most part, genuine surprises to independent observers, too.

Good news in the sense of better than planned outturns often came from the revenue side. As ratios to GDP (which are largely unaffected by errors in macroeconomic forecasts) revenues frequently outperformed plans. However, strong revenue performance often represented the last resort to compensate for expenditure overruns. In the years 1996–97, the unplanned increase in revenues made possible Italy's qualification for EMU. In the following decade the tax burden remained broadly stable, though virtually all plans targeted a reduction. As a result, a much-desired reduction in the size of the state and in the tax burden failed to materialize, ultimately owing to negative surprises (overruns) on the expenditure side.

European authorities have recently concurred that a major policy lesson stemming from the current crisis is the need to improve Member States' domestic fiscal frameworks. A set of minimum requirements is being defined, which covers accounting, statistical and forecasting issues, numerical rules, medium-term budgetary frameworks, and comprehensive coverage of public finances. A regular assessment and peer review of domestic fiscal frameworks is also envisaged to evaluate other desirable (though nonbinding) features.[23] Our analysis highlights the importance of domestic fiscal frameworks and suggests that Italy may significantly benefit from adhering to the indications agreed upon at the European level.

Acknowledgments

We are grateful to the editor for extensive support and advice; we also thank David Heald, Lusine Lusinyan, and Ricardo Velloso for very useful comments and Enrico Bonamici for excellent editorial assistance. The views expressed in this chapter are those of the authors and do not necessarily reflect those of the Banca d'Italia.

Notes

1. The short life of governments was a factor in 1988–2000, as only the government led by Romano Prodi lasted more than two years (May 1996–October 1998). In 2001–08, there were two consecutive governments led by Silvio Berlusconi (2001–05 and 2005–06) and the second government led by Romano Prodi lasted two years (May 2006–May 2008).

2. Indeed, this is consistent with previous studies that highlighted chronic difficulties in restraining current expenditures, only temporarily overcome during the special effort to meet the Maastricht criteria in the run-up to euro entry (see Balassone et al., 2002 and 2008; and Marino, Momigliano and Rizza, 2008). Looking at the time period following the one covered by our analysis, it is worth noticing that in 2009 and 2010—in the exceptional circumstances created by the crisis, including the strong pressure coming from financial markets—the control on expenditure was more effective than in the past.

3. For a comprehensive overview of the numerical fiscal rules in force in the EU countries and an assessment of their impact on budgetary outcomes, see Ayuso-i-Casals et al. (2007).

4. The 2001 Economic and Financial Programming Document, also presented by the Berlusconi Government, was rushed in only a few weeks after the government took office, with considerable uncertainty regarding the true state of public finances.

5. The first macroeconomic plan was the "Italian Long-Term Economic Program: 1948–49 to 1952–53" (or "Tremelloni Plan") devised in connection with the 1948 "European Recovery Plan" or ("Marshall Plan").

6. Article 81 of the Italian Constitution states that "Any [. . . .] law involving new or increased expenditures must specify the means to meet these expenditures."

This provision was intended to exclude the possibility of deficit financing new legislation, but for a long time it was not effectively implemented. With Law 362 and the strengthening of Parliamentary regulations, Article 81 became a more effective constraint, though still not water-tight (see Salvemini, 2003).

7. The plan presented in 1996 is included in the pre-EMU group because its main objective was to meet the Maastricht criteria. The decision to accelerate fiscal consolidation, aiming at a deficit below 3 percent of GDP already in 1997, was taken in the fall of 1996. The plan presented in 1997 largely assumed Italy's qualification to EMU.

8. If we exclude the EFPD presented in 1994, for which the outturn for 1997 was used to assess performance against the Maastricht criteria, the average slippage was 2 percent of GDP, about half the planned improvement (Figure 6.3).

9. Average of the forecasts published in the initial days of April and October (www. consensuseconomics.com/download/G7_Economic_Forecasts.htm.); the EFPDs were usually presented at the end of May or in June. For 1998–2005, cumulative growth forecast over $t + 1$ and $t + 2$ in EFPDs was on average 0.9 p.p. higher than in the European Commission Autumn forecasts, which in turn was 1.3 p.p. higher than outturns.

10. The budget semi-elasticity to output measures the change in the budget balance (as a ratio to GDP) arising from a 1 percent change in real GDP. Estimates by the OECD and the European Commission, as well as our own (based on the method described in Bouthevillain et al., 2001), set the Italian budget semi-elasticity to output close to 0.5.

11. As Giuliano Amato, Treasury Minister in 1988 put it, "The calling to [. . .] heal the Italian economy from the plague of inflation, we fulfilled it. Now there's another mission: it is to free this economy from public debt" (Amato, 1990, p. 48).

12. Corriere della sera, March 22, 1998. "Italia nella moneta unica con sei impegni."

13. We adjust the data to take account of one-off factors that could bias comparison between targets and outturns. The three main adjustments relate to the receipts from Universal Mobile Telecommunications Service (UMTS) licenses in 2000, the cancellation of the railway company's debt and the impact of a European Court of Justice decision on Value Added Tax (VAT), both in 2006.

14. Which of the two comparisons is relevant would require a case-by-case analysis, as it depends on whether statistical revisions concerning year t made after $t + 1$ were the result of unanticipated changes to statistical rules, or the response of statistical authorities to window dressing. Both factors played a role in the period. On the one hand, after the launch of EMU, the statistical protocol of reference for European fiscal rules changed from the 1979 to the 1995 version of the European System of Accounts (ESA) and Eurostat released opinions clarifying the interpretation of provisions in the protocol. On the other hand, evidence of window dressing in several EU countries is found, by Milesi-Ferretti (2003); Milesi-Ferretti and Moriyama (2004); Von Hagen and Wolff (2004); Koen and van den Noord (2005); and Balassone, Franco, and Zotteri (2006 and 2006).

15. Lower than expected primary spending in 2002 stemmed from sales of public real estate that were not originally planned and that were accounted for as negative expenditures.

16. There is no reference to the general government in the 1994 EFPD. The definition of Public Sector adopted in Italy at the time was close to that of general government (it included local governments and social security institutions), though slightly wider (it also included some state owned enterprises).

17. For an account of Italy's run-up to EMU, see Spaventa and Chiorazzo (2000), Degni et al. (2001) and Balassone et al. (2002).

18. The tax reform was part of a set of structural measures to increase potential and effective GDP growth by half a percentage point per year. The plan did not include an explicit target for capital expenditure, but it was clear that the Government mostly meant to cut current expenditures.

19. Such as those in the recent constitutional reform in Germany or in the Swiss system of fiscal rules on which the former draws substantially.

20. See Ljungman (2008) and references therein.

21. On the role of independent fiscal authorities see Debrun, Hauner, and Kumar (2007). Calmfors (2010) provides an account of the actual operation of such an independent authority, the Swedish Fiscal Policy Council.

22. On bias in government macrofiscal forecasts, see Milesi-Ferretti and Moriyama (2004) and Jonung and Larch (2004, 2006).

23. See Van Rompuy (2010) and European Commission (2010).

CHAPTER 7

Japan: Fiscal Adjustment Plans and Macroeconomic Shocks

Keiko Takahashi and
Kiichi Tokuoka

Introduction

Japan's gross government debt as a share of Gross Domestic Product (GDP) has been the largest among advanced economies for over a decade. As Figure 7.1 shows, the government debt–to-GDP ratio had steadily risen since the late 1970s, with primary deficits posted almost every year. Application of a formal criterion grounded in the academic literature to assess fiscal sustainability (based on whether increases in public debt lead policymakers to respond by improving the primary balance) would suggest that fiscal policy has not been sustainable since the 1990s, though in reality investors retain confidence in Japan's public finances, as evidenced by low interest rates and abundant financing.[1] Japan's fiscal adjustment efforts in recent years have faced major setbacks and have not been able to arrest the accumulation of public debt.

The purpose of this chapter is to examine to what extent and why fiscal adjustment has not proceeded as intended in Japan, focusing in particular on the reasons behind "unexpected" changes relative to original intentions. On that basis, this chapter will aim to provide lessons for the design and implementation of fiscal adjustment plans, including dealing with unexpected (and unavoidable) economic changes.

The approach followed in this chapter starts from the identification of *ex-ante* fiscal adjustment plans based on the following criteria:

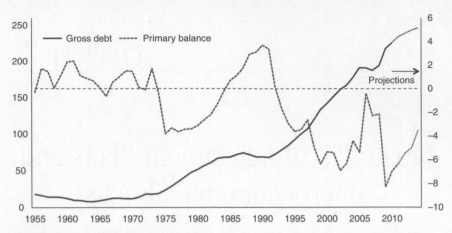

FIGURE 7.1 General Government Gross Debt and Primary Balance (in percent of GDP)

Sources: Cabinet Office, Japan (data before Fiscal Year (FY) 1969 are estimates), and World Economic Outlook (IMF.)

- Large planned reductions in fiscal deficits.
- Officially announced targets for fiscal consolidation and plans for achieving such targets articulated in, for example, special legislation or medium-term fiscal strategies.
- The formulation of adjustment plans and projections over multiple years: such projections can be viewed as target paths and compared with actual paths.

On that basis, this chapter focuses on two episodes: (i) the 1997 Fiscal Structural Reform Act; and (ii) a series of closely related fiscal adjustment attempts starting in FY2002—namely, the January 2003 medium-term fiscal framework, the FY2006 Basic Policies (annual policy guidelines), and the January 2007 medium-term fiscal framework.[2]

The 1997 Fiscal Structural Reform Act

After the asset price bubble burst in the early 1990s, expansionary fiscal policies were introduced to shore up economic activity. Between FY1992 and FY1995, seven fiscal stimulus packages were enacted through supplementary budgets. Consequently, the overall fiscal balance of the general government (excluding the social security fund) deteriorated from nearly zero in FY1990 to a deficit of 7 percent of GDP in FY1995 and

FY1996, bringing the gross debt–to-GDP ratio to around 100 percent at the end of FY1996.

In 1996, the economy appeared to have finally emerged from a long recession. The economic recovery from the post-bubble recession started in October 1993, but its pace had been relatively slow with signs of positive spillovers to the household sector observed only in 1996. A temporary surge in activity between late 1996 and the first quarter of 1997 largely reflected the lagged effects of interest rate cuts and the yen's depreciation, as well as frontloaded consumption ahead of a pre-announced consumption tax hike.[3]

In view of emerging signs of economic recovery, the fiscal stance embedded in the 1997 initial budget reflected a switch from expansion to consolidation. Fiscal structural reform was one of six priority reform initiatives[4] of then–Prime Minister Hashimoto. Ahead of the FY1997 budget discussion, the cabinet introduced the Fiscal Restructuring Targets, which included a reduction of the overall fiscal deficit of the general government (excluding the social security fund) to below 3 percent of GDP by FY2005 and a halt in the issuance of "deficit-financing bonds (bonds issued to finance current expenditures)." The 1997 initial budget constrained general expenditure growth significantly below projected nominal economic growth in order to achieve a primary surplus. On the revenue side, the consumption tax rate was raised from 3 percent to 5 percent in April 1997;[5] the temporary individual income tax cuts that had been in place since FY1994 were suspended in FY1997; finally, copayments for medical treatments were raised. The yield of these measures was estimated at 1.8 percent of GDP.

The political leadership undertook intensive discussions through 1997 on the Fiscal Structural Reform Act, which was eventually passed by the Diet in November of that year. The Council on Fiscal Structural Reform established in January 1997 and headed by the Prime Minister took the lead in the discussions. In March 1997, the Council approved five principles for the reform[6] and moved forward the target date from FY2005 to FY2003. Based on those principles, expenditure cuts by major policy area were approved by Cabinet in June 1997. Subsequently, the Fiscal Structural Reform Act was enacted in November 1997 in order to provide legislative support to the previously announced fiscal targets and expenditure cut measures. At that time, however, signs were emerging that the economy was slowing (see Figure 7.2).[7] Banking sector problems in late 1997 and the Asian financial crisis, which started in July 1997, contributed to the recession through their effects on external demand and on domestic credit conditions. These negative shocks were largely unexpected, with the policy emphasis placed mainly on the fiscal structural reforms in the wake of increasing public debt and demographic aging.

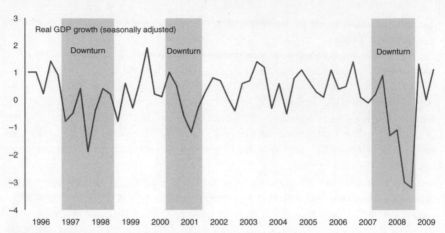

FIGURE 7.2 Real GDP Growth (year-on-year percent change)

Source: Cabinet Office.

Note: Cabinet Office decides business cycle dating based on index of coincident indicators.

Adjustment Plan and Objectives

Although the Fiscal Structural Reform Act was short-lived, it is useful to examine its design and objectives, taking into account the information available to policymakers at that time. The Act was Japan's first medium-term fiscal adjustments plan since World War II, spurred by strong political leadership in the wake of government debt increases and the fiscal consolidation efforts in other advanced economies, particularly in Europe in the run-up to the introduction of the Euro.

Upon its approval, the 1997 Fiscal Structural Reform Act featured:

- Medium-term fiscal targets. The Act aimed to: (i) reduce the fiscal deficit of the general government (excluding the social security fund) to no more than 3 percent of GDP by FY2003; and (ii) reduce the issuance of deficit-financing bonds every year and discontinue it by FY2003.
- Expenditure cut measures. Quantitative targets (caps) were set by major policy area for the period between FY1998 and FY2000 (regarded as the "intensive reform period").
- The plan sought to reduce the general government's fiscal deficit (excluding the social security fund) by an annual average of 0.6 percent of GDP over 6 years. This was to be achieved through expenditure cuts and additional future policy measures ("further required adjustment"), which were not announced at the time the plan was approved (see Table 7.1).

TABLE 7.1 The 1997 Fiscal Structural Reform Act: Plans and Outturns (Central government, in percent of GDP)

| | Plan(p) | | | Actual(a) | | | Actual improvement relative to plan | | |
| | | | | | | | FY2003a−FY2003p = FY2003 actual minus FY2003 planned | Δa−Δp = Actual improvement minus planned improvement | Of which: FY1997a−FY1997p = FY1997 actual minus FY1997 preliminary estimate from plan ("base effect") |
	FY-1997p	FY-2003p	Δp	FY-1997a	FY-2003a	Δa			
Revenues	12.0	12.0	0.0	11.1	9.5	−1.7	−2.5	−1.7	−0.8
Tax revenue	11.4	11.5	0.1	10.5	8.8	−1.7	−2.7	−1.8	−0.9
Cyclical	0.2	0.0	−0.2	0.4	−0.5	−0.9	−0.5	−0.7	0.2
Structural	11.2	11.5	0.3	10.1	9.3	−0.8	−2.2	−1.1	−1.1
Other revenue	0.6	0.5	−0.1	0.6	0.7	0.1	0.2	0.1	0.1
Expenditures	14.3	13.5	−0.8	14.3	15.1	0.9	1.7	−1.7	0.0
Primary	12.0	11.5	−0.5	12.2	13.6	1.4	2.1	−1.9	−0.2
Interest	2.3	2.0	−0.3	2.1	1.6	−0.5	−0.4	0.2	0.2
Further required adjustment	0.0	1.2	1.2	—	—	—	—	—	—
Overall balance	−2.3	−0.3	2.0	−3.1	−5.7	−2.6	−5.4	−4.6	−0.8
Primary balance	0.0	1.7	1.7	−1.1	−4.1	−3.1	−5.8	−4.8	−1.1
Structural primary balance	−0.2	0.5	0.7	−1.5	−3.6	−2.1	−4.1	−2.9	−1.3

Sources: "Medium-Term Fiscal Projection" (Ministry of Finance, January 1998) and authors' estimates.

The Act legislated numerical targets on initial budgets by major policy area (such as social security, public investment, and education), for which reform strategies and numerical expenditure cut targets were made explicit for the period between FY1998 and FY2000. Numerical targets were set in a way to ensure that priority expenditure recorded positive growth rates, whereas substantial cuts were scheduled for certain areas whose expenditure had already risen rapidly, such as public investment. As a result, policy-related expenditure ("general expenditure")[8] would be reduced for FY1998 (from the FY1997 initial budget) and be contained thereafter. Various long-term programs for public investment, agricultural and rural developments, and defense were reviewed.

Although specific expenditure ceilings were made explicit, medium-term projections suggested that additional measures would still be needed to underpin the targeted fiscal adjustment. In January 1998, a "Medium-Term Fiscal Projection" for the central government was submitted to the Diet, based on the fiscal targets and expenditure-cut measures stipulated in the 1997 Fiscal Structural Reform Act.[9] The projections relied on the following assumptions:

- Nominal GDP growth rates ranging between 1.75 and 3.5 percent[10]
- Estimated tax revenue impact of measures included in the January 1998 annual tax reform
- Implementation of the measures envisaged in the Act for policy-related expenditure ("general expenditure") in FY1998, such as, no increases in FY1999 and FY2000, and three alternative paths from FY2001 onward with annual expenditure increases of zero, one, and two percent, respectively

The medium-term projections, however, still showed large gaps between the projected and targeted fiscal balances, even under the assumption of a zero increase in policy-related expenditure from FY2001 onward. These gaps were presented as a "required fiscal adjustment" to be achieved by either revenue increases or further expenditure cuts.

The government's inability to explicitly identify measures needed to achieve the targeted fiscal adjustment should be understood in the context of the underlying economic conditions and uncertainty about the strength of the economic recovery. Although private consumption recovered in the third quarter of 1997 after the unwinding of the earlier surge ahead of the April consumption tax hike, negative shocks of the Asian financial crisis and the domestic banking crisis, in the same year, increased uncertainty for the economic outlook. Consequently, short-term forecasts of economic growth by the government and other institutions were revised downward during 1997 and 1998 (see Table 7.2). The nominal GDP growth assumption of a

TABLE 7.2 Comparison of Economic Forecasts by Different Institutions

Forecast	Publication		Real GDP Growth (percent)	
			1997	1998
Consensus Forecast[a]	May	1997	1.7	2.4
(Private institutions)	October	1997	1.2	1.7
	December	1997	0.9	1.1
	January	1998	0.2	1.0
IMF World Economic Outlook	May	1997	2.2	2.9
	October	1997	1.1	2.1
	December	1997	1	1.1
	May	1998	0.9	0
Economic Outlook[b]	January	1997	1.9	–
(Japanese government)	January	1998	0.1	1.9
	October	1998	−0.7	−1.8

Forecast	Publication		Nominal GDP Growth (percent)	
			1997	1998
Economic Outlook[b]	January	1997	3.1	–
(Japanese government)	January	1998	0.9	2.4
	October	1998	0.3	−1.8

[a]A consensus forecast is a simple average (mean) of individual predictions by about 20 private institutions collected by Consensus Economics.
[b]Fiscal year basis.

range between 1.75 and 3.5 percent in the medium-term fiscal projections was taken from the government's economic and social plan formulated in December 1995. Given the changes in economic conditions in 1997, this medium-term growth assumption was already overtaken by events at the time when the plan was drafted.

Results—Deviations from the Plan

This section looks at how and on what grounds the Act was amended and then suspended and examines to what extent targeted fiscal variables (the fiscal balance and issuance of debt-financing bonds) deviated from the original plans, and why.

AMENDMENT AND SUSPENSION OF THE ACT Soon after the enactment of the Fiscal Structural Reform Act, shocks from the domestic financial crisis came to the fore, including bankruptcies of four financial institutions.

The domestic credit crunch worsened business confidence and reduced investment and employment. The government responded by announcing 0.5 percent of GDP in income tax rebates, which were included in the FY1997 supplementary budget, and by frontloading public works. The FY1998 initial budget, announced at the same time as the FY1997 supplementary budget, was still contractionary, reflecting expenditure cuts mandated by the Fiscal Structural Reform Act. However, as the recession deepened further in early 1998, pressures for additional fiscal stimulus intensified. In April 1998, immediately after passage of the FY1998 initial budget, a stimulus package of 3 percent of GDP was announced.

The Fiscal Structural Reform Act was amended in May 1998 to allow flexibility in the face of deteriorating economic conditions. The authorities needed to amend the Act to maintain its consistency with the April 1998 stimulus package. In the amendment, the target date of medium-term fiscal objectives was extended from FY2003 to FY2005. In addition, the amendment relaxed the constraint on the issuance of deficit-financing bonds in the case of natural disasters or severe economic conditions as defined in the amendment. The spending ceilings on each expenditure category were not revised except for abandoning the 2 percent increase ceiling for social security–related expenditure.

During the course of FY1998, the fiscal stance shifted again toward expansionary. Prime Minister Hashimoto resigned in July 1998 after a defeat in an Upper House election. New Prime Minister Obuchi embarked on expansionary fiscal policy relying heavily on bond issuance. A package equivalent to about 5 percent of GDP was announced in November 1998, including cuts in personal and corporate income taxes, increased credit guarantees for bank loans to Small and Medium Enterprises (SMEs), temporary consumption vouchers, and a further boost to public works spending.

The Fiscal Structural Reform Act was suspended in December 1998 to implement fiscal stimulus, but it was stipulated that the suspension could be lifted when the economy recovered. Discussions in the Diet suggested that the government did not set a particular plan or schedule to resume the Act. The government acknowledged that it would be necessary to undertake fiscal consolidation in the near future, but focused on addressing the economic slowdown and financial system problems. The Act was never reinstated.

DEVIATIONS IN FISCAL AND MACROECONOMIC OUTTURNS FROM PLANNED PATHS

In FY1998, the general government fiscal deficit (excluding the social security fund) turned out at 7.5 percent of GDP, larger than its targeted level by nearly 3 percentage points. With growth lower than projected, cyclical revenues came in below expectations; moreover, the perceived need for stimulus to boost the economy resulted in discretionary tax cuts and higher spending. Actual tax revenues were lower than the initial budget level by

2 percent of GDP reflecting both discretionary tax cuts and unexpectedly low nominal economic growth, while actual general expenditures were higher by 1.5 percent of GDP (see Figure 7.3). With the adoption of an expansionary fiscal stance in FY1999, tax revenue continued to drop in the face of still negative nominal economic growth, while expenditure continued to increase with the November 1999 stimulus package.

DECOMPOSITION OF DEVIATIONS This section decomposes the deviation of actual fiscal balances from the targeted path between FY1998 and FY2003 in revenues and expenditures, both cyclical and structural, focusing on the central government's general account, for which real-time medium-term fiscal projections are available.[11]

APPROACHES TO DERIVE CYCLICAL AND STRUCTURAL (CYCLICALLY ADJUSTED) COMPONENTS Deviations in the fiscal balance can be decomposed into cyclical and structural (cyclically adjusted) components. A standard approach, used appropriately in other chapters, is to compute cyclical and cyclically adjusted components using output gap estimates and tax elasticities, both real-time and actual. For the purposes of this chapter, however, we instead use government records (such as government publications and minutes) to identify policy actions and their ex-ante estimated impacts.[12] We treat these as discretionary (structural) components and derive cyclical components as residuals. This approach allows us, for example, to benefit from the authorities' detailed knowledge of tax structures and elasticities, which in Japan's case differ considerably from Organization for Economic Cooperation and Development (OECD) averages (see ahead).

CONTRIBUTIONS OF CYCLICAL AND DISCRETIONARY TAX REVENUES AND EXPENDITURE Both cyclical and discretionary tax reductions, as well as higher stimulus-related expenditures, played a large role in derailing the fiscal balance off the targeted path. Figure 7.4 shows the decomposition of the deviation of actual fiscal balances into: (i) cyclical tax revenue; (ii) discretionary tax revenue; (iii) other revenue; (iv) primary expenditure; and (v) interest payments. Also reported is the "further required fiscal adjustment," which the authorities explicitly included in the plan (i.e., further planned adjustment for which measures would have to be identified at a later stage). By subtracting the impact of tax reforms adopted after the plan (discretionary tax revenue changes) from total tax revenue deviations from the targeted levels, we infer the deviations due to cyclical components. By contrast, we regard all primary expenditure changes as discretionary, assuming a zero expenditure elasticity for simplicity.

On the revenue side, large income tax cuts compounded the impact of weak economic conditions. In the course of FY1998, the government implemented additional temporary personal income tax cuts.[13] In FY1999, the

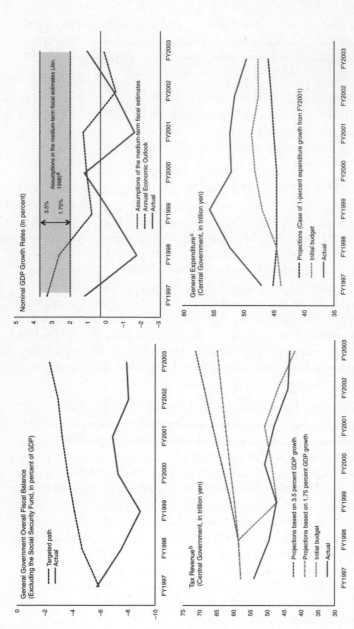

FIGURE 7.3 The 1997 Plan: Deviations in Fiscal and Macro Variables

Sources: Cabinet Office and Ministry of Finance (the Medium-term Fiscal Projections, January 1998).

[a]The government's Annual Economic Outlook published in January each year.

[b]The tax revenue includes revenue collected into the General Account. It includes stamp revenue.

[c]General Account basis. MOF's Medium-term Fiscal Projections show two other cases of 2 percent and zero expenditure growth from FY2001. General expenditure excludes interest payments and Local Allocation Tax grants. The initial budget amount does not include carryover from the previous year.

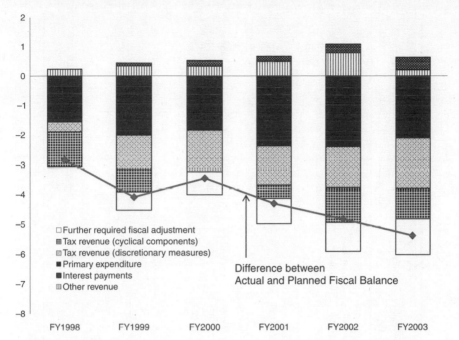

FIGURE 7.4 The 1997 Plan: Deviations in Fiscal Adjustment (Decomposition of Deviations in Overall Fiscal Balance of Central Government, in percent of GDP)

Sources: Ministry of Finance (the January 1998 medium-term fiscal projections, and actual data) and authors' estimates.

Note: The general account of the central government.

government adopted additional tax cuts in personal and corporate income taxes on top of Proportional Tax Reductions (which were renewed every year until FY2006). Revenue loss from the FY1999 package was estimated to be about 1 percent of GDP per year. Furthermore, large tax incentives were introduced between FY1999 and FY2003, for example, to boost investment (including residential) and support SMEs. Figure 7.4 shows large cyclical tax losses caused by unexpected economic changes in most years.

On the expenditure side, a series of stimulus packages raised primary spending. Between FY1998 and FY2002, no less than eight stimulus packages that required supplementary budgets were introduced (see Table 7.3).[14] Deviations in expenditures from the plan reflected not only these supplementary budgets, but also more expansionary budgets in FY1999–2002 than originally envisaged under the plan.

FINDINGS AND LESSONS The experience with the 1997 adjustment plan shows the importance of changes in economic growth and other macroeconomic and financial shocks. The plan was derailed quickly both through

TABLE 7.3 Stimulus Packages (from FY1998 to FY2002)

	FY1998		FY1999		FY2000	FY2001		FY2002
Announcement	April 1998	November 1998	June 1999	November 1999	October 2000	October 2001	December 2001	December 2002
Major components	Temporary tax cuts Public works	Public works Tax cuts (from FY1999) Financial measures Cash transfers	Employment measures	Public works Financial measures	Public works Financial measures	Employment measures Financial measures	Public works	Public works Financial measures
Project size								
(in percent of GDP)	3.2	4.8	n/a	3.4	2.2	0.3	0.8	0.9
(in trillion yen)	16	24	n/a	17	11	1.3	4.1	4.4
Supplementary budget (the general account)	**June 1998**	**December 1998**	**July 1999**	**December 1999**	**November 2000**	**November 2001**	**February 2002**	**January 2003**
(in percent of GDP)	0.9	1.5	0.1	1.3	0.8	0.2	0.5	0.6
(in trillion yen)	4.6	7.6	0.5	6.5	3.9	1.0	2.6	3.0
Central government bond issuance approved in supplementary budget								
(in percent of GDP)	1.2	2.4	0.0	1.5	0.4	0.3	0.0	1.0
(in trillion yen)	6.1	12.3	0.0	7.6	2.0	1.7	0.0	5.0
of which, deficit-financing bonds								
(in percent of GDP)	0.4	1.6	0.0	0.7	0.0	0.3	0.0	0.5
(in trillion yen)	2.0	7.8	0.0	3.7	0.0	1.4	0.0	2.6

Sources: Ministry of Finance and authors' estimates.

the direct impact of a slowdown in economic activity (and problems in the banking system) on fiscal revenues and through a change in policy priorities from fiscal consolidation to stimulating economic activity. In fact, a strong political leadership had catalyzed the initial fiscal structural reform, as shown by the introduction of explicit and medium-term expenditure ceilings by spending category. However, as economic conditions deteriorated, policymakers had to politically commit to stimulating the economy.[15] In the event, once fiscal stimulus was in place, it may have become entrenched.

The design of the fiscal adjustment plan reflected underlying concerns regarding growth developments. Expenditure ceilings did not bind actual spending but only limited initial budget levels compared to those in the previous year. In addition, the necessary measures to achieve the fiscal targets had not been fully, explicitly identified at the inception of the plan. These design features may have contributed to large deviations in fiscal adjustment from the initial plan. Yet it may be argued that the design itself was such as to permit these deviations because of widespread concern regarding the need to boost growth. Moreover, economic agents may have seen this and may have pressed for additional fiscal stimulus programs.

To some extent, deviations from the plan were also associated with macroeconomic assumptions already overtaken by events. Macroeconomic assumptions did not incorporate the more recently available economic information. The economy in 1997 was hit by negative shocks from the Asian financial crisis and the domestic banking crisis whose impact on the economy had not yet been fully understood. With such uncertainty, particularly with a strong downward risk, a fiscal adjustment plan could have had backup scenarios, such as an escape clause, in the case of negative economic shocks.[16]

Medium-Term Fiscal Adjustment Plans: Fiscal Year 2002 and the Following

In the intervening years, growth remained elusive or lackluster and the debt ratio continued rising steadily. Against this background, Prime Minister Koizumi, who was inaugurated in April 2001, put fiscal structural reforms back on the agenda, advocating structural reforms under the slogan of "no growth without reforms." As a first step, he committed to limiting Japanese Government Bond (JGB) issuance of the general account in the central government to no more than ¥30 trillion (6 percent of GDP) for the FY2002 budget. At the same time, and in recognition of the fragile economic recovery, the government passed two supplementary budgets in late FY2001.

The January 2002 medium-term fiscal framework[17] envisaged that the government would achieve a primary surplus in the early 2010s if policy efforts and favorable economic growth materialized. Such medium-term fiscal framework delineated the government's basic strategies for five years from FY2002 to FY2006 for structural reforms and economic and fiscal policies.[18] It focused on expenditure reforms to improve the quality of spending; enhanced spending control of central and local governments against the background of rising social security spending; and sought to improve efficiency of public works. Under the framework, general government expenditure (in percent of GDP) would be capped at the FY2002 level (37.6 percent of GDP) through FY2006. The framework envisioned a primary surplus of the general government (excluding the social security fund) in the early 2010s mainly through lower central and local governments' spending and supported by sustained economic growth. In June 2002, the authorities' Basic Policies—the annual guidelines for fiscal policy and reform initiatives—officially set a primary surplus in the early 2010s as a target. In January 2003, the medium-term fiscal framework was updated.

Given the weakness of economic activity, the authorities avoided committing to specific measures without firmer evidence of the recovery. The recovery that started in January 2002, while lasting for more than five years, was fragile in the early years, with real GDP growth of only 0.1 percent in 2002, and a contraction in the first half of 2003 (see Figure 7.2). Pessimism on the economic outlook remained, with persistent deflation and structural weaknesses, such as high private sector debt and nonperforming loans. Against this background, the authorities were sensitive about potentially adverse impacts of fiscal consolidation on the economy, haunted by the traumatic experience in 1998. Therefore, they preferred to preserve more flexibility in fiscal policy implementation, by postponing the adoption of specific and unduly ambitious measures until FY2005,[19] when the economy was recovering from the soft patch in 2004.

As the recovery took hold, the focus of policy discussions shifted to the design of the expenditure-tax mix in a fiscal adjustment package. From the beginning of 2005, the authorities started intensive discussions to formulate expenditure-tax reforms given the difficulty of relying only on expenditure cuts in light of the large fiscal adjustment needed. In designing such reforms, they gave priority to expenditure cuts to limit an increase in the tax burden, being aware of the public's perception that there was still room for cutting "wasteful" spending. The government emphasized that economic growth and fiscal consolidation should be pursued in tandem.

Based on these discussions, the FY2006 Basic Policies specified the timing for achieving a primary surplus and numerical ceilings on major expenditure categories. The FY2006 Basic Policies (approved in July 2006) set targets to achieve (and thereafter maintain) a primary surplus by FY2011 and reduce the debt-to-GDP ratio toward the mid-2010s.

ADJUSTMENT PLANS AND OBJECTIVES Starting in January 2002, the medium-term fiscal framework[20] was institutionalized in annual policymaking. It operated in tandem with the Basic Policies, a Cabinet decision prior to budget preparation on major macroeconomic and structural policies to be reflected in the following fiscal year budget. Fiscal consolidation plans were thus encapsulated in such policy frameworks and related documents.

The five-year medium-term fiscal framework was rolled over every year. For analytical purposes, this section looks selectively at the details of two sets of medium-term fiscal adjustment plans: (i) the January 2002 and 2003 medium-term fiscal frameworks; and (ii) the FY2006 Basic Policies and the January 2007 medium-term fiscal framework. The two subperiods were characterized by different policy approaches. In the first subperiod, policy intentions were almost entirely on the expenditure side, but the government did not have specific numerical targets by expenditure category. By contrast, in the second subperiod, numerical expenditure ceilings by category were identified and, at the same time, the need for tax-enhancing efforts was highlighted (although this was not translated in specific policy measures nor taken into account in the projections), while still placing greater emphasis on expenditure cuts. Key features of the two sets of fiscal adjustment plans include:

1. The January 2002 and 2003 medium-term fiscal frameworks
   - Medium-term fiscal targets in the 2002 framework.
      (i) The size of government measured by general government expenditure as a percent of GDP should be kept at or below the FY2002 level through FY2006 (the medium-term framework period)—implying that expenditure excluding the social security fund would be cut given rising social security costs.
      (ii) A primary surplus of the general government (excluding the social security fund) would be achieved in the early 2010s (assuming further consolidation efforts beyond the framework period and sustained economic growth).
   - Measures in the 2002 framework. Fiscal structural reforms included: prioritizing spending; improving efficiency of public works; and better use of outsourcing and Public Finance Initiative (PFI). For major expenditure categories, the following consolidation efforts were assumed:
      (i) Public works: prioritizing and improving efficiency to reduce them through FY2006 to the levels prevailing before the late 1990s.
      (ii) Social security: containing the level to the extent possible by implementing health care reform.

    (iii) Personnel expenses: containing the level to the extent possible by reducing the number of civil servants.

    (iv) Other general expenditures: containing by prioritizing and thorough reviewing.

■ January 2003 medium-term fiscal framework was the first update to the overall policy framework. It largely maintained the medium-term targets and measures set out in the 2002 framework, although in light of weaker economic growth, near-term fiscal targets were rendered less ambitious.

The government planned adjustments to the primary balance by about 0.5 percent of GDP per year, almost entirely through primary expenditure cuts (see Table 7.4). More expenditure cuts were planned through local governments than the central government (see Figure 7.5), reflecting the reform of intergovernmental fiscal relations under discussion at that time.[21] The reform aimed to achieve fiscal consolidation and to increase the efficiency of local government expenditure by (i) reducing subsidies for specific local projects; (ii) transferring tax resources from the central to local governments; and (iii) reducing the total amount of the local allocation tax (non-earmarked transfers) from the central government.

2. The FY2006 Basic Policies and the January 2007 medium-term fiscal framework

As the economic recovery became robust from 2005 onwards, fiscal adjustment paths were moved forward as documented in the FY2006 decision:

■ Medium-term fiscal targets announced in the FY2006 Basic Policies. The overarching targets were twofold:

    (i) Achieving a primary surplus of the general government (excluding the social security fund) by FY2011.

    (ii) Reducing the debt-to-GDP ratio by the mid-2010s by maintaining a primary surplus.

■ Measures in the FY2006 Basic Policies. The required fiscal adjustment (relative to the authorities' baseline) to achieve a primary surplus by FY2011 was estimated at ¥16.5 trillion (3 percent of GDP). The authorities presented options for fiscal adjustment through the "Integrated Expenditure-Revenue Reform." An important principle was that the impact of adjustments would be minimized if thorough expenditure cuts were undertaken before considering tax increases. Expenditure measures amounting to ¥11.4-14.3 trillion were identified; the rest of the required adjustment was to be covered by revenue measures (the expenditure cuts planned through FY2011 are in Table 7.5). To make the plans consistent with economic developments, the expenditure cut plans were to be reviewed every fiscal

TABLE 7.4 The January 2003 Medium-Term Fiscal Framework versus Outturns (in percent of GDP)

	Actual (*t*) FY2002*p*	Plan (*p*) FY2007*p*	Δ*p*	Actual (*a*) FY2007*a*	Δ*a*	Overperformance (actual relative to plan) FY2007*a*−FY2007*p* = FY2007 actual *minus* FY2007 planned
Revenues	**20.5**	**19.7**	**−0.8**	**21.7**	**1.2**	**2.0**
Tax revenue	15.9	15.4	−0.5	17.8	1.9	2.4
Cyclical	0.3	0.0	−0.3	1.7	1.5	1.7
Structural	15.6	15.4	−0.2	16.1	0.5	0.7
Other revenue	4.6	4.3	−0.3	3.9	−0.7	−0.4
	24.7	21.8	−2.9	22.0	−2.7	0.2
Primary expenditure	**24.7**	**21.8**	**−2.9**	**22.0**	**−2.7**	**−0.2**
Residuals[a]	−1.4	−0.8	0.6	−0.9	0.4	−0.1
Primary balance	**−5.6**	**−2.9**	**2.7**	**−1.2**	**4.4**	**1.7**
Structural primary balance	−4.5	−2.1	2.4	−2.0	2.5	0.0

Sources: Cabinet Office and authors' estimates.

[a]Residuals partly reflect expenditure of central government special accounts, which are not included in primary expenditure.

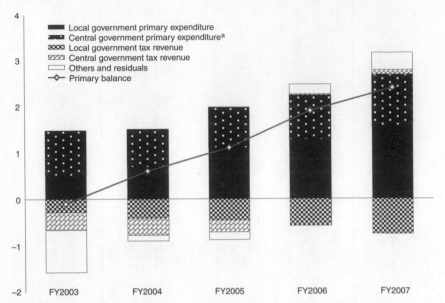

FIGURE 7.5 The 2003 Plan: Planned Cumulative Improvement in Primary Balance (General government, excluding the social security fund, in percent of GDP)

Sources: Cabinet Office and authors' estimates.

[a]Excludes local allocation tax grants (transfers from central government to local government).

year until FY2011. No specific revenue measures were identified (or committed to) in the FY2006 Basic Policies.

- The January 2007 medium-term fiscal framework was in line with the FY2006 Basic Policies. It showed an annual primary balance adjustment of 0.4 percent of GDP on average (see Table 7.6). The plan relied on expenditure cuts (about 2 percentage points of GDP over five years) and also expected cyclical tax increases. Although the government acknowledged that revenue-enhancing efforts would be required to achieve a primary surplus by FY2011, no revenue-enhancing measures were specified. Instead, assumed revenue increases were entirely cyclical, based on underlying macroeconomic assumptions foreseeing an upfront economic recovery based on growth-enhancing strategies advocated by Prime Minister Abe.[22,23] Accordingly, fiscal adjustments were also expected to be front-loaded, while the target year of achieving a primary surplus was basically unchanged from the previous year's plan. The underlying projections envisaged an adjustment by more than 1 percent in FY2007 followed by modest yearly adjustments of 0.2 percent of GDP on average through FY2011.

TABLE 7.5 The FY2006 Basic Policies: Expenditure Reforms through FY2011

| (in trillion yen) | FY2006 | FY2011 | | | Applications to budget and related reforms |
		Baseline	Reform	Adjustments	
Social Security	31.1	39.9	38.3	1.6	Further prioritizing and improving efficiency of medical benefits
Personnel Expenses	30.1	35	32.4	2.6	Further reforms both in the number of civil servants and salary structures.
Public Investment	18.8	21.7	16.1–17.8	3.9–5.6	Public works–related expenditure (general account): 1%–3% reduction; by continuous efforts (3% per year in nominal terms) of cost reductions, prioritization, and improvement of efficiency Local government–led public works: 1%–3% reduction
Others	27.3	31.6	27.1–28.3	3.3–4.5	Science and Technology: +1.1%—in line with economic growth ODA: 2%–4% reduction
Total	107.3	128.2	113.9–116.8	11.4–14.3	

Sources: The 2006 Basic Policies for Economic and Fiscal Management and Structural Reform (approved in the Cabinet on July 7, 2006).

Notes: The amounts above (in trillion yen) are the total amounts of expenditure cuts by central and local governments (national accounts based). Targeted growth rates for each category are applicable to central government's general expenditure budget. Those for local government–led public works are for the local budget plan (prepared by the Ministry of Internal Affairs and Communications).

Results—Deviations from the Plan

Following the same methodology used for the previous episode, this section looks at actual developments in the main fiscal target—the primary surplus of the general government (excluding the social security fund) and other fiscal and macroeconomic variables. It examines to what extent they deviated from the plans, and why.

DEVIATIONS IN FISCAL AND MACROECONOMIC OUTTURNS FROM PLANNED PATHS[24]

Primary Balance   Fiscal outturns between FY2004 and FY2006 were better than planned despite an initial rise in fiscal deficits in FY2002–FY2003. The primary deficit surged in FY2002 on account of a fall in tax revenues and the implementation of stimulus packages. However, the primary balance improved between FY2004 and FY2006 at a faster pace (about 1.3 percent of GDP annually, on average) than targeted (about 0.7 percent of GDP annually), reflecting strong tax revenue (see Figure 7.6). After these fast improvements, the primary balance caught up with the initially planned level for FY2006.

After FY2007, the primary balance deteriorated sharply due to the global recession, moving substantially off the targeted path. The improvement in the primary balance in FY2007 was much smaller (only 0.2 percent of GDP) than planned, reflecting lower tax revenues. Following the global financial crisis, Japan experienced sharp revenue shortfalls and the government provided a series of sizable stimulus packages (over 5 percent of GDP altogether). Consequently, the primary deficit rose to 8 percent of GDP in FY2009 (see Figure 7.6).

TABLE 7.6 The January 2007 Medium-Term Fiscal Framework (in percent of GDP)

	Plan			
	FY2006	FY2007	FY2011	Planned adjustment (FY2011–FY2006)
Revenues	**21.8**	**21.9**	**21.1**	**−0.7**
Tax revenue	17.5	18.6	18.4	0.9
Cyclical	0.0	1.1	0.9	0.9
Structural	17.5	17.5	17.5	0.0
Other revenue	4.3	3.3	2.7	−1.6
Primary expenditure	**22.2**	**22.2**	**20.1**	**−2.1**
Residuals[a]	−1.2	−0.3	−0.7	0.5
Primary balance	**−1.7**	**−0.6**	**0.2**	**1.9**
Structural primary balance	−0.5	−1.4	0.0	0.5

Sources: Cabinet Office and authors' estimates.

[a]Residuals partly reflect expenditure of central government special accounts, which are not included in primary expenditure.

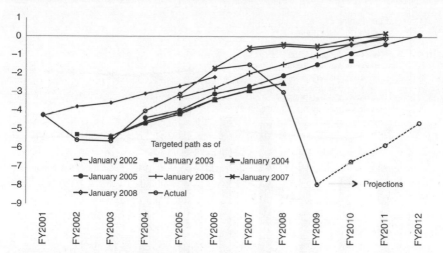

FIGURE 7.6 Planned and Actual Primary Balance (General government, excluding the social security fund, in percent of GDP)

Sources: Cabinet Office and authors' estimates.

Tax Revenue   Deviations in tax revenues were particularly large in both directions. Tax revenue outperformed their planned (or budget) levels between FY2003 and FY2006 (see Figure 7.7). The fact that tax revenue increased at a faster pace than nominal GDP growth suggests the existence of higher tax elasticities than those derived from the long-term relationship between revenues and the output gap, and highlights the difficulties in estimating short-term elasticities. In contrast, while the 2007-revised plan assumed higher tax-to-GDP ratios than previously projected by more than 1 percent of GDP, actual tax revenues were hit heavily by the economic slowdown. This upward revision in the tax-to-GDP ratio took place despite the absence of specific revenue measures. Also, despite the government's earlier commitment to increase its contributions to the National Pension in FY2009, no revenue measures were implemented (see Box 7.1).

Expenditures   While planned and actual expenditures continued on a downward trajectory through FY2006, general expenditure–to-GDP ratios (both of the central and local governments) were well above expectations in each of FY2002–FY2005, but were gradually reduced and eventually below the targeted level for FY2006. For an important subcomponent (i.e., public-works-related expenditure), actual spending generally exceeded budget levels, partly owing to large carryovers from previous years (see Figure 7.8).

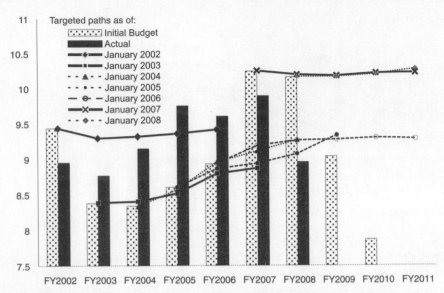

FIGURE 7.7 Planned and Actual Tax Revenue (Central government, in percent of GDP)

Source: Cabinet Office.

Note: The above tax revenue includes tax and stamp revenues that are collected into the General Account.

Box 7.1: Tax Revenue Volatility and Tax Elasticity*

Large unexpected deviations in actual tax revenue under the medium-term fiscal framework were an important factor behind both the improvement in the primary balance during FY2004–FY2006 and its subsequent deterioration during the global financial crisis. While a larger responsiveness of taxes to sharp output downturns than suggested by the long-run revenue elasticities is commonly observed in other countries (Sancak, Velloso, and Xing, 2010), this phenomenon may be associated with Japan's tax revenue structure, which is skewed toward direct taxes. For example, income taxes (corporate and personal) account for 57 percent of total tax revenues, whereas consumption taxes have been only 28 percent of total taxes in Japan. By contrast, income taxes and consumption taxes are on average 48 percent and 43 percent of total taxes (in 2007), respectively, in the OECD countries. Moreover, Japanese corporate income tax and to a lesser degree, personal income tax exhibit relatively high cyclical sensitivity, as measured by the income tax elasticity with respect to the output gap. In particular, the corporate income tax elasticity of Japan (1.65) is among the highest in the OECD countries:[25]

(*continued*)

(continued)

Tax Revenue Composition and Tax Elasticities

		Income Taxes	Property Taxes	Consumption Taxes
Japan	Share of total tax revenue	57%	15%	28%
	Tax elasticity	Personal Tax: 1.17 Corporate Tax: 1.65	–	1
OECD average	Share of total tax revenue	48%	9%	43%
	Tax elasticity	Personal Tax: 1.26 Corporate Tax: 1.50	–	1

Notes: The 2007 data are from the Ministry of Finance (Japan) and OECD. Tax elasticities with respect to output gap, Girouard and Andre (2005).
*Box prepared by Jaejoon Woo.

Macroeconomic Variables Nominal GDP was overestimated, owing to larger than projected deflation more than offsetting positive surprises for economic real growth rates (see Figure 7.9). Between FY2004 and FY2006, actual real economic growth surpassed the authorities assumptions, which were conservative (e.g., relative to the IMF's World Economic Outlook (WEO), see Table 7.7). However, the changes in the annual GDP deflator were negative, averaging less than minus one percent since FY2002, with deviation from projections by a large margin. That led to lower than expected nominal GDP growth, in particular, from FY2005 to FY2007.

GOVERNMENT'S REACTIONS TO THE GLOBAL FINANCIAL CRISIS As in most other advanced economies, the global recession derailed the Japanese authorities' fiscal consolidation plan. Although the fiscal stance embedded in the FY2008 initial budget was originally broadly neutral, a large stimulus package in response to the global recession together with a sharp decline in tax revenues led to a surge in fiscal deficits, pushing the government's commitment of achieving a primary surplus by FY2011 out of reach. In the medium-to long-term macroeconomic and fiscal strategies published in January 2009,[26] the government acknowledged that its commitment to achieve a primary surplus by FY2011 was not realistic anymore, while still referring to the target of stabilizing and then reducing the debt-to-GDP ratio by the mid-2010s. On revenue reforms, the authorities outlined a medium-term commitment for revenue and social security reforms,[27] which called for—conditional on economic recovery—new legislation by FY2011.

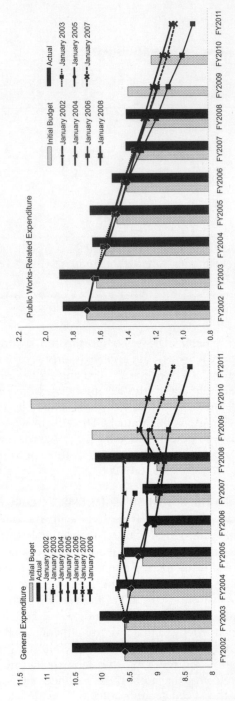

FIGURE 7.8 Planned and Actual Expenditure (Central government, in percent of GDP)

Sources: Cabinet Office and Ministry of Finance.

Notes: The above expenditure is on a General Account basis. Initial budget does not include carryover from the previous year. The FY2009 initial budget includes a one-off factor (transfer from a special account).

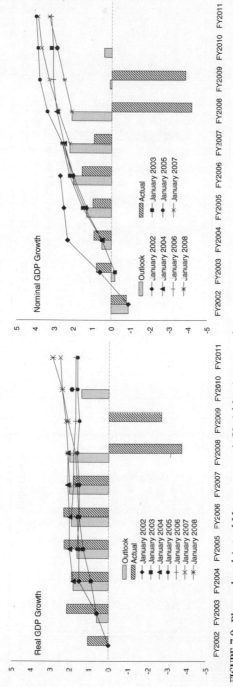

FIGURE 7.9 Planned and Actual Macroeconomic Variables (percent change)

Source: Cabinet Office.

TABLE 7.7 Comparison of Economic Forecasts by Different Institutions

Forecast	Publication		Real GDP Growth (percent)					
			2002	2003	2004	2005	2006	2007
Consensus forecast[a]	January	2002	−1.2	0.7	0.8			
(Private institutions)	January	2003		0.4				
IMF WEO	October	2001	0.2	2.0	3.4	3.6	3.6	2.9
	April	2002	−1.0	0.8	2.2	2.9	2.9	2.5
	September	2002	−0.5	1.1	2.5	2.6	2.5	2.3
	April	2003	0.3	0.8	1.0	1.7	2.2	
Medium-term projection[b]	January	2002	0.0	0.6	1.5	1.5	1.6	
(Japanese government)	January	2003	0.9	0.6	0.9	1.3	1.5	1.6

Forecast	Publication		Nominal GDP Growth (percent)					
			2002	2003	2004	2005	2006	2007
Medium-term projection[b]	January	2002	−0.9	0.6	2.3	2.5	2.7	0.0
(Japanese government)	January	2003	−0.6	−0.2	0.5	1.5	2.2	2.6

[a] A consensus forecast is a simple average (mean) of individual predictions by about 20 private institutions collected by Consensus Economics.
[b] Fiscal year basis.

In light of rapidly deteriorating fiscal positions, the FY2009 Basic Policies (released in June 2009) announced new medium-term fiscal targets including: (i) halving the primary deficit within 5 years excluding temporary stimulus packages; (ii) achieving a primary surplus (excluding the social security fund) within 10 years; and (iii) stabilizing the debt-to-GDP ratio (excluding the social security fund) by the mid-2010s and putting it on a downward path during the early 2020s.[28] In June 2010, the (new) government announced a fiscal management strategy, setting a target of achieving a primary balance by FY2020.

Decomposition of Plans' Deviations

This section presents a more stylized decomposition of deviations of the actual primary balance from the targeted path.

In the subperiod starting in FY2003,[29] a cyclical tax recovery led to positive deviations in the primary balance. Most of the overperformance in the primary balance (1.7 percent of GDP) through FY2007 came from cyclical tax revenue increases (see Table 7.4 and Figure 7.10), which were much stronger than in the plan—corporate tax revenues were especially buoyant. Structural tax revenue increases turned significant during FY2006–FY2007, with the phasing out of an earlier personal income tax cut.

In the subperiod starting in FY2007, the primary balance started to deviate significantly from the plan, following the onset of the global financial crisis, in FY2008, and further widened in FY2009 (see Figure 7.10). This was mainly due to cyclical tax declines and the substantial stimulus spending, which reached 5 percent of GDP for FY2009 and FY2010 altogether.

Conclusion

The experience of fiscal adjustments that started in FY2002 was built on some of the lessons learned from the 1997 episode. The newly introduced five-year rolling frameworks helped to make fiscal adjustment plans more resilient to macroeconomic shocks. While both episodes displayed large deviations from the original plans, which were triggered by economic crises, in the latter episode the government was able to maintain medium- to long-term fiscal consolidation objectives, rather than abandoning them. However, substantial modifications could not be avoided due to the unprecedented downturn from the global financial crisis. Going forward, an important objective is to further improve the design and implementation of plans to permit flexibility in the face of economic shocks while preserving the plans' medium-term targets and credibility.

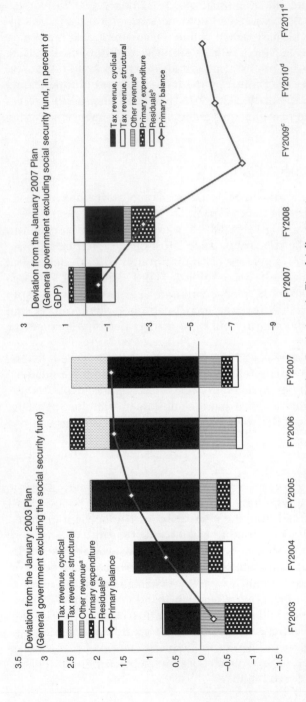

FIGURE 7.10 The January 2003 Plan and the January 2007 Plan: Deviations in Fiscal Adjustment

Sources: Cabinet Office and authors' estimates.

[a]Includes revenue other than tax, such as fees.

[b]Residuals partly reflect deviations from planned expenditure in central government special accounts (planned levels were not announced).

[c]Cabinet Office's estimate.

[d]Cabinet Office's projections.

Despite some improvement, these recent fiscal adjustment plans were still affected by similar issues as those experienced in the context of the 1997 adjustment plan. In both cases, revenue-enhancing measures had not been made explicit and expenditure ceilings were neither binding nor result-oriented. More specifically, while the government acknowledged the need to implement revenue measures, in order to secure stable funding for the increased government contributions to the National Pension, it did not spell out specific measures;[30] and frequent large supplementary budgets and carryovers of public investment continued to allow spending in excess of planned expenditure levels.

Moreover, in hindsight, the government's plans and their implementation could have been more ambitious when economic conditions were improving. Larger than expected fiscal adjustment at an early stage was supported by cyclical increases in taxes, but the pace of adjustment slowed down once economic activity decelerated. Given the large size of public debt, fiscal adjustment needs to take place throughout business cycles. Thus, a fiscal adjustment plan needs to take into account the impact of both recessions and booms on the fiscal position, and needs to be implemented without jeopardizing growth or overly stimulating the economy.

Japan's experience emphasizes the importance of built-in mechanisms to achieve targeted fiscal adjustments while dealing with unanticipated economic changes. The following could be considered to make fiscal adjustment plans more effective:

- Articulating more explicitly the pace and timing of adjustments and the supporting of (properly identified) measures
- Defining indicators in cyclically adjusted terms to reduce pro-cyclical bias
- Limiting the use of supplementary budgets to well-defined cases (e.g., natural disasters, annual entitlement expenditure adjustments)
- Adopting a medium-term budget (or expenditure) framework[31] to strengthen expenditure control

In particular, high tax revenue volatility needs to be managed with medium-term fiscal adjustment. The difficulty of estimating short-term tax elasticities highlights the need for a mechanism to manage volatile tax revenue in a fiscal adjustment plan. Large fluctuations in tax revenue, which may have been magnified by Japan's tax structure with high proportions of direct taxes, are considered to be related not only to GDP fluctuations but also to other factors such as a change in the composition of GDP, asset price fluctuations, and the amount of loss carried forward by corporations. Therefore, designing a built-in mechanism to manage unexpected cyclical tax windfalls/shortfalls with medium-term fiscal adjustment plans could be considered.

Appendix 7A: The Bohn Fiscal Sustainability Test[32]

Intuitively, Bohn's (1998) test asks to what extent primary surpluses have risen in response to increases in the public debt ratio. Specifically, the test examines fiscal sustainability by regressing fiscal primary balances against public debt and other determinants of primary balances. A positive coefficient on debt suggests fiscal sustainability in a sense that fiscal policy is responding to the accumulation of public debt by improving primary balance so that an inter-temporal budget constraint can be satisfied.

A regression for the Bohn fiscal sustainability test is expressed in the form,

$$PB_t = \alpha + \beta \cdot D_{t-1} + \gamma \cdot Z_t + \varepsilon_t \qquad (1)$$

where PB_t is the primary balance relative to nominal GDP; D_{t-1} is the debt-to-GDP ratio at the end of the previous period; Z_t is a set of non-debt determinants of the primary balance; and ε_t is an error term. Based on Barro's (1979) tax-smoothing model, Bohn (1998) and other literature that apply the Bohn fiscal sustainability test assume non-debt determinants of primary surplus (Z_t) to be temporary government spending, $GVAR$, and business cycle fluctuation in GDP, $YVAR$. Therefore, equation (1) can be rewritten as,

$$PB_t = \alpha + \beta \cdot D_{t-1} + \gamma_1 \cdot GVAR + \gamma_2 \cdot YVAR + \varepsilon_t \qquad (2)$$

Table 7A.1 reports the result of regressions for the Bohn fiscal sustainability test using Japan's general government data from 1947 to 2009. The data used in this Appendix are drawn from the National Accounts of Japan (the Economic and Social Research Institute of Cabinet Office, Japan) for 1955–2009, and the Hundred-Year Statistics of the Japanese Economy for 1946–1954. Fiscal data (gross debt, primary balance, and real expenditure) used in this Appendix are for the general government beginning in 1955 and, prior to that date, for the combined central and local governments. (The approximation involved in this change in coverage is not macroeconomically significant.)

As non-debt determinants, we use the output gap and the government expenditure gap, following Mendoza and Ostry (2008). The coefficients on D_{t-1} from the test for the whole period are significantly negative, implying that over 1947–2009 as a whole, fiscal policy has not been sustainable in a sense that the government did not improve the primary balance in response to increases in the debt level.

In an attempt to pinpoint, more specifically, subperiods during which fiscal policy according to this test was (un)sustainable, the same regression was estimated recursively for (a) all possible 25-year windows within

TABLE 7A.1 Bohn Fiscal Sustainability Test[a]

Sample	1947–2009			
Dependent variable	General government primary balance (in percent of GDP)[b,d]			
	I	II	III	IV
Constant	0.808	0.891	0.840	0.913
	(1.639)	(1.910)	(1.863)	(2.132)
	[0.107]	[0.061]	[0.068]	[0.037]
D_{t-1}[b]	−0.030	−0.031	−0.030	−0.031
	(−5.481)	(−5.892)	(−6.020)	(−6.443)
	[0.000]	[0.000]	[0.000]	[0.000]
Output gap[c]		0.273		0.245
		(2.688)		(2.615)
		[0.009]		[0.011]
Government expenditure gap[c]			−0.317	−0.295
			(−3.342)	(−3.269)
			[0.001]	[0.002]
Adj. R[b]	0.366	0.444	0.480	0.542

[a] *Sources:* Cabinet Office, Japan, Hundred-Year Statistics of the Japanese Economy, and authors' estimates.
[b] Debt-to-GDP ratio at the end of the previous year.
[c] Output and government expenditure gaps are percent deviations from Hodrick-Prescott trends of (in real terms).
[d] All estimates are OLS with annual data; ( ) = t-statistics; [ ] = p-value

1947–2009; and (b) all possible subperiods beginning in 1947. The estimated slope coefficients on D_{t-1} and corresponding P-values are reported in Figure 7A.1. In recent history, the only subperiods in which the slope coefficient on the debt ratio is positive and statistically significant (i.e., the P-value is 0.05 or below) are those beginning in the mid-1960s and ending in the mid-1990s. On this basis, the test would have signaled fiscal sustainability at risk at least since the mid-1990s.

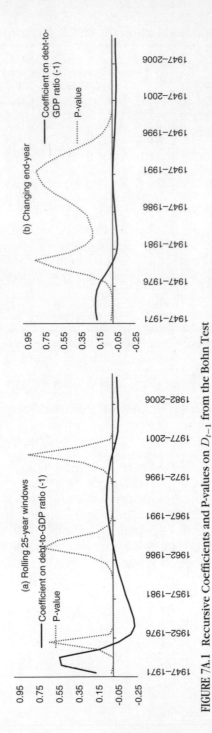

FIGURE 7A.1 Recursive Coefficients and P-values on D_{t-1} from the Bohn Test

Note: Sample periods over which the Bohn regression is estimated are reported on the horizontal axis.

Appendix 7B: Timeline of Medium-Term Fiscal Adjustment Plans in Japan

I. The 1997 Fiscal Structural Reform Act

Nov 1997 *Fiscal Structural Reform Act.* The general government deficit (excluding the social security fund) was targeted to fall below 3 percent of GDP by FY2003.

May 1998 *The Act was amended.* The target year of fiscal balance was rolled back to FY2005.

Dec 1998 The Act was suspended.

II. Medium-Term Fiscal Adjustment Plans—FY2002 and Following

Jan. 2002 *January 2002 Medium-Term Fiscal Framework (five-year plan).* The framework provided projections to achieve a primary surplus for the general government (excluding the social security fund) in the early 2010s based on a *desirable policy* scenario.

June 2002 *FY2002 Basic Policies (annual policy guideline).* The government set a target of achieving a primary surplus for the general government in the early 2010s.

Jan. 2003 *January 2003 Medium-Term Fiscal Framework (first update).*

July 2006 *FY2006 Basic Policies.* The government targeted to (i) achieve a primary surplus for the general government (excluding the social security fund) by FY2011 and (ii) stabilize the debt-to-GDP ratio toward the mid-2010s. The Basic Policies included a five-year expenditure reduction plan.

June 2009 *FY2009 Basic Policies.* The target date specified in the FY2006 Basic Policies was postponed.

Acknowledgments

The authors are grateful to Jaejoon Woo for insightful comments and valuable inputs, to Bumpei Miki for excellent assistance in the collection of data, and to Mauricio Villafuerte, Kenneth Kang, and the editor for guidance and suggestions. The authors also appreciate valuable comments from and discussions with Masatsugu Asakawa, Shigeru Ariizumi, Yukinobu Furuta, and Atsuko Takahashi, and insights from Koji Yano and Hideki Takada at an early stage of the project.

Notes

1. Methodology developed by Bohn (1998). See Appendix 7A for a description and results.

2. Japan had announced fiscal consolidation targets in the 1980s, such as the FY1982 zero ceiling and the FY1983 "minus ceiling"—setting a negative growth rate in budget requests from line ministries—as a means of ending the issuance of deficit-financing bonds. However, these efforts undertaken in the 1980s are excluded from the analysis, in light of the absence of a medium-term framework. For issues related to fiscal adjustment in Japan, see also Miyazaki (2006) and Tanaka (2003).

3. International Monetary Fund, Japan-Staff Report for Article IV Consultation (1998).

4. Hashimoto's initiatives encompassed reforms in: (i) administration, (ii) social security, (iii) economic structure, (iv) financial system, (v) education, and (vi) fiscal policies.

5. The increase in the consumption tax rate had been enacted in November 1994 for implementation starting in FY1997, together with permanent individual income tax cuts, which started in FY1995 in the wake of still fragile economy.

6. The five principles were: (i) aiming to achieve the Fiscal Restructuring Targets as early as possible, and no later than FY2005; (ii) during the "intensive reform period" between FY1998 and FY2000, placing numerical targets on major expenditure cuts; (iii) reducing general expenditure in the FY1998 budget compared to the level in FY1997; (iv) reconsidering long-term programs such as public works to be substantially cut and not creating any new long-term programs; and (v) containing the national burden rate (the ratio of burdens from tax and social security contributions plus fiscal deficits to national income) below 50 percent.

7. The former Economic Planning Agency (reorganized as part of the Cabinet Office in 2001) officially declared in June 1998 that the economy had peaked in May 1997. Business cycle dating in Japan is performed on the basis of an index of coincident indicators.

8. In the Japanese context, general expenditure is total expenditure (in the general account) minus debt service and minus tax allocation grants to local governments.

9. A "medium-term fiscal projection" was submitted annually by the Ministry of Finance to the Budget Committee together with the draft Budget. The projection covered the general account of the central government (excluding special accounts).

10. That range was based on the analysis in the "Economic and Social Plans for Structural Reform" (Cabinet decision in December 1995).

11. Although the Fiscal Structural Reform Act was abolished a year after its introduction, there is much to be learned by comparing actual outcomes with initial plans embedded in the Act. Indeed, this is an example of the novel information gained using this book's approach, which captures failures as well as successes.

12. Estimates of tax reform impacts on tax revenue are published in the document of Cabinet decision of an annual tax reform.

13. The total amount of temporary personal income tax cuts (including local resident tax cuts) in FY1998 was equivalent to 0.8 percent of GDP.

14. Not all the budgeted stimulus was used, but this still contributed to sizable expenditure overruns vis-à-vis the original 1997 plan.

15. In the press conference on December 17, 1997, upon his return from the Association of Southeast Asian Nations (ASEAN) summit, Prime Minister Hashimoto stated that he had made it explicit in the summit that Japan would not trigger a worldwide recession and, in this context, he had determined to implement a tax stimulus of ¥2 trillion through the FY1997 supplementary budget.

16. In this context, showing strong commitments attached to the Fiscal Structural Reform Act was preferred instead of announcing an escape clause, while considering possible stimulus within the scope of the Act.

17. This five-year rolling framework entitled "Structural Reform and Medium-Term Economic and Fiscal Perspectives" was announced in January 2002, in the course of FY2001 (the fiscal year runs from April to March) prior to the FY2002 budget discussion in the Diet. Medium-term macroeconomic and fiscal projections were provided by the Cabinet Office as a quantitative reference for the framework.

18. For fiscal structural reforms including achievement of a primary surplus, the medium-term fiscal framework considered a longer period going beyond FY2006.

19. For each yearly budget between FY2003 and FY2005, the authorities aimed to contain the general account expenditure and its policy-related "general expenditure" of the central government to levels of previous years.

20. The five-year macroeconomic and fiscal projections were prepared by the Cabinet Office. Previously, the Ministry of Finance had provided the medium-term fiscal estimates, whereas the former Economic Planning Agency (the current Cabinet Office since 2001) had submitted medium-term macroeconomic plans.

21. For details on local government finances and intergovernmental fiscal relations, and reform discussions, see Iakova and Komori (2004, IMF Selected Issues).

22. The Abe administration (September 2006–September 2007), which succeeded the Koizumi administration, emphasized the growth-enhancing approach. Accordingly, the underlying macroeconomic assumptions published in January 2007 reflected the high-growth orientation.

23. The medium-term macroeconomic and fiscal strategy published in January 2007 presented two scenarios—"Growth scenario" and "Risk scenario." The former relied on optimistic assumptions such as a favorable growth–interest rate differential, near zero, between FY2008 and FY2011 on average. The latter involved a less favorable growth environment. The strategy, however, did not spell out which (combination) of the "growth" and "risk" scenarios seemed more likely to materialize.

24. In terms of ratios to GDP, as presented in Figures 7.7 and 7.8, an unexpected (lower or higher) economic growth will usually affect mainly the expenditure ratio, because government expenditure is mostly exogenous. On the other hand, government revenues generally fluctuate in line with economic activity, and thus the revenue-to-GDP ratio is less affected by changes in economic growth.

25. There are substantial difficulties with obtaining consistent cross-country estimates on consumption tax elasticities, so Girouard and Andre (2005) assume the

elasticity of unity for the OECD countries. On the other hand, Sancak et al. (2010) obtain an estimate of 1.12 for Value Added Tax (VAT) revenue elasticity for the group of advanced economies in a cross-country regression. (However, Japan is not included in their analysis.)

26. This replaced the previous medium-term plans, extending the covered period.

27. Cabinet decision, "Medium-Term Program for a sustainable social security system and its stable funding," December 24, 2008.

28. No numerical targets for the debt-to-GDP ratio were specified.

29. The analysis focuses on the January 2003 plan as the targeted path.

30. The government outlined a medium-term commitment for revenue and social security reforms, which called for new legislation by FY2011 to be implemented in a phased manner through the mid-2010s.

31. For example, expenditure ceilings by major policy area stipulated in the 1997 Fiscal Structural Reform Act and the expenditure cut plans adopted in the FY2006 Basic Policies could be regarded as a medium-term budget (or expenditure) framework.

32. Appendix prepared by Keiko Takahashi.

CHAPTER 8

The Performance of Large Fiscal Adjustment Plans in the European Union: A Cross-Country Statistical Analysis

S. Ali Abbas, Fuad Hasanov,
Paolo Mauro, and Junhyung Park

Introduction

In this chapter, we turn to systematic statistical analysis of past fiscal adjustment plans—including both ex-ante design features and ex-post outcomes. While the case studies presented in the previous chapters provided in-depth analysis of consolidation attempts in individual countries, here we cast the net wider to cover all the EU countries over the past two decades. We are thus unable to delve into as much detail as the case studies did regarding the motivation for the plans and their design, the composition of the various measures, or political and institutional nuances. However, we gain considerably in terms of data coverage and numerical analysis rigor, thus complementing the results found in the previous chapters. In some ways, the case studies may resonate more strongly for policymakers who are looking for lessons from the concrete experience of other countries, whereas formal statistical analysis may be more convincing to academic or professional economists. From our perspective, we find it reassuring that several key messages come through clearly in both the case studies and the statistical analysis.

As mentioned in this book's Introduction, previous cross-country statistical analyses identified successful fiscal adjustment episodes, for the most part, on the basis of the largest observed improvements in the government debt or the overall fiscal balance.[1] As in the remainder of this book, we focus instead on large fiscal adjustment plans identified as the largest ex-ante intended reductions in headline and cyclically adjusted budget deficits. Thus in this chapter we start from *ex-ante* planned fiscal adjustments, rather than actual *ex-post* fiscal outturns. We analyze policymakers' intentions embedded in the plans' design. We then study the implementation of large fiscal adjustment plans, tracking ex-post outcomes compared with ex-ante plans, and seek to unveil the factors underlying deviations of outcomes from plans. For instance, we look at the extent to which macroeconomic variables such as economic growth deviated from those projected at the time when the plans were drawn up.

By focusing on ex-ante plans in the context of a systematic statistical analysis, however, this chapter connects also with more recent studies that analyze the credibility and implementation record of announced budgets using "real-time" fiscal data. This literature has also focused on countries in the European Union, because of the availability of relatively standardized convergence or Stability and Growth Pact (SGP) programs (Strauch et al., 2004; Beetsma and Giuliodori, 2008; Cimadomo, 2008; Beetsma et al., 2009; and von Hagen, 2010). The focus of these studies has been on identifying the determinants of the size and direction of planned fiscal policy changes (such as starting fiscal position, stage of economic and political cycle) and of the factors affecting their implementation across all budgetary plans. These studies have argued that (i) implementation of budgets has generally been weak in the EU; (ii) implementation has been weaker for more ambitious fiscal adjustment plans, which are typically drawn up to signal competence ahead of elections, and/or when the initial deficit is high;[2] and (iii) implementation has been aided by positive growth surprises and strong fiscal institutions.

As our motivation in conducting this empirical analysis is similar to that of the "large fiscal adjustments" literature, but appealing methodological features can be drawn from the "fiscal policy credibility" literature, we bring together helpful elements from both approaches. We focus on episodes of *large* (defined ahead) planned fiscal adjustments, whereas previous studies in the "fiscal policy credibility" literature considered together not only attempts at large and small fiscal consolidations but also fiscal expansions— episodes that we consider to be fundamentally different in nature. We evaluate large fiscal adjustment plans over a *medium-term* (three-year) horizon, whereas the "fiscal policy credibility" literature worked primarily at the *annual* frequency.[3] Our focus on large medium-term plans is motivated by the current policy context where many countries are preparing multiyear strategies for large fiscal consolidation to bring debt down from historic post-crisis levels. Moreover, adjustments planned over several years may better capture medium-term fiscal policy goals than a one-year plan whose construction and outcomes are likely contaminated by various short-term factors. Finally, we work with a longer sample period—beginning in 1991—than previous studies did.

The main findings of our empirical analysis on the design and implementation of plans are as follows:

- On *design*, we find that large planned adjustments typically envisaged a greater role for expenditure cuts than tax increases (indeed in a majority of cases, tax *reductions* were planned). Of the one-third of plans that envisaged revenue increases, less than half were anchored in tangible tax policy measures, but in most of these cases, the measures were implemented and resulted in significant revenue increases that were generally sustained beyond the plan horizon. Most plans were based on assumptions of improving macroeconomic conditions, although growth projections were not found to be optimistic relative to International Monetary Fund (IMF) staff forecasts published in the *World Economic Outlook* (WEO) at the time. Plans were noticeably more ambitious when the initial deficit was above the 3 percent of Gross Domestic Product (GDP) Maastricht criteria, and in the run-up to European monetary union (EMU).

- On *implementation*, we find that, on average, three-fourths of the planned adjustments were realized, but that the composition of adjustments often differed from plans, with revenue overperformance offsetting expenditure overruns. Implementation was not adversely affected by plan ambition. There is only partial evidence that carrots such as EMU accession and sticks such as the European Union's Excessive Deficit Procedure (EDP) strengthened adherence to plans; the evidence does not survive in regressions where other factors, especially growth surprises, are controlled for. Growth surprises in fact turn out to be the most important factor underlying deviations of plans from outcomes: for every one percentage point in higher than expected growth, the overall balance improves by 0.5 percent of GDP. Base effects (surprise revisions in the initial fiscal balance) are followed by small changes in end-point fiscal balance targets and thus imply large effects on implementation measured by outcomes versus plans with respect to the improvement in the fiscal balance. Implementation is greater in the presence of stronger national fiscal rules, less fractionalized parliaments, and larger improvements in government stability.

In the remainder of this chapter, we discuss data, methodology, and results. The first section discusses the data and methodological issues, including the construction of a sample of 66 large adjustment plans in the EU from the universe of convergence and SGP programs published during 1991–2007. The next section reports summary statistics on the design and implementation of the plans in this sample, and provides descriptive statistics and plots on major variables of interest. The following section presents our main econometric results on potential drivers of plan implementation such as initial macro-fiscal conditions, the ambition of the planned consolidation, macroeconomic surprises, policy reaction to news, and institutional and political variables. The Conclusion completes the chapter with key policy issues.

Data, Sample Selection, and Methodology

Our starting point is the universe consisting of 229 convergence and SGP programs prepared by 25 EU countries during 1991–2007: of these, the 175 post-1998 plans were drawn from the website of the European Commission's Economic and Financial Affairs General Directorate (DG ECFIN); the remaining 54 pre-1998 plans were sourced from country authorities, libraries, and the IMF's own archives. As the time span of plans published in 2006 and later overlaps significantly with the global financial crisis—whose impact would unduly dominate and skew the results of any systematic statistical analysis of this type—we focus on the 178 published plans before end-2005. For these plans we extracted all available time series information on key macro-fiscal variables—notably the estimates for year t (the year of the plan's publication), reported outturns for year $t - 1$, and projections for years $t + 1$, $t + 2$, and $t + 3$. The fiscal variables include headline balances, revenues, primary expenditures, interest payments, and public debt levels. Macroeconomic variables comprise real and nominal GDP growth rates and levels, inflation, and interest rates. We also recovered plan information on cyclically adjusted balances for the plans for which it was available (about one-half of the plans), and supplemented that information with our own computations of the cyclically adjusted balance, which we undertook using carefully constructed real-time output gaps—that is, using only the information that would have been available to contemporary observers (see Appendix 8A). We drew ex-post data for the same variables from the European Commission's annual macroeconomic (AMECO) database.

Starting from the 178 pre-2006 plans (corresponding to all shaded cells in Table 8.1), and defining as "large planned fiscal adjustments" those that envisaged a cumulative adjustment in the headline fiscal balance of more than 1 percent of GDP in the following three years, we identified a total of 100 large fiscal adjustment plans (shown in dark gray shaded cells in Table 8.1). Finally, for each country, plans with more than two overlapping years were dropped, yielding our sample of 66 large planned headline balance improvements.[4]

TABLE 8.1 Selection of 66 Large Fiscal Adjustment Plans from the Universe of Plans

	1991	1992	1993	1994	1995	1996	1997	1998	1999	2000	2001	2002	2003	2004	2005
Austria										•					•
Belgium		•				•			•					•	
Cyprus														•	
Czech Republic						•							•		•
Germany			•			•		•			•		•		•
Denmark				•		•		•							
Estonia															
Greece		•		•				•		•		•		•	
Spain							•		•					•	
Finland			•		•	•	•		•					•	
France						•		•				•			•
Hungary															
Ireland							•							•	
Italy	•										•		•		•
Lithuania															•
Luxembourg															
Latvia															
Malta														•	
The Netherlands	•			•										•	
Poland															
Portugal	•		•				•		•		•		•		•
Sweden					•		•						•		•
Slovakia														•	
Slovenia															
United Kingdom					•		•						•		•

Universe of plans   Greater than 1% adjustment   • Large Nonoverlapping Plans

As can be gleaned from Table 8.1, 27 of the 66 plans were published prior to 1998. As the ECFIN website only posts plans published from 1998 onward, these earlier plans have not been looked at in detail in the fiscal policy credibility literature. Yet, they are of great interest, particularly because they include countries/years characterized by large fiscal adjustments, including in the run-up to EMU. Of these, 17 plans were prepared during 1992–96, of which 12 plans aimed at delivering deficits below 3 percent of GDP by 1997 (the test year for the first round of EMU accession).

Having identified the plans we'll work with, we now discuss two key steps involved in defining fiscal adjustment and tracking implementation:

1. *Defining fiscal adjustment.* We define the ex-ante planned adjustment as the projected percentage point increase in the fiscal balance–to-GDP ratio between years t and $t + 3$ as reported in the year t plan. The corresponding ex-post adjustment is defined as the actual percentage point increase in the fiscal balance–to-GDP ratio between years t and $t + 3$ as reported in the final data (the 2009 AMECO vintage).[5] In addition to the overall fiscal balance and its revenue and expenditure components, we also track adjustment in the cyclically adjusted primary balance, subdivided into cyclically adjusted revenues and primary expenditures.

2. *Measuring implementation.* We use two measures of plan implementation: (a) an implementation *ratio*, which, for each plan, scales the *actual* observed three-year cumulative improvement in the fiscal balance–to-GDP ratio to the corresponding planned improvement; (b) an implementation *error*, which, for each plan, subtracts the planned three-year cumulative improvement in the fiscal balance–to-GDP ratio from the corresponding actual improvement. Perfect implementation would be implied by an implementation ratio of 1 or, equivalently, an implementation error of zero. Of course, overperformance of plans (implementation ratio greater than 1, or implementation errors greater than zero) is also feasible.

An advantage of using the implementation *ratio* is that it appropriately scales actual performance to the plan's fiscal adjustment ambition (planned improvement in the fiscal balance) and is thus comparable across plans in a nonregression framework (see Descriptive Analysis), that is, where ambition is not otherwise controlled for. An advantage of using the implementation *error* is the ease of interpretation it affords in a regression framework, as its units are percentage points of GDP. We, therefore, use this measure in our formal regressions (see Regression Analysis), where ambition is appropriately controlled for.

Descriptive Analysis

In this section, we present summary statistics to shed light on key design aspects of the plans in our sample, aggregate statistics on the plans' implementation, and some descriptive analysis on potential drivers of implementation.

Plan Design

A quick look at the share of the plans in our sample that display certain features reveals a wide mix, making for interesting comparisons, and begins to provide a sense of the results that will be confirmed through more systematic analysis in the next sections:

Various Plan Features	Proportion of 66 Plans (in percent)
Dated pre-1998	41
Where initial deficit >3 percent of GDP	56
Where initial debt >60 percent of GDP	59
Prepared in run-up to EMU	23
During which there was a change in government	47
With >50% adjustment in year 1	23
Projecting output gap increase	77
With >50% adjustment from spending side	87
Stipulating revenue effort backed by measures	17

As noted earlier, two-fifths of the plans are pre-1998. Over half of the plans were prepared in the context of initial deficits or debts above the Maastricht-prescribed ceilings of 3 and 60 percent of GDP, respectively. Moreover, although this would not always have been known at the time the plans were drawn up, a change in government during the three-year adjustment horizon occurred in about half the cases. Less than a quarter of the plans envisaged frontloaded adjustment (i.e., more than half of the adjustment occurring in the first year).

Three-quarters of the plans in our sample projected an improvement in macroeconomic conditions as measured by the output gap (i.e., the percentage deviation of actual real output from potential) over the plan horizon. This is not surprising given that one of policymakers' key objectives is to foster economic growth and that EMU entry or broader European integration bore the promise of economic gains. Figure 8.1 shows that real GDP growth rate assumptions embedded in the plans were not overly optimistic, on average, and that for the most part they were close to IMF staff projections published in the contemporary issues of the WEO (most observations

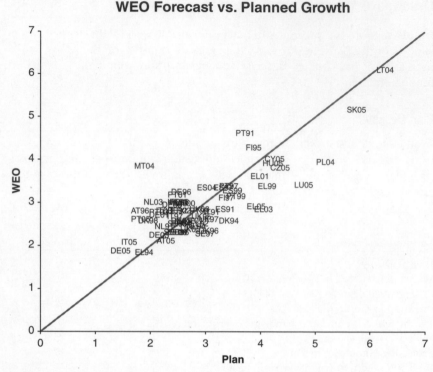

FIGURE 8.1 WEO Growth Forecasts versus Plan Growth Rates (percent per annum, annualized from three-year cumulative)

are close to the 45 degree line).[6] Thus, ex-post growth surprises relative to plan must be ascribed to true macroeconomic uncertainty rather than any systematic projection bias (see also IMF, 2009).

Planned adjustments were more ambitious the higher the initial deficit, although the relationship appears to be more relevant at higher deficit levels. Figure 8.2 reports this bivariate association separately for plans formulated when the initial deficit was larger than the EMU-prescribed limit of 3 percent of GDP (dark circles and solid regression line) and for plans formulated when the initial deficit was already below the 3 percent limit (fainter circles and dashed regression line). Greater ambition was significantly associated with larger initial deficits (with a slope coefficient above 0.6), but only when these were above 3 percent. When initial deficits were below 3 percent, the association with plans' ambition is essentially nil. These general patterns in policymakers' planning behavior are somewhat reassuring, because a necessary condition for fiscal sustainability is that fiscal effort/performance be stronger when the initial fiscal position is weaker.[7]

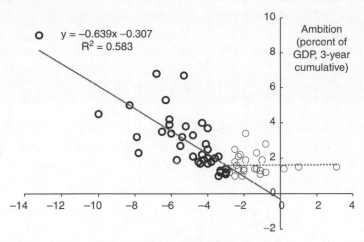

FIGURE 8.2 **Plan Ambition versus Initial Balance**

The plans' composition in terms of the expenditure-revenue measure mix overwhelmingly favored expenditure cuts over revenue increases. Almost 90 percent of the plans envisaged that more than half of the adjustment would come from spending cuts (as shares of GDP). Moreover, almost two-thirds of the plans envisaged that revenues would be cut as a share of GDP, thus requiring cuts in expenditure ratios in excess of the total adjustment in the fiscal balance:

Revenue and Expenditure Composition of 66 Plans (in percent)

		Expenditure		
		Increase	Decrease	Total
Revenue	Increase	10	27	37
	Decrease	0	63	63
		10	90	100

Also noteworthy is the fact that of the one-third of plans stipulating increases in the revenue-to-GDP ratio, only about ten plans were grounded in well-specified tax policy changes (such as rate increases or elimination of clearly identified tax exemptions); the rest mentioned improvements in revenue administration and tax compliance, efforts against tax evasion, or generic base-widening. Thus, less than one-sixth of our large planned consolidations envisaged deliberate increases in revenue ratios grounded in well-specified measures.

This leads to an alternative perspective on large, revenue-based, fiscal adjustments that had been identified as such by the traditional strand of literature using ex-post outcomes. For example, almost all of the episodes in Alesina and Ardagna (1998) feature an increase in revenues by at least 1 percentage point of GDP; and two-thirds of the observed fiscal effort in large consolidations identified by Alesina and Ardagna (2009) came from the revenue side.

How can one make sense of the different roles of revenues when contrasting ex-anteversus ex-post-based definitions of large fiscal adjustments? As we will show below, in their ex-ante plan design, policymakers intended to rely on expenditure cuts rather than revenue increases (indeed, in several cases they hoped to cut spending sufficiently to make room for tax cuts, too), but the ex-post composition of adjustment turned out different than expected: as spending was cut less than planned, policymakers had to rely on (often temporary) revenue increases to a greater extent than they had initially intended, often reneging on tax cut promises.

Plan Implementation

Table 8.2 sets out the main results on outcomes versus plans in our sample, by looking at averages across the 66 episodes in the sample. Implementation was generally good: on average, the planned improvement in the headline (overall) balance was 2.5 percent of GDP over three-year horizons, and the actual improvement was 2 percent of GDP, yielding an implementation

TABLE 8.2 Summary Statistics for Plan Implementation—By Fiscal Variable

	Variable	ΔPLAN	ΔACTUAL	Implementation RATIO = ΔACTUAL/ ΔPLAN (1 is perfect)	Implementation ERROR = Δ ACTUAL minus ΔPLAN (0 is perfect)
in percent of GDP	Overall balance	2.5	2.0	0.8	−0.5
	Revenues	−0.1	0.5	−	0.6
	Expenditures	−2.6	−1.5	0.6	1.0
	Primary	−2.1	−0.9	0.4	1.2
	Interest	−0.5	−0.7	1.3	−0.1
	Primary balance	2.0	1.3	0.7	−0.7
in percent of potential GDP	Cyclically adjusted primary balance	1.6	0.9	0.5	−0.7
	Cyc.Adj. revenues	−0.4	0.5	−	0.9
	Primary expenditures	−1.9	−0.3	0.2	1.6
	Memo: Cyclical revenues	0.2	0.5	2.5	0.3

error of −0.5 percent of GDP. The implementation ratio (i.e., the ratio of actual to planned improvement in the overall balance) was 0.8. Filtering out the impact of higher than planned interest bill savings causes the implementation ratio (for the primary balance) to decline somewhat to 0.7, still a fairly high degree of implementation.

However, the composition of actual adjustments differs substantially from that envisaged under the plans, with policymakers not fully delivering on the promised ambitious primary expenditure cuts or the accompanying tax reductions. Specifically, on average, the plans envisaged cuts in primary spending ratios by 2.1 percent of GDP and achieved cuts amounting only to 0.9 percent of GDP. Revenues compensated in part, with an overperformance of 0.6 percent of GDP. Although the observed decline in the interest bill was largely anticipated, this item accounted for a further positive surprise of 0.1 percent of GDP. On the whole, although the plans envisaged four-fifths of the adjustment from primary spending cuts and the remainder from interest bill savings, in reality less than half of the adjustment came from primary spending cuts, with revenues accounting for one-quarter and the remainder from interest bill savings.

Considering implementation in cyclically adjusted terms (the bottom panel of Table 8.2, with all variables expressed in percent of potential GDP), three observations stand out. First, the implementation ratio is slightly lower (0.5) than for the headline variables. (In other words, as mentioned previously, cyclical conditions turned out somewhat better than expected— cyclical revenues overperformed by 0.3 percent of GDP.) Second, using cyclically adjusted variables and potential (rather than nominal) GDP as a scaling variable further reduces the relative contribution of expenditure reductions to the overall adjustment. Although primary expenditure cuts were intended to be more than sufficient for the planned reduction in the cyclically adjusted balance, on an ex-post basis primary expenditure cuts accounted for a small portion of the actual adjustment, whereas increases in cyclically adjusted revenues contributed almost two-thirds of the adjustment in the cyclically adjusted primary balance. This large contribution from cyclically adjusted revenues arose from an overperformance of almost 1 percentage point of GDP against the plans.

What factors did this unexpected overperformance of cyclically adjusted revenues stem from? Although a complete answer would require further analysis, we offer four considerations. First, on the whole, governments implemented the measures they had specified in the plans: to the extent we were able to check the implementation record of tax policy measures, few were delayed or dropped, but also few were added. (On this point, see also the case studies for the G-7 countries in Europe.) Second, efforts to widen the tax base and improve compliance seem to have had some payoff, despite the rather vague manner in which they were outlined in the plans.

Third, several EU countries relied on one-off revenues, especially at critical moments in the run-up to EMU (see, for example, the case studies for France and Italy). Fourth, and in our view most important, a sizable portion of the overperformance reflected non-policy-related revenue increases stemming from temporary factors, such as unusually strong asset market performance, which standard cyclical adjustment methods are unable to filter out. In particular, several EU countries benefited from booming stock markets and housing price bubbles, which yielded large revenue increases prior to the global crisis that began in 2008 but, in hindsight, proved to be clearly of a temporary nature.[8]

Isolating Determinants of Success

We begin our exploration of the potential determinants of the degree of implementation of the plans with simple bivariate charts, to be followed in the next section by a more formal multivariate regression analysis. Specifically, we consider the possible role of the size of the planned fiscal policy change (plan ambition); the strength of fiscal rules; the starting fiscal position; surprises in economic growth and inflation; and political and electoral variables.

PLAN AMBITION   The plans' degree of ambition might in principle be related to the implementation ratio: one might speculate, for example, that highly ambitious plans are less likely to be implemented in full. A simple scatter plot of actual versus planned adjustment (over the plans' three-year horizon) in our sample finds no support for this hypothesis (see Figure 8.3). The bivariate regression coefficient (excluding the five influential observations shown in gray) is 0.8, that is, the same as the implementation ratio reported in Table 8.2, indicating that the implementation ratio is no different for more ambitious plans.[9]

"STICKS": FISCAL RULES   Although there is a fervent debate in the economics profession and among policymakers on the pros and cons of fiscal rules, it would seem reasonable to expect the presence of strong fiscal rules to be associated with better implementation of government plans.[10] In our definition of fiscal rules, we include both national rules enshrined in law (which necessitate fiscal correction once fiscal indicators approach or breach certain thresholds) and well-defined supranational rules, such as the EU's Maastricht corrective and dissuasive arms (deficit below 3 percent of GDP and debt below 60 percent of GDP, respectively). The violation of these norms and rules is typically associated with reputational costs, but in some cases also triggers penalties.

The strength of national fiscal rules (measured by the fiscal rules strength index (FRSI), compiled by the European Commission's DG

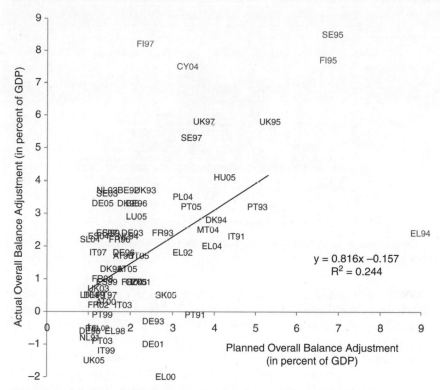

FIGURE 8.3 Actual versus Planned Adjustment (Ambition) (in percent)

ECFIN—see its website for a complete description) seems to translate robustly into plan implementation. Figure 8.4 shows the distribution of overall balance implementation ratios, both for cases where the intensity of rules (in terms of design and enforcement) was strong (shaded) and where it was weak (white).[11] Stronger rules are associated with better plan implementation.

In contrast, EU wide rules do not seem to have had much impact on the degree of implementation of plans. Indeed, Figure 8.5 reveals a mixed pattern at best: implementation ratios for plans prepared when initial debts were above the 60 percent of GDP limit (shaded) is not noticeably different than for plans prepared when debts were already below 60 percent. For plans prepared when deficits were above 3 percent of GDP (shaded) the frequency distribution of implementation ratios is somewhat shifted to the right compared with plans prepared when deficit ratios were already below the 3 percent limit, but this is not a statistically significant difference. This said, as shown previously, the deficit limit of 3 percent of GDP may well have had an important impact on the degree of ambition of the plans, an issue we explore further later in this chapter.

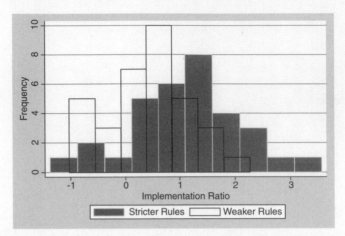

FIGURE 8.4 Does the Strength of Fiscal Rules Matter? (Stricter rules correspond to shaded histogram.)

"CARROT": EMU ACCESSION Table 8.3 captures the dynamics of plan implementation in the run-up to EMU accession. Because the "test date" for assessing Euro eligibility was December 31, 1997, plans formulated in 1994 were the most critical, as they had to deliver a deficit below 3 percent of GDP by end-1997.[12] However, the 1995 and 1996 plans would also have been important, due to their proximity to the test date and the fact that EMU would only become effective at the beginning of 1999. We can clearly see the surge in planned overall balance improvement from 3 to 5 percent of GDP in 1994, and tapering off thereafter. Actual improvements followed a similar path, but always undershot planned improvements, despite stronger than expected growth. Even for the Euro-critical 1994 plans, only two-thirds of the envisaged adjustment materialized (the corresponding implementation error was −2 percent of GDP). This did not compromise the attainment of the 3 percent of GDP deficit target for 1997 because (i) the degree of ambition of the planned adjustment was set high enough to provide a "slippage cushion"; and (ii) the average 1994 deficit was revised down by more than 1 percent of GDP in 1995 but the deficit target was maintained. Thus, the plan implementation in the run-up to EMU does not appear exceptionally strong or different, once plan ambition, growth surprises, and base effects are taken into account.[13]

GROWTH AND INFLATION SURPRISES Adverse economic growth surprises may be expected to worsen implementation ratios, through both a direct channel (weak growth implies low revenues) and an indirect channel (policymakers' preferences shift away from fiscal adjustment and toward fiscal stimulus). Conversely, positive growth surprises, through similar reasoning,

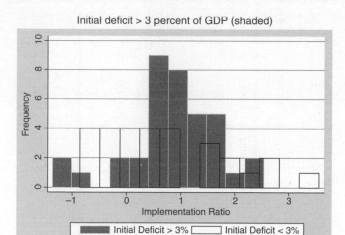

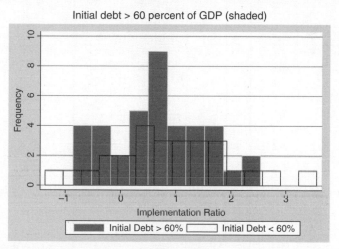

FIGURE 8.5 Distribution of Implementation Ratios for Sub-Samples Based on
Maastricht Criteria

Note: Non-shaded distributions refer to the plans drawn up when the initial debt was
below 60 percent of GDP (bottom panel) and plans drawn up when the initial deficit
was below 3 percent of GDP (top panel).

may be expected to lead to better implementation of announced plans. Figure 8.6 indeed suggests a strong positive association between implementation errors and growth surprises.

The association is statistically significant at the conventional levels. The
estimated slope coefficient, 0.3, is close to what one would expect if the only

TABLE 8.3 Plan Design and Implementation in the Run-up to EMU (overall balance in percent of GDP; overlapping plans included; means reported)

Vintage	Plan			Actual			Actual minus Plan			
	Year t	Year $t+3$	Improvement	Year t	Year $t+3$	Improvement	Year t	Year $t+3$	Improvement	Growth surprise
1993	−6.0	−3.2	2.8	−5.8	−3.6	2.2	0.2	−0.4	−0.6	−0.5
1994	−7.4	−2.5	5.0	−5.5	−2.5	3.0	1.9	0.0	−2.0	1.5
1995	−4.9	−0.4	4.5	−5.6	0.0	5.6	−0.8	0.4	1.2	1.2
1996	−3.5	−0.9	2.7	−3.6	−0.2	3.4	0.0	0.7	0.7	1.8
1997	−2.2	−0.1	2.1	−2.2	1.6	3.8	0.0	1.7	1.7	2.5
1998	−1.6	−0.2	1.3	−2.1	−1.3	0.8	−0.6	−1.1	−0.6	0.8
1999	−1.0	0.4	1.4	−1.4	−1.5	−0.1	−0.4	−1.9	−1.5	−1.1

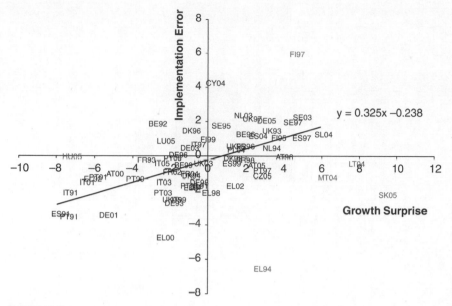

FIGURE 8.6 Implementation Error and Growth Surprise (in percent)

impact of growth surprises onto the implementation error were the direct impact on revenues.[14]

Whether the effect of growth surprises works symmetrically (i.e., with the same coefficient for both positive and negative growth surprises) is an interesting question to explore. One might expect, for example, that policymakers could plausibly spend some or all of a positive growth surprise as long as the headline deficit targets are preserved, whereas they might allow the automatic stabilizers to operate fully and even respond with stimulus measures to negative growth surprises. (In other words, policymakers might be tempted into procyclical fiscal policy in unexpected boom years but might want to use fiscal policy as a countercyclical tool against unexpected economic downturns.)

The behavioral response to growth surprises could also be cast in terms of incentives to undertake "structural" fiscal effort (i.e., improvements in the cyclically adjusted fiscal balance) and how these are affected by growth surprises. On the one hand, an unexpected boom might afford greater political space to push through unpopular reforms; on the other hand, the incentive for fiscal adjustment through painful measures might weaken if headline balances are already improving "effortlessly" as a result of positive growth surprises. On balance, these opposing effects might well exactly offset each other.

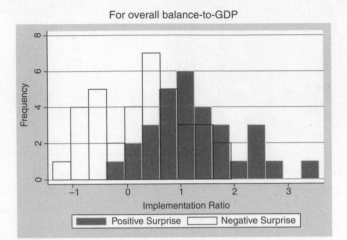

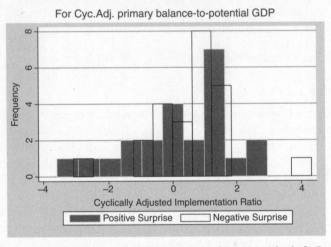

FIGURE 8.7 Implementation Ratios with Negative and Positive (shaded) Growth Surprises

By comparing frequency histograms for the implementation ratios associated with positive versus negative growth surprises, Figure 8.7 shows that growth surprises clearly have a strong impact on implementation ratios for the headline fiscal balance (top panel), but bear little relationship with implementation ratios for the cyclically adjusted primary balance (bottom panel). This is consistent with the view that indeed the behavioral responses to growth surprises described in the previous paragraph do approximately offset each other.

At moderate inflation rates, positive inflation surprises would be expected to favorably impact fiscal adjustment via the bracket creep effect on the tax side (inflation leads taxpayers to move into higher tax brackets if these are not adjusted in a timely manner) and the real ex-post compression effect on the spending side (if spending is set in nominal terms and nominal GDP unexpectedly rises because of inflation, then spending-to-GDP ratios fall).[15] Turning to the data, there is essentially no link between inflation surprises and plan implementation. A possible explanation for the absence of an inflation-boost for implementation could be the generally low level of inflation (around 3 percent per annum) prevailing in the European Union during the last two decades. As inflation volatility (and uncertainty) is usually associated with the level of inflation, the mean inflation surprise (in annual absolute terms) was also small during this period—a mere 0.3 percentage point, less than one-third the size of the mean absolute growth surprise. Moreover, as we work at the three-year horizon, policymakers wishing to do so had ample time to respond to inflation surprises by adjusting tax brackets and nominal spending levels.

REVISIONS TO INITIAL FISCAL POSITION ("BASE EFFECT") Large and unexpected data revisions are a fact of life for many policymakers. In the context of multiyear plans and their implementation, such data revisions, especially to the initial fiscal position, can have a significant effect on adjustment needs and incentives. For illustration purposes, consider a scenario in which the estimated fiscal balance for year t (the starting position for a three-year adjustment plan) is revised upward (i.e., unexpectedly improves) by 1 percent of GDP in year $t + 1$. Policymakers could respond in several ways to this "news": if they wish to maintain unchanged the originally set fiscal balance target for year $t + 3$, they will lower their fiscal effort in the plan's outer years by 1 percent of GDP; but if they seek to preserve the amount of fiscal adjustment envisaged over the life of the plan, they will raise their fiscal balance target for year $t + 3$ by 1 percent of GDP. In the former case, the implementation error (defined as actual minus originally planned adjustment) would fall by 1 percent of GDP, whereas in the latter case the implementation error would not be affected by news of the revision.

The mean absolute base effect (for the year t fiscal balance–to-GDP ratio) in our sample of 66 plans is in fact 0.9 percentage points. This is sizable, by comparison to the average planned adjustment, for example (2.5 percent of GDP). On average, about half of the base effect showed up in plan documents within one year. This means that policymakers would have typically had sufficient basis and time to recalibrate their fiscal effort in the plan's outer years, had they wished to do so. Although negative base effects occurred more frequently than positive ones in our sample (three-fifths versus two-fifths), their average magnitude was similar. In principle, policymakers' response to positive base effects could well differ from their response to negative base effects. The logic underlying this possible asymmetry could be that policymakers may be inclined to "spend" fully a positive revision to the initial deficit (thus, the implementation error would worsen by the amount of the revision), while insufficiently compensating for negative base effects (the implementation error would remain unchanged). This hypothesis will be explored ahead in a formal regression framework.

POLITICAL VARIABLES   Several political factors might contribute to determining the plans' degree of implementation. We focus here on two potentially important political variables for which sufficient data and intuitive hypotheses are available:

- *Change in government during the plan period*—which would generally be expected to weaken implementation, because new governments would likely be less committed to their predecessors' plans.
- *Parliamentary fractionalization*—a high average level of parliamentary fractionalization over the plan period would likely be associated with weakened ability to implement large/painful fiscal adjustments.[16] In what follows, parliamentary fractionalization is measured as the probability that two deputies randomly drawn from the legislature will belong to different parties. (The data for this variable are collected from the World Bank's Database of Political Institutions, 2010 vintage).

Figure 8.8 explores these hypotheses through simple charts, contrasting plan implementation for cases with (shaded) versus cases without changes in government (bottom panel); and for cases with higher parliamentary fractionalization (shaded) versus cases with lower parliamentary fractionalization. No clear pattern emerges in these bivariate exercises—at best, one can say that changes in government or higher fractionalization do not seem to hamper plan implementation. We will explore political factors further in a multivariate setting, given the need to control for other factors.

Regression Analysis

The previous descriptive analysis has shed preliminary light on possible determinants of plan implementation using simple bivariate relationships (illustrated, for the most part, through distributions of implementation "ratios" for subsets of the sample). We now turn to our more formal regression analysis, where we investigate the determinants of "implementation errors"

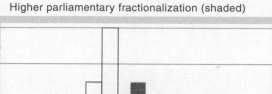

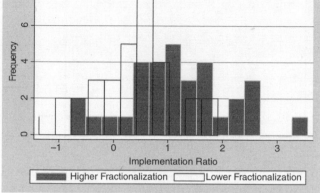

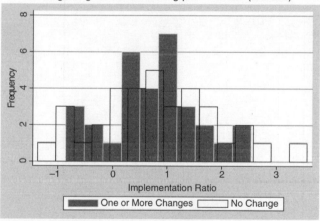

FIGURE 8.8 **Plan Implementation Ratios for Sub-Samples of Political Variables**

(i.e., actual minus planned adjustment, all scaled by GDP) in a multivariate setting.[17]

In line with the discussion in the previous section, we explore several explanatory variables. In the first and simpler set of estimates (corresponding to Table 8.4), we focus on five core variables (discussed ahead). Additional institutional and political variables—as well as the asymmetric effects of positive and negative growth surprises (and base effects) on plan implementation—are then explored in more detailed estimates (corresponding to Tables 8.5 and 8.6).

TABLE 8.4 Baseline Regressions with Core Variables

Dependent Variable: Implementation error = actual minus planned adjustment

VARIABLES	Fixed Effects			FE Instrumental Variables		
	(1)	(2)	(3)	(4)	(5)	(6)
Overall balance base effect	-0.61***	-0.61***	-0.53**	-0.82***	-0.85***	-0.53***
	(0.17)	(0.16)	(0.19)	(0.22)	(0.24)	(0.13)
Initial fiscal balance	-0.26		-0.38	-0.27*		-0.39**
	(0.22)		(0.24)	(0.16)		(0.18)
Real GDP growth surprise	0.34***	0.34***	0.12	0.52***	0.53***	-0.029
	(0.059)	(0.059)	(0.13)	(0.088)	(0.094)	(0.079)
Plan ambition	-0.37	-0.19	-0.29	-0.29	-0.14	-0.29
	(0.47)	(0.32)	(0.47)	(0.33)	(0.29)	(0.33)
Deviation of initial deficit from 3% of GDP level		0.18			0.24	
		(0.18)			(0.19)	
Time dummies			Yes			Yes
Observations	66	66	66	66	66	66
R-squared	0.456	0.422	0.662	0.367	0.320	0.177

Notes: Robust standard errors in parentheses.
***$p < 0.01$, **$p < 0.05$, *$p < 0.1$.

TABLE 8.5 Additional Regressions with Political Variables and Asymmetries

Dependent Variable: Implementation error = actual minus planned adjustment

VARIABLES	(1)	(2)	FE Instrumental Variables (3)	(4)	(5)	(6)
Overall balance base effect	-0.32***		-0.83***	-0.84***	-0.68***	-0.87***
	(0.22)		(0.22)	(0.21)	(0.21)	(0.22)
Initial fiscal balance	-0.27*	-0.27*	-0.31	-0.39**	-0.30**	-0.30*
	(0.16)	(0.16)	(0.19)	(0.16)	(0.13)	(0.17)
Real GDP growth surprise	0.52***	0.50***		0.49***	0.45***	0.50***
	(0.388)	(0.089)		(0.080)	(0.088)	(0.087)
Plan ambition	-0.29	-0.26	-0.33	-0.40	-0.46	-0.29
	(0.33)	(0.32)	(0.33)	(0.32)	(0.28)	(0.34)
Positive overall balance base effect		-0.92***				
		(0.34)				
Negative overall balance base effect		-0.71**				
		(0.31)				
Positive growth surprise			0.37			
			(0.29)			
Negative growth surprise			0.58***			
			(0.16)			
Fiscal rule strength				0.61**		
				(0.30)		
Change in government stability					3.07***	
					(1.12)	
Parliamentary fractionalization						-3.62*
						(2.09)
Observations	66	66	65	66	66	65
R-squared	0.367	0.380	0.375	0.426	0.493	0.382

Notes: Robust standard errors in parentheses.
*** p < 0.01, ** p < 0.05, * p < 0.1.

235

TABLE 8.6 Regressions with Outliers Removed

Dependent Variable: Implementation error = actual minus planned adjustment

VARIABLES	Fixed Effects				FE Instrumental Variables			
	(1)	(2)	(3)	(4)	(5)	(6)	(7)	(8)
Overall balance base effect	-0.70***		-0.82***	-0.72***	-0.87***		-1.22***	-0.85***
	(0.20)		(0.21)	(0.20)	(0.20)		(0.34)	(0.18)
Initial fiscal balance	-0.14	-0.13	-0.19	-0.30**	-0.15*	-0.14	-0.30**	-0.30***
	(0.11)	(0.12)	(0.11)	(0.13)	(0.091)	(0.097)	(0.12)	(0.10)
Real GDP growth surprise	0.38***	0.37***		0.34***	0.54***	0.52***		0.45***
	(0.056)	(0.049)		(0.048)	(0.092)	(0.090)		(0.064)
Plan ambition	-0.0044	0.033	-0.076	-0.26	0.11	0.14	-0.16	-0.15
	(0.19)	(0.21)	(0.19)	(0.18)	(0.16)	(0.16)	(0.20)	(0.15)
Positive overall balance base effect		-1.64***				-1.69***		
		(0.47)				(0.47)		
Negative overall balance base effect		-0.46**				-0.64**		
		(0.18)				(0.25)		
Positive growth surprise			0.21**				-0.087	
			(0.090)				(0.30)	
Negative growth surprise			0.48***				0.82***	
			(0.066)				(0.23)	
Fiscal rule strength				0.41*				0.38**
				(0.23)				(0.16)
Change in government stability				2.68***				2.25***
				(0.82)				(0.70)
Parliamentary fractionalization				-0.47				-1.18
				(2.64)				(1.67)
Observations	58	58	58	57	58	58	58	57
R-squared	0.582	0.611	0.602	0.713	0.496	0.534	0.437	0.665

Notes: Robust standard errors in parentheses.
*** p < 0.01, ** p < 0.05, * p < 0.1.

The five core variables are as follows:

Explanatory Variables and Methodology

1. *Initial fiscal balance*, measured by the year *t* overall balance (in percent of GDP). A larger initial balance (i.e., a better starting fiscal position) might be expected to be associated with worse implementation of fiscal adjustment plans.
2. *Fiscal balance base effect*, measured by the ex-post revision of the initial overall fiscal balance (in percent of GDP). An upward revision in the initial balance would reduce the need for adjustment effort, and could thus worsen implementation.
3. *Real GDP growth surprise*, measured by the percentage point difference between the cumulative actual and planned growth rates over the three-year plan horizon (or, equivalently, the percentage point surprise in third-year output). In the absence of an active response by policy-makers, the direct effect on the headline fiscal balance would be essentially equal to the automatic stabilizers (i.e., approximately the percentage point surprise in third-year output times the share of total revenues in GDP).[18]
4. *Plan ambition*, measured by the planned improvement in the fiscal balance between year *t* and year $t + 3$ (in percent of GDP). This explores whether more ambitious plans face challenges in implementation.
5. *Deviation of initial deficit from 3 percent of GDP* (the Maastricht/EDP threshold), measured in percentage points of GDP (and set to zero when the initial deficit ratio is below 3 percent). A larger deviation of the initial deficit from the 3 percent of GDP limit would induce greater urgency to undertake corrective fiscal action and thus be associated with stronger implementation.

The nature of our sample (unbalanced panel with 22 countries) and explanatory variables requires us to address some methodological issues. (The remainder of this paragraph is important from a technical standpoint, but can be skipped with no loss of continuity by the nontechnical reader.) As in most estimations based upon panels of countries, it is likely that both the dependent variable and the explanatory variables are correlated with unobserved country characteristics. To avoid this problem, we use the standard technique of controlling for country characteristics (that do not change over time) by using the panel fixed effects (FE) estimator (with robust standard errors). Moreover, one might reasonably be concerned about two-way causation between the dependent variable (unexpected improvement in the headline fiscal balance) and the surprise in economic growth—one of the explanatory variables.[19] To avoid the resulting bias, we use instrumental variable estimation (FE-IV). Specifically, we use the average of other countries' real GDP growth surprises to instrument for the growth surprise of country i (this is similar to Beetsma and others, 2009). In intuitive terms, the identifying assumption is that the only channel through which other countries' GDP growth surprises are related to the implementation error is through the GDP growth surprise in the country in question; and the implementation error in an individual country has essentially no impact on other countries' GDP growth surprise.

Regression Results

The baseline regressions in Table 8.4 suggest that base effects and the growth surprises are the key drivers of implementation errors (deviations of actual from planned fiscal adjustment). The initial fiscal balance seems to play a role. Other potential explanatory variables, including plan ambition or the deviation of the initial deficit ratio from 3 percent, did not turn out to be significant.

The *base effect* turns out to be significant in all the regressions with its coefficient varying between −0.5 and −0.8. The fairly large magnitude of this coefficient would seem to suggest that policymakers do not adjust their initially set deficit *targets* by much in the face of revisions to the initial fiscal balance, and so it is the fiscal *consolidation* that ends up adjusting relative to plan. In other words, if the initial balance is revised upward (downward) by 1 percent of GDP, actual implementation would fall (rise) by one-half to four-fifths of the revision. In some specifications, the coefficient is not statistically different from −1. In those cases, the null hypothesis that policymakers stick to the original overall balance target cannot be rejected. Note that the previous interpretation implicitly assumes that the coefficient is symmetric for positive and negative base effects, an assumption that we probe further ahead.

For the *growth surprise*, the coefficient is about 0.3 with FE and 0.5 with FE-IV. This means that a 1 percentage point increase in the cumulative three-year growth surprise leads to an increase in the implementation error in the range of 0.3–0.5 percent of GDP. This is consistent with an average government size of about 40 percent of GDP in our sample, and an approximately unit elasticity of revenues with respect to GDP. Later, we investigate if the coefficient is similar in the case of positive and negative surprises. Importantly, the inclusion of time (individual year) dummies causes the effect of the growth surprise to disappear in both sets of regressions (see Table 8.4, columns 3 and 6). This is to be expected, given that growth across EU countries is largely driven by common factors. Turning to the difference between the size of the coefficients across FE and FE-IV, the smaller FE coefficient is consistent with the downward bias that would arise from reverse causality, and the magnitude of the shift suggests that instrumenting for it is important.

The coefficient on *initial fiscal balance* varies between -0.25 and -0.4 and, although not consistently significant, has an intuitive interpretation: when policymakers face higher initial deficits (as seen at the time of the plan's inception) they respond with extra effort to reduce plan implementation errors. On average, this implies lower implementation errors by 0.25–0.4 percentage point of GDP for every 1 percent of GDP widening in the initial overall deficit. This estimate is similar to those reported in previous studies in the fiscal policy credibility literature.

The lack of significance of other regressors also has important implications. That *plan ambition* turns out to be an insignificant predictor for implementation suggests that deviations of outcomes from plans are—on average, controlling for other determinants—similar for more ambitious fiscal adjustment plans as they are for less ambitious plans.[20] Lack of significance of the coefficient on *initial deviations from the 3 percent deficit limit* indicates that EU-wide fiscal rules, while relevant for plan ambition (as shown earlier) do not substantially strengthen the plans' implementation once they have been designed.[21]

Having analyzed the core explanatory variables, we now turn to somewhat more complicated regression specifications. In Table 8.5, we explore specifications that allow for asymmetries in the impact of base effects and growth surprises, and the role of institutional and political variables.

Allowing for different coefficients for positive and negative base effects (column 2), we find the absolute value of the coefficient on positive (favorable) base effects to be higher than on negative ones, though the difference is not statistically significant (but will be statistically significant when observations deemed unduly influential through a standard procedure are removed—see ahead). On average, a 1 percent of GDP positive base effect, other things equal, worsens plan implementation by 0.9 percent of GDP, whereas a 1 percent of GDP negative base effect improves implementation by 0.7 percent of GDP. In other words, if the initial fiscal balance is found to be better than originally estimated when the plan was drawn up, the fiscal balance outcome at the end of the three years is almost unchanged; whereas if the initial fiscal balance is revised to be, say, 1 percent of GDP worse than estimated when the plan was drawn up, the deficit at the end of the three years is only 0.3 percent of GDP worse than would otherwise have been the case. These results appear to lend some support to the hypothesis that a favorable surprise about the initial fiscal position likely induces further fiscal laxity to a greater extent than an unfavorable surprise induces additional fiscal austerity.

There is also tentative (not statistically significant) evidence of asymmetry in the response to positive and negative growth surprises (column 3). The estimates suggest that policymakers essentially allow the automatic stabilizers to operate against the background of positive growth surprises (specifically, a 1 percentage point positive surprise in output by the end of the third year is associated with a 0.4 percentage point of GDP improvement in the fiscal balance). When growth surprises on the negative side, however, the headline fiscal balance deviation from plans worsens by 0.6 percentage point of GDP, implying that policymakers undertake discretionary stimulus in addition to letting the automatic stabilizers operate fully. Note that the fiscal slippage is in fact greater for negative (than positive) growth surprises, which contrasts with the pattern obtained in the case of base effects (the slippage was smaller in the case of unfavorable base revisions). However, this appears intuitive, as policymakers are likely to undertake countercyclical fiscal measures in the face of a weaker than anticipated economy, whereas no such imperative or incentive exists in the case of a negative base effect.

We also find some tentative evidence that institutional and political variables play a role. The three variables that seem to matter (are statistically significant at the conventional levels) are national fiscal rules intensity, the change in government stability, and the degree of parliamentary fractionalization. Specifically, we find that a one-point increase in the EU DG ECFIN's fiscal rules stringency index (or a one-standard-deviation increase that would take us from Hungary to Sweden), improves the implementation error by 0.6 percent of GDP (column 4). For changes in government stability (based upon the annual average share of veto players dropping out of government during the plan horizon, drawn from the World Bank's Database of Political Institutions, 2010 vintage) the results are also significant (column 5). If the share of veto players dropping out were increased from 0 to 20 percent, plan implementation would improve by 0.3-0.4 percent of GDP. For parliamentary fractionalization (the probability that two deputies picked at random will be of different parties—an increase indicates higher fractionalization), a one-standard-deviation increase is associated with a 0.4 percent of GDP weakening in implementation (column 6).[22]

We checked the robustness of our results through several exercises, including: dropping influential observations identified as such by a standard automated procedure; using overlapping plans; and using alternative definitions of "large" fiscal adjustment plans. The results are broadly similar when (see Table 8.6) running the same regressions on a sample that excludes influential observations.[23] As a matter of fact, the asymmetries in the impact of positive versus negative base effects (columns 2 and 6) and positive versus negative growth surprises (columns 3 and 7) become statistically significant. However, parliamentary fractionalization loses its significance.

We also used the overlapping sample of about 100 observations and found broadly similar results except that the evidence on asymmetry of coefficients was weaker. In addition, the results are not materially altered when using a cutoff of 0.5 percent of GDP (instead of 1 percent of GDP) to define large fiscal adjustment.

Finally, it is good practice to list all variables analyzed in one's research. Variables we considered beyond those on which we already reported in detail in this chapter include the following: the direction/momentum of change in fiscal balances, debt, growth, and real exchange rate at the time of plan inception; additional political variables (changes in government, number of years left in office, degree of polarization between the ruling party and other parties); and institutional characteristics (bureaucratic quality, corruption, law and order, and democratic accountability). For the most part, we found statistically insignificant coefficients for these variables, once the main variables discussed in the body of the chapter were included in the regressions.

Conclusion

In this chapter, we analyzed the design and implementation of large fiscal adjustment plans in the European Union during 1991–2008. We explored plan features as well as the impact of macroeconomic and fiscal conditions, and political and institutional variables, on plan implementation. Our main results are as follows.

Plans' Degree of Ambition

- Planned adjustments are more ambitious the higher the initial deficit is. However, this relationship appears to be relatively weak when initial deficit levels are low (such as below 3 percent of GDP). This is somewhat reassuring, because it is consistent with the view that, on average, policymakers seek to ensure fiscal sustainability.
- In general, implementation of plans was reasonably good and was not adversely affected by plan ambition.

Macroeconomic Factors and Revisions to Fiscal Data

- Growth surprises improve implementation of plans strongly (1 percent higher growth improves implementation by 0.5 percent of GDP). There is some evidence of asymmetry: the improvement in the fiscal balance stemming from positive growth surprises is approximately in line with the automatic increase in revenues, whereas negative growth surprises are associated with a larger worsening in the fiscal balance (compared with plans), suggesting that governments undertake stimulus measures in addition to letting the automatic stabilizers work.
- Growth forecasts are largely unbiased and close to consensus, so any growth surprises are largely unpredictable. This suggests that the main value added of fiscal councils may lie in other areas than providing an independent growth forecast.

- Inflation surprises do not matter, perhaps because inflation (and uncertainty) was low during the sample period.
- Favorable revisions to the initial overall fiscal balance seem to have little impact on the final fiscal balance (and in some estimates even lead to a worse fiscal balance than would otherwise have been the case). In the case of adverse revisions, the final fiscal balance is worse by 0.5 percent of GDP for each percent of GDP by which revisions worsen the initial fiscal balance.

Composition of Fiscal Adjustment

- *Ex-ante* plans are primarily expenditure-led, but *ex-post* implementation is more balanced. Revenue increases play an important role ex-post, although observed overperformance does not always reflect structural effort. In fact, only one-sixth of the plans envisaged revenue increases grounded in concrete tax policy measures. Most of these measures were implemented and resulted in revenue-to-GDP increases that were largely preserved beyond the plan horizon. Still, revenue increases reflected also one-off measures and temporary factors stemming from developments (such as asset price booms) not captured by the usual corrections for the economic cycle.
- In an interesting rejoinder with past studies on large fiscal adjustments based upon ex-post data, these findings lead us to take a more benign perspective regarding the durability of revenue-based adjustments. Indeed, when revenue-based adjustments are truly intended by policymakers and grounded in reforms, they may have better chances of being durable than one might infer from experiences that included unintended revenue increases that ultimately proved to be of a temporary nature.
- The composition of planned adjustment does not seem to drive success or failure in implementation.

Institutional and Political Factors

- EMU-related carrots and sticks have not always been effective, although there is some evidence that the run-up to EMU accession drove more ambitious design and better implementation, especially for plans published in 1994–1996.
- The strength of national fiscal rules/institutions improves implementation; supranational fiscal rules (specifically the EDP) matter at the design stage, but not the implementation stage.
- Better implementation is significantly associated with less fractionalized parliaments and greater improvements in government stability, but not with changes in government.

These results have considerable policy relevance going forward. If the past is to be any guide, five observations seem to be especially relevant for the daunting fiscal adjustment that many advanced countries will have to undertake in the years ahead. First, the absence of a correlation between the degree of ambition in planned adjustment and the plans' degree of implementation suggests that policymakers need not plan conservatively simply out of a concern that more ambitious adjustments would not be implemented. Second, the major impact of economic growth surprises on implementation points to the need to spell out in the plans appropriate policy responses to possible growth surprises. Third, the large impact of revisions to initial fiscal data highlights not only the importance of high-quality data and timely monitoring, but also the need to reinforce adjustment measures in the event that the starting point is found to be worse than expected. Fourth, the past challenges faced in implementing large expenditure cuts and the corresponding role of unplanned revenue increases calls for a redoubling of efforts to ensure that spending targets are respected and careful consideration of whether tax reforms or other lasting revenue measures would also be appropriate. Fifth, the positive results regarding national fiscal institutions—such as strength, compliance, and enforcement of fiscal rules— is suggestive of the role such an institution can play. We return to these issues in this book's concluding chapter, Chapter 9.

Appendix 8A: Data Issues and Cyclical Adjustment

Core Dataset

The fiscal and macroeconomic variables for plans published in 1998–2007 were drawn from European Commission's SGP documents, compiled and provided by Beetsma and others (2009).[24] This dataset was extended to 1991 using 39 hard copies of convergence plans. Unlike post-1998 convergence plans, the pre-1998 documents are published at different times of the year. Convergence plan documents were usually published in June or later months of year T (defining the starting position) with a fiscal adjustment horizon spanning years $T + 1$, $T + 2$, and $T + 3$. However, in certain cases, publications were between January and May (inclusive), so that the publication year was more appropriately seen as corresponding to $T + 1$ rather than T. In each case, the October WEO vintage of year T was used for the purposes of calculating the output gap.[25]

Cyclical Adjustment

The cyclically adjusted variables, if not available in the Plan documents, were generated by assuming a revenue elasticity of 1, and an expenditure elasticity of zero with respect to the output gap.

$$\underbrace{\frac{R}{Y^P}}_{\text{total}} = \underbrace{\frac{R}{Y}}_{\text{structural}} + \underbrace{\frac{R}{Y}\frac{y - y^P}{y^P}}_{\text{cyclical}}$$

where R is nominal revenues; Y and Y^P are nominal GDP and nominal potential GDP, respectively; $(y - y^P)/y^P$ is the output gap, with y and y^P denoting real GDP and real potential GDP, respectively.[26] Of the 66 plans comprising our main sample, 22 included information on both the output gap and structural primary balance as a share of GDP;[27] these variables were retrieved directly from the convergence and SGP program documents. In these cases, structural revenues were computed by adding primary expenditures to the structural primary balance all in percent of GDP, thus leveraging the full information on elasticities imbedded in the Plan's structural computations. In the remaining cases, the structural and cyclical revenues, both as a share of nominal and potential GDP, were computed using output gap estimations from a Hodrick-Prescott (HP) filter.

The HP-filter smoothes a real GDP series that is constructed as shown next. For each convergence plan, the entire historic series of real GDP preceding the projection year T is taken from the corresponding WEO vintage. Then, real GDP series is extrapolated over the projection period (T to $T+3$) by using the real growth rates for that period presented in the Plan documents, and over ten more years after $T+3$, by assuming the year $T+3$ growth rate as the long-run growth rate. A smoothing parameter of 200 is chosen to minimize the average absolute difference between the output gaps reported in the plans and the output gaps estimated using the HP-filter.

TABLE 8A.1 Methodology for Calculation of Structural Variables

	Structural Primary Balance	Output Gap	Calculation for Structural Revenue in Percent of Potential GDP
Case A	Available in Plan	Available in Plan	Structural primary balance + Primary expenditure; scaling to potential GDP using "Plan" Output Gap
Case B	Available in Plan	n.a.	Structural primary balance + Primary expenditure; scaling to potential GDP using "HP-Filter" Output Gap
Case C	n.a.	n.a.	Equals Plan Revenue-to-GDP ratio; "HP-Filter" Output Gap needed to back out Cyclical Revenues in percent of potential GDP

Ex-post data on structural revenues and potential GDP are taken from the European Commission's AMECO database. Any missing gaps were filled using ex-post WEO data (see Table 8A.1).

Appendix 8B: Timeline for European Monetary Integration (1990–2009)

1990	Launch of the first stage of EMU: closer economic policy coordination and the liberalization of capital movements.
1991	Agreement to the five Maastricht convergence criteria (including deficit <3% of GDP and debt <60% of GDP) to participate in EMU.
1994	Start of the second stage of EMU: creation of the European Monetary Institute (EMI). Member States required to fulfill by end-1997 the five Maastricht criteria. Plans for fiscal consolidation must show deficit <3% of GDP and debt <60% of GDP at end-1997.
1995	Madrid EU summit: The single currency is named the *euro*, and the scenario for the third stage of EMU—the introduction of the euro—is set out.
1997	The SGP agreed to at the Amsterdam EU summit, to ensure budgetary discipline among the likely EMU members. SGP gave teeth to Excessive Deficit Procedure (applying to countries with deficits exceeding 3% of GDP). A requirement for members and aspirers to submit to ECOFIN, annually, Stability programs or Convergence programs, respectively, is introduced.
May 1998	The European Council agrees to launch the third stage of EMU on Jan 1, 1999 and announces that 11 states meet the criteria to adopt the single currency: Belgium, Germany, France, Ireland, Italy, Luxembourg, the Netherlands, Austria, Portugal, and Finland. European Central Bank replaces the EMI as of 1 June 1998.
Jan 1, 1999	Start of the third stage of EMU: the euro is launched as the single currency for 11 Member States. However, the euro only exists as a virtual currency.
Jan 1, 2001	Following compliance with the Maastricht criteria, Greece becomes the 12th country to join the euro area.
Jan 1, 2002	Euro banknotes and coins are introduced in the 12 euro-area Member States.
Spring 2005	SGP revised following concerns about pro-cyclical fiscal policy in the EU. Country-specific medium-term objectives (MTOs), cast in terms of cyclically adjusted balances, are set.
Jan 1, 2007	Slovenia becomes the 13th member of the euro area in 2007.
Jan 1, 2008	Cyprus and Malta bring the number of euro-area members to 15.
Jan 1, 2009	The euro celebrates its first 10 years, and welcomes its 16th member—Slovakia.

Acknowledgments

We are grateful to Roel Beestma and Andrea Schaechter for valuable comments and suggestions, and to Katia Chen, Alica Dzelilovic, and Patricia Quiros for collecting the plans from various archival sources.

Notes

1. The focus of those studies was on whether fiscal adjustments are longer lasting and more successful in eliciting a non-Keynesian growth response when they rely on expenditure cuts rather than on tax hikes. For advanced economies, such studies have emphasized the possibility that spending-led adjustments (especially cuts in public employment, public wages, and transfers) are more durable and more successful in terms of their growth aftereffects, including due to favorable supply-side effects. For emerging economies, revenue-based adjustments were also found to be helpful, especially where the initial revenue/GDP ratio was low.

2. The level of initial debt and "structural" balance do not affect ambition in the overall fiscal balance. In other words, the *corrective* arm of the SGP (excessive deficit procedure) has been more successful in inducing fiscal corrections than the *preventive* (neutral fiscal stance over the cycle) and *dissuasive* arms (debt/GDP should not exceed 60 percent).

3. Previous studies have compared the planned adjustment in $t + 1$ with actual adjustment in $t + 1$, or the planned "year-on-year" adjustment in $t + 2$ with the actual "year-on-year" adjustment in $t + 2$. We compare three-year cumulative planned adjustments with three-year cumulative outcomes.

4. We also conducted a parallel exercise, where the sorting of plans was done based on planned improvement in the *structural primary balance–to-potential GDP* ratio. For this purpose, we used a threshold improvement of 0.5 percentage points of potential GDP (close to the median improvement in the ratio of the structural primary balance to potential GDP) to define large planned adjustments. This gave us 74 plans, of which 48 were nonoverlapping (as defined previously). The results for this sample were broadly similar to those described in this chapter, and are not reported for the sake of brevity.

5. By extracting all ex-ante information from a single plan document, and all ex-post information from a single AMECO vintage, we limit the impact of base effects (i.e., revisions to initial deficit data) and changes in accounting definitions *within* the ex-ante or the ex-post data (though such differences may emerge *between* ex-ante and ex-post data).

6. A *t*-test on the deviations of economic growth rates assumed under the plans from WEO growth rates published around the same time did not reject the null hypothesis that the distribution of these deviations was centered on zero. A test of forecast unbiasedness further confirmed that plan growth forecasts were unbiased relative to "actual" growth rates.

7. More precisely, the primary fiscal balance must be improved in response to increases in the public debt–to-GDP ratio (Bohn, 1998).

8. By contrast, revenue increases anchored in tangible planned tax policy changes appear to be more durable. In 8 out of the 10 cases where tax policy was discernibly tightened, more than half of the resulting increase in the revenue-to-GDP ratio endured three years beyond the end of the plan horizon.

9. Thus we do not confirm the findings put forward by previous studies according to which more ambitious plans were less likely to be implemented, using shorter sample periods at the one-year frequency. Note also that the slope coefficient in our reported regression (Figure 8.3) is approximately 0.8 also when we include the influential observations identified using the DFBETA procedure in STATA.

10. Indeed, the proponents of fiscal rules usually argue that rules improve fiscal discipline through lower debt and deficit targets and greater compliance with such targets. Those who oppose fiscal rules point instead to the challenges involved in setting targets that appropriately reflect the economic cycle (i.e., fiscal rules lead to procyclical fiscal policy) and to increased incentives toward meeting targets through the use of accounting stratagems. Thus, many opponents of fiscal rules would probably agree that rules increase the likelihood of abiding by governmental plans. Conversely, many proponents of fiscal rules would accept that even if fiscal rules were found to improve implementation of plans, this would not settle the overall case for or against fiscal rules in their favor.

11. Median rule strength was used as the relevant cutoff to divide the sample.

12. Appendix 8B presents a timeline for European monetary integration with key dates for fiscal policy highlighted.

13. Testing the dummy for the euro accession or pre-97 period, we do not find any statistically significant effect.

14. With revenues averaging 40 percent of GDP in our country sample and unitary elasticity of revenues with respect to GDP, the coefficient would be 0.4. A slightly smaller coefficient would reflect countercyclical fiscal measures.

15. At very high inflation rates, the so-called Keynes-Oliveira-Tanzi effect would set in, whereby the real value of tax revenues falls as inflation rises. This is not relevant for the countries in our sample over the past two decades.

16. High parliamentary fractionalization would also be expected to lead to conservative growth projections. In fact, the government would seek to avoid negative growth surprises, which in turn would necessitate renegotiating the fiscal adjustment plan—a cumbersome process with a fractionalized parliament. This effect would tend to lead to positive growth surprises (von Hagen, 2010).

17. Specifically, the implementation error is defined as the difference between the actual adjustment (the difference of the *actual* overall fiscal balance–to-GDP ratio between years $t + 3$ and t) and the planned adjustment (the difference of the *planned* overall balance between years $t + 3$ and t). A positive implementation error, therefore, corresponds to an overperformance in adjustment relative to the plan. A negative implementation error implies weaker than planned adjustment. As we switch from implementation ratios to implementation errors, we control for plan ambition. Using implementation errors in a regression setting has two advantages: first, marginal effects are scaled in percent of GDP, making for

intuitive results; second, implementation errors are the standard dependent variable in regression-based analyses undertaken by the fiscal policy credibility literature, thus facilitating comparison with previous studies.

18. For example, a 2 percentage point positive output surprise in the plan's third year in an economy where the ratio of revenues to GDP is 40 percent would result in an "automatic" improvement in the headline fiscal balance by 0.8 percentage points of GDP.

19. To better understand this "endogeneity" problem, consider an actual improvement in the overall balance that manifests itself in a higher implementation error (dependent variable). Insofar as the fiscal improvement (tighter aggregate demand) exerts the expected Keynesian effects on actual output, the real GDP growth surprise (explanatory variable) would tend to be lower. This would lead to bias in the estimation.

20. This finding also challenges the conclusion of earlier studies—based on annual data for a shorter sample period—that ambitious plans are associated with weak implementation (Beetsma and others, 2009).

21. As the initial fiscal balance and the deviation of the initial fiscal deficit from the 3 percent limit are strongly correlated, we avoid colinearity by never including them in the same regression.

22. Note that this intuitive result is obtained after controlling for growth surprises which, as discussed earlier, were likely to be more positive in coalition setups because of the built-in incentive associated with projecting conservatively (avoiding the cost of renegotiating the fiscal program in the event of a negative surprise).

23. We used the DFBETA procedure in STATA to identify influential observations displaying large effects on regression coefficients. The eight influential observations from a regression with the full sample of 66 were: Austria (2000), Greece (1992, 1994, 2000), Finland (1995, 1997), and the United Kingdom (1997, 2005).

24. The nine variables are: headline balance, revenue, expenditure, interest payments, and debt (all in percent of GDP); nominal and real growth, and inflation (in percent); and the GDP deflator.

25. A special exception was made for the United Kingdom, whose pre-1998 documents reported figures for fiscal years (ending March 31), rather than calendar years. For instance, the UK convergence plan published in March 1997 included an estimated fiscal outturn for 1996–97 (year T) and projections for the next three fiscal years: 1997–98, 1998–99 and 1999–2000 ($T+1$, $T+2$, and $T+3$, respectively). When migrating to calendar year basis, the 1996–97 outturn was booked to 1997 and the Spring 1997 WEO vintage used for structural balance computations.

26. When expressed as a ratio of nominal GDP, the equivalent equation is: $\frac{R}{Y} = \frac{R}{Y}\frac{y^P}{y} + \frac{R}{Y}\frac{y-y^P}{y}$.

27. In six additional cases, only the structural primary balance was reported.

CHAPTER 9

Conclusion

This book started from the premise that, although current circumstances may differ from those of the past, useful lessons regarding fiscal adjustment plans can be learned from historical experience, and that it is important to analyze not only success stories but also failures. Policymakers designing and implementing plans today can glean keys to success and pitfalls to avoid by putting themselves in the shoes of their predecessors—that is, by taking the perspective of past policymakers with the information available at the time, and tracing what went right and what went wrong "as it happened." Similarly, investors and the public at large can better gauge whether new plans being proposed have good chances of success when their own judgment is grounded in a better understanding of past plans and their outcomes.

The experience of the past few decades, as reviewed in the case studies for the G-7 countries (Chapters 1–7) and the cross country statistical analysis for a sample of large fiscal adjustment plans for the European economies (Chapter 8), shows that plans face sizable risks and often encounter substantial implementation difficulties along the way. Unexpected declines in economic growth, upward revisions to the initial fiscal deficit, changing priorities, lack of support among the general public, poor plan design, all have the potential to derail fiscal adjustment plans. Conversely, when favorable economic and political conditions emerge, objectives are often met or exceeded, even when plans envisage ambitious reductions in deficits and debts.

Indeed, one overarching message from this book is that the risks surrounding fiscal adjustment plans are large and stem primarily from powerful economic shocks. Thus, the design of plans and supporting budgetary institutional features needs to incorporate sufficient flexibility to accommodate—at least in part—sizable shocks. At the same time, this needs to be done in a manner that is spelled out upfront and that preserves the credibility of the medium-term fiscal adjustment objectives. In part these are technical matters, which we further develop below. Beyond the technical aspects, however, these are also political matters as the policy response to shocks will need to be acceptable to the public at large. This requires governments to communicate effectively to the public not only their proposed strategy under a set of reasonable assumptions about future economic developments, but also how governments will respond to unforeseen circumstances. Public awareness from the very beginning of the underlying rationale for fiscal adjustment and of how various types of shocks will be dealt with will ultimately help attain the adjustment objectives.

Our review of past experience also reveals that some shocks are far more important than others. Indeed, the most powerful determinant of whether fiscal adjustment plans succeed is economic growth. When growth turns out above expectations, so do revenues, and meeting the plans' fiscal targets becomes far easier. Conversely, when growth falls short of expectations, weakening revenues are frequently a source of deviations of fiscal outcomes from targets. Moreover, weak growth often leads governments to shift their priorities away from fiscal adjustment and toward fiscal stimulus. Among other factors underlying deviations of outcomes from plans, revisions to initial deficits also stand out: when the starting point is worse than initially assumed, governments often find it more challenging to attain the fiscal balance targets they had set for themselves.[1]

More generally, our results point to the primacy of economic shocks over and above political factors. In fact, although this was not a central objective of our project, we also learned that there is no straightforward relationship between political variables—especially, changes in government—and the chances that fiscal adjustment objectives will be met. Implementing fiscal adjustment plans as promised does not make governments more likely to lose power. In the case studies, we found few instances in which changes in government or in its composition posed risks to the implementation of adjustment. Moreover, political factors (measured by variables such as the fractionalization of the parliament among various political parties) played a limited role in explaining the extent to which plan targets were met. This is not to say that politics is unimportant. On the contrary, politics does matter. But what seems most relevant is not so much the strength of a government's majority in parliament; rather, it is the broad public's understanding of the need for adjustment, and its support for debt and deficit reduction and for the measures through which it is to be achieved. In some ways, this is a positive message, in the sense that even politically weak governments can undertake adjustment if they succeed in shaping public opinion through reasoned arguments.

Key Findings: What Failed and What Worked in Past Attempts at Fiscal Adjustment

Turning to more specific methodology and results, our analysis in the previous chapters addressed the design and implementation of large fiscal adjustment plans (tracking *ex-post* outcomes compared with *ex-ante* plans and the factors underlying such deviations), for case studies of each of the G-7 countries. Specific ex-ante consolidation attempts in those countries were selected based on the large size of planned adjustment, formal and public commitment to adjust, detailed formulation, and medium-term perspective. We complemented our case studies by a systematic cross-country statistical analysis drawing on the three-year "convergence" or "stability and growth" programs produced by EU countries during 1991–2007 (ultimately covering 66 "large fiscal adjustment plans" that envisaged a general government balance improvement of at least 1 percent of Gross Domestic Product (GDP) cumulative over the three-year period). On this basis, we obtained findings in three dimensions: (i) rationale for and design of the envisaged fiscal adjustment; (ii) degree of implementation and underlying macroeconomic factors; and (iii) political and institutional determinants of the implementation record.

Rationale for and Design of Fiscal Adjustment Plans

We obtain novel results on the rationale for, and intended design of, fiscal adjustment plans and their underlying macroeconomic assumptions.

RATIONALE The motivation behind fiscal consolidation plans in the G-7 economies has evolved over time. Adjustments in the 1970s and early 1980s were focused on reducing fiscal deficits in an effort to tackle macroeconomic imbalances, such as rising inflation and external current account deficits (e.g., France, Germany, and the United Kingdom). Since the mid-1980s, the underlying motivation has shifted toward issues of medium- and long-run fiscal sustainability, and plans have usually been introduced in response to high or rising public debts. Refinancing concerns have not been a major factor in the countries we examined, but in some cases (e.g., Canada in the 1990s, Italy in the run-up to European Monetary Union (EMU)) rising interest costs and spreads relative to neighboring countries were a motivating factor. In Europe, a common driving force underlying fiscal adjustment attempts has been the process toward the establishment and operation of the EMU, with the Maastricht criteria, the Stability and Growth Pact, and the Excessive Deficit Procedure serving to focus policymakers' and the public's attention on adjustment targets.

ENVISAGED COMPOSITION OF FISCAL ADJUSTMENT Most plans focused on spending cuts, consistent with the relatively large initial size of government in the advanced economies we analyze, particularly in Europe. Indeed, in our cross-country analysis based upon a sample of 66 large fiscal adjustment plans in the European Union, the vast majority of plans envisaged that more than half of the adjustment would come from spending cuts (as shares of GDP). Moreover, almost two-thirds of the plans envisaged that revenues would be reduced as a share of GDP, thus requiring cuts in expenditure ratios in excess of the total planned adjustment in the fiscal balance. Of the one-third of plans stipulating increases in the revenue-to-GDP ratio, only ten plans were grounded in well-specified tax policy measures. This leads to an alternative perspective on large, revenue-based, fiscal adjustments that had been identified as such by previous studies relying on ex-post outcomes. Indeed, that traditional strand of literature had identified a large share of fiscal adjustment episodes as "revenue-based." Our analysis of ex-ante plan design reveals that few adjustments had been intended as revenue-based by their originators, though that is how several adjustments turned out ex-post.

MACROECONOMIC ASSUMPTIONS Macroeconomic assumptions underlying adjustment plans, both in the case studies and in the cross-country analysis, were mostly in line with those of independent observers (such as *Consensus Forecasts* and the International Monetary Fund's *World Economic Outlook*). In other words, any surprises in economic growth (see ahead) and other macroeconomic variables were largely surprises not just for the plans' designers, but for all observers.

Implementation Record and Underlying Macroeconomic Factors

By combining our results on policymakers' intentions and on actual developments, we cast new light not only on the determinants of the implementation record, but also on the very notion of "success" in fiscal adjustment.

IMPLEMENTATION RECORD AND DEGREE OF AMBITION The implementation record of the plans analyzed in both the case studies and the cross-country analysis was mixed. For the 66 plans in the EU sample, the average annual planned improvement in the structural fiscal balance was equivalent to 1.7 percent of GDP (cumulative over the three years), whereas the outturn was a 0.9 percent improvement. On a positive note, actual implementation was not weakened by greater ambition: higher planned adjustment was associated with higher actual adjustment, one-for-one, on average. This evidence suggests that it is "okay to plan big," because ambitious plans do tend to produce more adjustment than do more modest ones.

REVENUE-EXPENDITURE MIX IN OUTCOMES VERSUS PLANS   In most of the case studies, expenditure cuts did not materialize to the extent initially envisaged; by contrast, revenues often turned out above expectations, owing only in part to favorable cyclical developments. Our cross-country statistical evidence confirms these findings: although plans envisaged cuts in the ratio of structural primary spending to potential GDP of 1.8 percent on average, actual cuts amounted to 0.3 percent. Revenues exhibited a converse pattern—exceeding planned increases by over 1 percent of potential GDP. This revenue overperformance stemmed from the introduction of (often temporary) revenue measures to offset difficulties in implementing expenditure cuts (see, for example, the cases of France and Italy in the 1990s) or other temporary factors, such as unusually strong asset market performance, which standard cyclical adjustment methods are unable to filter out. In an interesting rejoinder with past studies on large fiscal adjustments based upon ex-post data, these findings lead us to take a more benign perspective regarding the durability of revenue-based adjustments. Indeed, when revenue-based adjustments are truly intended by policymakers and grounded in reforms, they may have better chances of being durable than one might infer based on experiences that included unintended revenue increases (as in the traditional literature), which ultimately proved to be of a temporary nature.

ROLE OF ECONOMIC GROWTH   Deviations of economic growth from initial expectations were a key factor underlying the extent to which intended consolidation targets were attained. Several adjustment plans (e.g., Germany in the 1970s; Japan in the late 1990s and in the 2000s) were derailed, sometimes immediately, by unexpected economic downturns. Lower growth had a direct negative impact on cyclical revenues (and, to a lesser extent, caused an increase in some expenditure items), thereby worsening the headline (unadjusted for the cycle) fiscal balance. In addition, it had an indirect impact by tilting the authorities' perception of the relative merits of fiscal consolidation versus fiscal stimulus. Conversely, the success of some plans was facilitated by higher than expected growth and asset price developments. In some cases, when strong growth was accompanied by booming stock markets and housing prices, revenues surprised on the upside to an even greater extent (e.g., the United States during its successful fiscal adjustment episode in the mid- to late 1990s). In the cross-country analysis, a one-percentage-point improvement in growth compared with expectations resulted, on average, in a 0.5 percent of GDP strengthening in the headline fiscal balance.

STRUCTURAL REFORMS   The case studies reveal that fiscal adjustment plans were more likely to meet their objectives when they were grounded in structural reforms. This was evident in Germany in the 1980s and 2000s, with structural reforms to the social welfare system; in the United Kingdom with

the "Lawson adjustment" of the 1980s, which curbed expenditures as part of
Prime Minister Thatcher's redefinition of the role of the state; and in Canada
in the 1990s, in the context of a repositioning of the role of the state supported by a comprehensive expenditure review. In contrast, plans that
eschewed reforms in the same countries failed to meet their targets. Similarly, in Japan, where adjustment objectives were not accomplished, plans
envisaged revenue increases but the underlying measures were not explicitly identified and in the end were not implemented.

Fiscal Institutions and Political Factors

Our results also point to specific aspects of fiscal institutions and political
factors that facilitate fiscal adjustment.

FEATURES OF FISCAL INSTITUTIONS   Several aspects of fiscal institutions influenced the degree of implementation of fiscal adjustment plans:

- *Monitoring of fiscal outturns and policy response to data revisions.*
  Shortcomings in these areas were an important factor especially in Italy,
  where a significant portion of the deviations of outturns from plans
  reflected upward revisions to the initial deficit and where subsequent
  medium-term plans failed to compensate for such revisions. In the
  cross-country analysis, if the initial fiscal balance was found to be better
  than originally estimated when the plan was drawn up, the fiscal
  balance outcome at the end of the three years did not improve relative
  to plan; whereas if the initial fiscal balance was revised to be, say, 1 percent of GDP worse than estimated when the plan was drawn up, the
  deficit at the end of the three years turned out 0.5 percent of GDP worse
  than would otherwise have been the case.
- *Binding medium-term limits.* Although the presence of medium term
  plans was one of the criteria for choosing the case studies reviewed, the
  extent to which they included binding limits on expenditures varied. As
  medium-term limits were gradually made more legally binding over
  time, actual compliance with spending targets improved. This pattern
  was most noticeable in the United States (where constraints on discretionary expenditure allowed a more rapid improvement in the fiscal balance in the context of favorable growth and asset price developments),
  France, and the United Kingdom.
- *Contingency reserves.* Some plans effectively used contingency reserves
  to build in space to cope with potential adverse shocks, accelerate the
  adjustment, or create room for reducing the tax burden in the event that
  no adverse shocks materialized. Contingency reserves played a role in

the extent to which fiscal adjustment targets were met in the United Kingdom and, to a lesser extent, Canada.

■ *Coordination across levels of government*. Although most adjustment plans were originally devised for the central government, several involved reductions in transfers to subnational governments or other public entities. The extent to which those entities undertook parallel fiscal consolidations was an important determinant of whether the general government balance improved (as in Canada) or challenges were encountered (France and the United Kingdom).

■ *Fiscal rules*. The cross-country statistical analysis found tentative evidence of a positive association between the intensity of national fiscal rules (as measured by existing indices) and the extent to which targets were met.

POLITICAL FACTORS As mentioned previously, the cross-country evidence yields mixed messages on the role of political factors: lower parliamentary fractionalization and perceptions of greater political stability are to some extent associated with better implementation of plans; however, implementation of ambitious plans was not associated with more frequent changes in government. The limited role played by changes in government and other political factors is an important finding. Other researchers obtain similar results using the traditional ex-post based methodology.[2] However, the question lingered whether their results would be overturned by an ex-ante approach, which would include in the sample not only successful fiscal adjustments in which governments stayed in power, but also fiscal adjustment attempts that might have been thwarted by the public's resistance, often resulting in changes in government. It turns out, we found, that concerns about a possible link between failed adjustment attempts and falling governments did not seem to be validated by the data.

PUBLIC SUPPORT FOR FISCAL ADJUSTMENT What comes out far more clearly from the case studies is the importance of public support. For example, opinion polls ahead of the mid-1990s consolidation in Canada showed broad public support for public debt reduction. The authorities took advantage of this to put in place a communication strategy to reinforce support for their adjustment plan. In Germany, a general shift in the economic policymaking paradigm in the 1980s (against active short-term demand management) and a reformist platform of the left-of-center party in the 2000s was favored by broad sections of the population, helping sustain fiscal adjustment.

Implications for Planned Adjustments

Drawing on these findings, what are the lessons for fiscal adjustment plan design and implementation in the years (and decades) ahead?[3]

Spelling out how Policies will Respond to Shocks

Current fiscal adjustment plans do not sufficiently spell out the envisaged policy response to shocks. As seen previously, shocks, especially to economic growth, often derail fiscal adjustment. Indeed, uncertainty regarding future macroeconomic developments may well be greater today than at the outset of past fiscal adjustment attempts. Plans thus need to explicitly incorporate mechanisms to deal with such shocks, permitting some flexibility while credibly preserving the medium-term consolidation objectives. Examples of helpful mechanisms include:

- *Multiyear spending limits.* To anchor the consolidation path, plans should include binding and well-defined ceilings for expenditures and their subcomponents, and would preferably be endorsed not just by the government but also by parliament. The ceilings could exclude items that are cyclical (e.g., unemployment benefits) or nondiscretionary (e.g., interest payments). In other words, the plans could set a medium-term path for those items that do not depend on the cycle, while permitting revenues and other cyclical items to respond to the cycle. To the extent that these developments are indeed cyclical, they would not pose a threat to medium-term adjustment objectives.
- *Cyclically adjusted targets* would let the automatic stabilizers operate in response to cyclical fluctuations. To ensure credibility, the methods used to adjust the fiscal variables for the cycle should be subject to outside scrutiny.
- *Realistic/prudent macroeconomic assumptions* would reduce the risk of missing the fiscal targets. Using more conservative assumptions relative to independent observers to leave a "prudence buffer" could be justified in a context of high uncertainty, but should be used sparingly in order not to reduce credibility. Our results showed that, for the samples we examined, macroeconomic assumptions in government plans were not overly optimistic compared with projections by independent observers; hence, this has not been an area of concern for the countries we examined.[4] Nevertheless, this could potentially be important going forward, at times when economic forecasts seem to be subject to greater than usual uncertainty.

Monitoring and Accountability

The design and implementation of plans is greatly facilitated by the availability of reliable and timely information. Indeed, fiscal targets and the measures needed to achieve them can be set sensibly to the extent that they are based on sound information regarding the initial state of the public finances.

Any revisions to the initial position should lead to fine-tuning the adjustment path while seeking to preserve the medium-term objectives. More precisely, in the event of upward revisions to the initial deficit, it would seem sensible to permit some deviation from deficit targets in the near term, while imposing a more rapid improvement in the fiscal balance thereafter, so as to stick with the initially set targets for the medium term. In the event of downward revisions to the initial deficit (better than initially estimated fiscal balance), it would seem appropriate to adjust the whole fiscal balance path, one-for-one, so as to attain the initially set medium-term target ahead of time. Once medium-term adjustment plans have been designed and announced, fiscal councils and peer-monitoring processes can validate the consistency between targets and the proposed measures to attain them, and can enhance accountability in implementing plans.[5]

Composition of Fiscal Adjustment

The revenue-expenditure mix of fiscal consolidation plans needs to reflect country-specific societal preferences and structural fiscal characteristics. Going forward, as in past fiscal adjustment plans, greater reliance on measures aimed at limiting expenditures would be consistent with the large size of the state in many advanced economies, especially in Europe. This said, in view of the large scale of required adjustment in the years ahead, it is likely that several advanced economies will also need to include some revenue-enhancing measures in their plans to stabilize and gradually reduce debt ratios to more prudent levels. Drawing on the experience with the implementation record of past plans, where revenue increases partly compensated for expenditure overruns, it would seem desirable to: (i) redouble monitoring efforts and enhance institutional mechanisms to ensure that expenditure ceilings are adhered to; and (ii) prepare additional high-quality measures and reforms on the revenue side, to be deployed in the event of expenditure overruns.

Structural Reforms

As shown by past experience, structural reforms are needed to underpin successful implementation of large fiscal adjustment plans. Both expenditure cuts and revenue increases have good chances of being durable if they are based upon well-thought-out reforms. In the years ahead, these reforms will need to include tackling the thorniest sources of spending pressures—those from pension and, especially, health entitlements. Other areas that remain relevant in many countries include the public administration and the social welfare system, where significant gains were made in the more successful episodes reviewed in our case studies.

Building Public Support

As noted above, public support for fiscal adjustment, rather than a comfortable parliamentary majority, was a key determinant of successful fiscal adjustments. Thus, a priority going forward will be to build public support through communication campaigns, undertaken by not only policymakers but also independent observers in institutions, think-tanks, and academia. Such efforts would aim at educating the general public about the rationale and the scale of the needed fiscal challenges, and at explaining the rationale for what can reasonably be achieved through reforms without overburdening taxpayers or unduly curtailing necessary public services.

Notes

1. Although the key risks that we identify in this book will be highly relevant in the years ahead, it is important to recall that additional types of risks may also be relevant but were not captured, given our focus on advanced economies (especially the largest economies) prior to the crisis that began in 2008. Indeed, we know from previous work by some of us (Cebotari and others, 2009)—also based upon an ex-ante versus ex-post approach and covering advanced and emerging economies—and from the experience of the recent crisis that banking crises and exchange rate crises should also be listed among the most important fiscal risks.

2. For a recent and thorough statistical analysis, see Alesina, Carloni, and Lecce (2010). In an older but no less compelling analysis based upon case studies, Boltho (1992) showed that minority, coalition, and frequently changing governments in several European countries were able to reduce debt and deficit ratios, thanks to support for fiscal adjustment by broad segments of the population.

3. Information on recently adopted fiscal adjustment plans for 2011 and beyond for the G-20 countries and some other advanced economies is provided in Bornhorst and others (2010).

4. Indeed, based on the evidence in the previous chapters, it would seem that verifying the realism of the government's macroeconomic forecasts would not be the key motivation underlying proposals for independent fiscal policy councils—which would, however, be valuable for other activities, such as confirming the validity of the government's estimates of the impact of new fiscal policy measures.

5. For example, in the European Union, the recently introduced "European semester" (a six-month period every year during which member states' policies will be reviewed to detect any inconsistencies and emerging imbalances) is expected to reinforce coordination while major budgetary decisions are still under preparation. This is a further step in the process whereby, as documented previously, European institutions have increasingly sought to foster fiscal adjustments by member countries.

References

Alesina, Alberto, and Silvia Ardagna. 1995. "Tales of Fiscal Adjustment," *Economic Policy* (Vol. 13, No. 27), pp. 489–545.

Alesina, Alberto, and Silvia Ardagna. 2009. "Large Changes in Fiscal Policy: Taxes Versus Spending," *NBER* Working Paper 15439.

Alesina, Alberto, and Roberto Perotti. 1998. "Fiscal Expansions and Adjustments in OECD Countries," *Economic Policy*.

Alesina, Alberto, Dorian Carloni, and Giampaolo Lecce. 2010. "The Electoral Consequences of Large Fiscal Adjustments," *Harvard University*, unpublished.

Amato, Giuliano. 1990. *Due anni al Tesoro*, Bologna, Il Mulino.

Auerbach, Alan J. November 1, 1999. "U.S. Fiscal Policy in a (Brief?) Era of Surpluses." Paper prepared for a panel discussion sponsored by the Center for Japan–U.S. Business and Economic Studies, NYU Stern School of Business.

Auerbach, Alan J. March 27–28, 2003. "Fiscal Policy, Past and Present." Paper prepared for the Brookings Panel on Economic Activity.

Auerbach, Alan J. June 2004, revised March 2005. "American Fiscal Policy in the Post-War Era: An Interpretative History." Paper presented at the Federal Reserve Bank of Boston's conference on "The Macroeconomics of Fiscal Policy."

Auerbach, Alan J., Jason Furman, and William G. Gale. 2008. "Facing the Music: The Fiscal Outlook at the End of the Bush Administration." Mimeo.

Auerbach, Alan J. January 2009. "U.S. Experience with Federal Budget Rules." *CESifo Dice Report*.

Ayuso-i-Casals, Joaquim, Diana Gonzalez Hernández, Laurent Moulin, and Alessandro Turrini. April 3–5, 2007. "Beyond the SGP: Features and Effects of EU National-level Fiscal Rules," *Fiscal Sustainability: Analytical Developments and Emerging Policy Issues*, proceedings of the 9th Banca d'Italia Workshop on Fiscal Policy, Perugia. www.bancaditalia.it/studiricerche/convegni/atti/fiscal_sustainability.

Balassone, Fabrizio, G. Cesaroni, G. Gisci, B. Mazzotta, F. Mocavini, and D. Monacelli. July 2008. "Fiscal Consolidation in an Evolving Institutional

Framework: The Italian Experience," paper prepared for the Ministry of Economy and Finance (General Accounting Department) conference on *Budget Discipline and Public Sector Efficiency*, Rome. http://www.rgs. mef.gov.it/_Documenti/VERSIONE-I/RGS-comuni/Eventi/WORKSHOP–2/ completo_080798_ENG.pdf.

Balassone, Fabrizio, Daniele Franco, Sandro Momigliano, and Daniela Monacelli. March 21–23, 2002. "Italy: Fiscal Consolidation and Its Legacy,"*The Impact of Fiscal Policy*, proceedings of the 4th Banca d'Italia Workshop on Fiscal Policy, Perugia.

Balassone, Fabrizio, Daniele Franco, and Stefania Zotteri. 2006. "EMU Fiscal Indicators: A Misleading Compass?" *Empirica* (No. 33), pp. 63–87.

Balassone, Fabrizio, Daniele Franco, and Stefania Zotteri. June 2006. "The Reliability of EMU Fiscal Indicators: Risks and Safeguards," Temi di Discussione, Banca d'Italia (No. 633).

Baldacci, Emanuele, Benedict Clements, Sanjeev Gupta, and Carlos Mulas-Granados. November 2006. "The Phasing of Fiscal Adjustments: What Works in Emerging Market Economies?" *Review of Development Economics*, Blackwell Publishing (Vol. 10, No. 4), pp. 612–631.

Baldacci, Emanuele, Benedict Clements, Sanjeev Gupta, and Erwin R. Tiongson. 2005. "What Sustains Fiscal Consolidations in Emerging Market Countries?" *International Journal of Finance and Economics* (Vol. 10), pp. 307–21.

Barro, Robert J. 1979. "On the Determination of Public Debt," *Journal of Political Economy* (Vol. 87, No. 5), pp. 940–971.

Beetsma, Roel and Massimo Giuliodori. 2008. "Fiscal Adjustment to Cyclical Developments in the OECD: An Empirical Analysis Based on Real-Time Data" CEPR Discussion Paper (6692), London, United Kingdom.

Beetsma, Roel, Massimo Giuliodori, and Peter Wierts. 2009. "Planning to Cheat: EU Fiscal Policy in Real Time," *Economic Policy* (Vol. 24, No. 60), pp. 753–804.

Berglund, Per Gunnar and Matias Vernengo. November/December 2004. "A Debate on the Deficit," *Challenge*, pp. 1–42.

Bladen-Hovell, Robin. 1996. "Fiscal Policy and the Budget," in Artis, Michael J. (ed.), *The U. K. Economy*, London: Oxford University Press.

Bohn, Henning. 1998. "The Behavior of U.S. Public Debt and Deficits," *Quarterly Journal of Economics* (Vol. 113, No. 3).

Boltho, Andrea. 1992. "Disavanzo pubblico e strategie di rientro in alcuni paesi europei," in "Il disavanzo pubblico in Italia," Part II, Ente Luigi Einaudi, Il Mulino, Bologna, Italy.

Bornhorst, Fabian, Nina Budina, Giovanni Callegari, Asmaa A. El-Ganainy, Raquel Gomez Sirera, Andrea Lemgruber, Andrea Schaechter, and Joong B. Shin. 2010. "A Status Update on Fiscal Exit Strategies," IMF Working Paper (No. 10/272).

Bourgon, Jocelyne. 2009. "Program Review: The Government of Canada's Experience Eliminating the Deficit, 1994-1999: A Canadian Case Study," The Centre for International Governance Innovation.

Bouthevillain, Carine, Philippine Cour-Thimann, Gerrit van den Dool, Pablo Hernandez de Cos, Geert Langenus, Matthias Mohr, Sandro Momigliano, and Mika Tujula. September 2001. "Cyclically-Adjusted Budget Balances: An Alternative Approach," European Central Bank, Working Paper (No. 77).

Buchanan, James M. and Richard E. Wagner. (1977). *Democracy in Deficit.* Academic Press, New York.

Buettner, Thiess and Bjoern Kauder. 2010. "Revenue Forecasting Practices: Differences across Countries and Consequences for Forecasting Performance," *Fiscal Studies* (Vol. 31, No. 3).

Cabinet Office, Japan, various issues, *Medium-Term Macroeconomic and Fiscal Projections.*

Calmfors, Lars. March 18–19, 2010. "The Swedish Fiscal Policy Council-Experiences and Lessons," paper prepared for the Conference on Independent Fiscal Policy Institutions, Budapest.

Cebotari, Aliona, Jeffrey M. Davis, Lusine Lusinyan, Amine Mati, Paolo Mauro, Murray Petrie, and Ricardo Velloso. 2009. "Fiscal Risks: Sources, Disclosure, and Management," IMF Fiscal Affairs Department, Departmental Paper No. 09/01.

Champsaur, Paul and Jean-Philippe Cotis. 2010. "Rapport sur la situation des finances publiques," report available at: lesrapports.ladocumentation francaise.fr/BRP/104000234/0000.pdf.

Cimadomo, Jacopo. 2008. "Fiscal Policy in Real Time," European Central Bank Working Paper No. 919, Frankfurt, Germany.

Commission des finances du Sénat. July 6, 2010. "Rapport d'information sur le débat d'orientation des finances publiques pour 2011."

Congressional Budget Office. May 2008. *Sources of the Growth and Decline in Individual Income Tax Revenues since 1994.* Washington, D.C.

Cottarelli, Carlo and Andrea Schaechter. September 1, 2010. "Long Term Trends in Public Finances in the G-7 Economies," IMF Staff Position Note.

Courchene, Thomas, J. 1997. "The International Dimension of Macroeconomic Policies in Canada." In *Macroeconomics Policy in Open Economies*, eds. M. U. Fratianni, D. Salvatore and J. von Hagen. Westport, Connecticut: Greenwood Press, pp. 495–537.

Courchene, Thomas, J. 2005. "Balanced Budgets: A Canadian Fiscal Value." Paper prepared for the International Conference: *The Long-Term Budget Challenge: Public Finance and Fiscal Sustainability in the G7.*

Crescenzi, Antonella (ed.). 2007. *I Documenti di Programmazione.* Rome, LUISS University Press.

Debrun, Xavier, David Hauner, and Manmohan Kumar. 2007. "Discretion, Institutions and Fiscal Discipline," in Manmohan Kumar and Teresa Ter-Minassian (eds.), *Promoting Fiscal Discipline*, International Monetary Fund, Washington, D.C.

Degni, Marcello, Nicoletta Emiliani, Francesca Gastaldi, Giancarlo. Salvemini, and Claudio Virno. 2001. *Il Riequilibrio della Finanza Pubblica negli anni Novanta*, Studi e Note di Economia, Quaderni, No. 7.

Economic Report of the President. Various issues. Washington, D.C.

European Commission. September 2005. "New and Updated Budgetary Sensitivities for the EU Budgetary Surveillance," Information Note for the Economic and Policy Committee, DG ECFIN.

European Commission. 2007. "How to Stick to Medium-Term Budgetary Plans," Part III of "Public Finances in EMU 2007," *European Economy* No. 3/2007, DG ECFIN, pp. 149–192.

European Commission. September 29, 2010. *Strengthening Economic Governance in the EU: Proposals for Council Regulations*.

Fedelino, Annalisa, Mark Horton, Anna Ivanova. 2009. "Computing Cyclically-Adjusted Balances and Automatic Stabilizers." IMF Technical Notes and Manuals 09/05, Fiscal Affairs Department.

Francese, Maura and Angelo Pace. 2008. "Italian Public Debt since National Unification: A Reconstruction of the Time Series," *Questioni di economia e finanza* (occasional papers) 31, Banca d'Italia.

Franco, Daniele. 1993. *L'espansione della spesa pubblica in Italia*, Il Mulino, Bologna.

Frankel, Jeffrey and Peter Orzsag. 2002. "Retrospective on American Economic Policy in the 1990s." In Frankel and Orzsag (eds.), *American Economic Policy in the 1990s*. MIT Press.

Giavazzi, Francesco, Tullio Jappelli, and Marco Pagano. 2000. "Searching for Non-Linear Effects of Fiscal Policy: Evidence from Industrial and Developing Countries," *European Economic Review* (Vol. 44), pp. 1259–89.

Giavazzi, Francesco and Luigi Spaventa. (eds.) 1988. *High Public Debt: The Italian Experience*, Cambridge University Press, Cambridge, England, U.K.

Girouard, Nathalie, and Christophe André. 2005. "Measuring Cyclically-Adjusted Budget Balances for OECD Countries," OECD Working Paper No. 434, Economics Department.

Government of Japan. June 2002. "Basic Policies for Macroeconomic Management."

Government of Japan. 2002. "Structural Reform and Medium-Term Economic and Fiscal Perspectives," and its revisions made in subsequent years (from 2003 to 2006).

Government of Japan. July 2006. "Basic Policies for Macroeconomic Management."

Government of Japan. 2007. "Direction and Strategy for the Japanese Economy," and its revisions made in 2008.

Greenspan, Alan. April 27, 2001. "The Paydown of Federal Debt." Remarks before the Bond Market Association.

Gupta, Sanjeev, Emanuele Baldacci, Benedict Clements, and Erwin R. Tiongson. 2005. "What Sustains Fiscal Consolidations in Emerging Market Countries?" *International Journal of Finance and Economics* (Vol. 10), pp. 307–21.

Hahm, Sung Deuk, Mark S. Kamlet, David C. Mowery, and Tsai-Tsu Su. 1992. "The Influence of Gramm-Rudman-Hollings Act on Federal Budgetary Outcomes, 1986–89," *Journal of Policy Analysis and Management* (Vol. 11, No. 2), pp. 207–234.

Iakova, Dora and Takuo. Komori. 2004. "Reform of Local Government Finances in Japan," Japan, selected issues, IMF.

Inspection Générale des Finances. April 2007. "Rapport sur la gestion pluriannuelle des finances."

International Monetary Fund. 2010a. "Will It Hurt? Macroeconomic Effects of Fiscal Consolidation," *World Economic Outlook*, Chapter 3, October.

International Monetary Fund. 2010b. *Fiscal Monitor*. November. Washington, D.C.

Jonung, Lars and Martin Larch. 2006. "Improving Fiscal Policy in the EU: The Case for Independent Forecasts," *Economic Policy* (Vol. 21, No. 47), pp. 491–534.

Jonung, Lars and Martin Larch. 2004. "Improving Fiscal Policy in the EU: The Case for Independent Forecasts," European Commission Economic Paper No. 210, DG ECFIN.

Keith, Robert. March 2004. *Budget Sequesters: A Brief Review*. Congressional Research Service Report for Congress.

Koen, Vincent and Paul van den Noord. 2005. "Fiscal Gimmickry in Europe: One-off Measures and Creative Accounting," OECD, Working Paper No. 417, Paris.

Kroszner, Randall S. 2003. "Is it Better to Forgive Than to Receive? An Empirical Analysis of the Impact of Debt Repudiation," University of Chicago Graduate School of Business.

Leidy, Michael. September 1998. "A Postmortem on the Achievement of Federal Fiscal Balance," IMF Staff Country Report No. 98/105.

Ljungman, Göesta. 2008. "Expenditure Ceilings: A Survey," IMF Working Paper 08/282.

Marino, Maria Rosaria, Sandro Momigliano, and Pietro Rizza. 2008. "A Structural Analysis of Italy's Fiscal Policies after Joining the Monetary Union: Are We Learning from Our Past?" *Public Finance and Management* (Vol. 8, No. 3), pp. 451–501.

Martin, Paul. 1996. "The Canadian Experience in Reducing Budget Deficits and Debt," *Federal Reserve Bank of Kansas City Economic Review*.

Martin, Paul. 2008. *Come Hell or High Water: My Life In And Out of Politics.* Mccleland & Stewart.

Martin, Paul. 2010. "Improvement in a Cold Climate," keynote speech for the Guardian Public Services Summit.

Masson, Paul and Michael Mussa. 1995. "Long-Term Tendencies in Budget Deficits and Debt." In *Budget Deficits and Debt: Issues and Options,* proceedings from a Symposium sponsored by the Federal Reserve Bank of Kansas City, Jackson Hole, Wyoming.

Mendoza, Enrique G. and Jonathan D. Ostry. 2008. "International Evidence on Fiscal Solvency: Is Fiscal Policy 'Responsible'?" *Journal of Monetary Economics.*

Milesi-Ferretti, Gian Maria. 2003. "Good, Bad or Ugly: On the Effects of Fiscal Rules with Creative Accounting," *Journal of Public Economics* (No. 88), pp. 377–94.

Milesi-Ferretti, Gian Maria, and Kenji Moriyama. March 21–23, 2004. "Fiscal Adjustment in EU Countries: A Balance Sheet Approach," in *Public Debt,* proceedings of the 6th Banca d'Italia Workshop on Fiscal Policy, Perugia.

Ministry of Finance, Japan. 1998. *Medium-Term Fiscal Projections.*

Miyazaki, Masato. 2006. "Framework for Fiscal Consolidation: Successes and Failures in Japan," *OECD Journal on Budgeting* (Vol. 6, No. 4).

Momigliano, Sandro and Pietro Rizza. 2007. "Temporary Measures in Italy: Buying or Losing Time?" in Magyar Nemzeti Bank (ed.), *Temporary Measures and Off-budget Activities.*

Moulin, Laurent. March 12, 2004. "Expenditure rules à la française: An assessment after five years," ECFIN country focus, Volume 1, No. 5.

Moulin, Laurent and Peter Wierts. 2006. "How Credible Are Multiannual Budgetary Plans in the EU?," proceedings of the Banca d'Italia workshop on fiscal indicators, March 30 to April 1.

Mühleisen, Martin. 2004. "Overview: Returning Deficits and the Need for Fiscal Reforms." In Martin Mühleisen and Christopher Towe (eds.), U.S. Fiscal Policies and Priorities for Long-Run Sustainability. IMF Occasional Paper 227, Washington, D.C.

Nelson, Edward and Kalin Nikolav. 2001. "U.K. Inflation in the 1970s and 1980s: The Role of Output Gap Mismeasurement," Working Paper No. 148. London: The Bank of England.

Orszag, Peter. July 25, 2007. *Issues in Reinstating a Statutory Pay-As-You-Go Requirement.* Statement before the Committee on the Budget, U.S. House of Representatives.

Reinhart, Carmen M. and Kenneth Rogoff. 2010. *This Time Is Different: Eight Centuries of Financial Folly.* Princeton University Press.

Reischauer, Robert D. 1990. "Taxes and Spending under Gramm-Rudman-Hollings," *National Tax Journal* (Vol. 43, No. 3, September).

Rubin, Robert and Jacob Weisberg. 2008. *In an Uncertain World*. Random House.

Salvemini, Giancarlo (ed.). 2003. "I guardiani del bilancio: Una norma importante ma di difficile applicazione" l'articolo 81 della Costituzione, Venice, Marsilio.

Sancak, Cemile, Ricardo Velloso, and Jing Xing. 2010. "Tax Revenue Response to the Business Cycle," IMF Working Paper, WP/10/71.

Sartor, Nicola (ed.). 1998. "Il risanamento mancato. La politica di bilancio italiana: 1986–1990." Rome, Carocci.

Spaventa, Luigi and Vincenzo Chiorazzo. 2000. "Astuzia o virtù? Come accadde che l'Italia fu ammessa all'Unione Monetaria," Donzelli Editore.

Strauch, Rolf, Mark Hallerberg, and Jürgen von Hagen. 2004. "Budgetary Forecasts in Europe: The Track Record of Stability and Convergence Programmes," European Central Bank Working Paper No. 307 (February). Also available as Economic Working Paper E2004/42, Centro de Estudios Andaluces, Sevilla, Spain.

Summers, Larry. October 1986. *Debt Problems and Macroeconomic Policies*. NBER Working Paper No. 2061. National Bureau of Economic Research, Massachusetts.

Tanaka, Hideaki. 2003. "Fiscal Consolidation and Medium-term Fiscal Planning in Japan," *OECD Journal on Budgeting* (Vol. 3, No. 2).

Tsibouris, George C., Mark A. Horton, Mark J. Flanagan, and Wojciech S. Maliszweski. 2006. "Experience with Large Fiscal Adjustments," IMF Occasional Paper 246.

United Kingdom Economics and Finance Ministry. 1997. *Fiscal Policy: Lessons from the Last Economic Cycle*. London: Her Majesty's Treasury.

Van den Noord, Paul. 2002. "Managing Public Expenditure: The U.K. Approach," OECD Economics Department Working Paper No. 341. Paris: Organization for Economic Cooperation and Development.

Van Rompuy. 2010. "Strengthening Economic Governance in the EU: Report of the Task Force to the European Council. www.consilium.europa.eu/uedocs/cms_data/docs/pressdata/en/ec/117236.pdf.

Von Hagen, Jürgen, Andrew H. Hallett, and Rolf Strauch. 2001. "Budgetary Consolidation in the EMU," *EC Economic Papers*.

Von Hagen, Jürgen. 2010. "Sticking to Fiscal Plans: The Role of Institutions," *Public Choice* (144), pp. 487–503.

Von Hagen, Jürgen and Guntram. B. Wolff. 2004. "What Do Deficits Tell Us about Debt? Empirical Evidence on Creative Accounting with Fiscal Rules in the EU," Discussion Paper No. 38, Deutsche Bundesbank.

About the Project Team

S.M. Ali Abbas is an economist in the International Monetary Fund's (IMF's) Fiscal Affairs Department. He has published on capital flows and government debt markets and recently co-compiled a comprehensive historical public debt database. Before joining the IMF, he pursued doctoral studies in Economics at Oxford University, after a two-year Overseas Development Institute fellowship in the Tanzanian treasury.

Toni Ahnert was in the IMF's Fiscal Affairs Department while this book was being written. He is a Ph.D. candidate at the London School of Economics and Political Science and affiliated with the Centre for Economic Performance. He obtained Master's degrees in Economics from Universitat Pompeu Fabra, Barcelona, and the University of Essex, U.K.

Fabrizio Balassone is a director in the Structural Economic Analysis Department at Banca d'Italia. He was previously Advisor to the Head of the General Accounting Office in Italy and worked at the IMF.

Christian Breuer is an economist in the Public Finance Department at the Ifo Institute for Economic Research in Munich and represents the Ifo Institute at the Working Group for tax revenue forecasts at the German ministry of finance. He obtained a Master's degree in Economics from Martin-Luther-University Halle-Wittenberg.

Jan Gottschalk is a macroeconomic advisor with the IMF's Pacific Financial Technical Assistance Centre; while this book was written he was with the Fiscal Affairs Department. Prior to joining the IMF, he was a researcher with the Kiel Institute for the World Economy and published journal articles on monetary policy and business cycle research. He obtained a Ph.D. degree in Economics from Kiel University, Germany.

Fuad Hasanov is an economist in the IMF's Fiscal Affairs Department. Previously he was Assistant Professor at Oakland University in Rochester, Michigan. He has published journal articles on economic growth, inequality, housing, and consumption. He holds a Ph.D. in Economics from the University of Texas at Austin.

Richard Hughes is a Deputy Division Chief in the Fiscal Affairs Department of the IMF. He was previously a Deputy Director in the Public Spending Directorate of Her Majesty's Treasury, where he led the 2007 Comprehensive Spending Review. He was educated at Harvard and Oxford Universities.

Anna Ivanova is an economist in the European department at the IMF. Previously she worked as an economist in the Fiscal Affairs and Middle East and Central Asia departments of the IMF and as a physicist in the Institute of Nuclear Problems in Belarus. She obtained her Ph.D. in Economics from the University of Wisconsin–Madison, Master's degree in Economic Development from Vanderbilt University, and Master's degree in Nuclear Physics from Belarussian State University.

Jiri Jonas is a senior economist in the IMF's Fiscal Affairs Department. Previously he was the Czech Republic representative at the IMF Executive Board, and served as an advisor to the Minister of Finance. He obtained a Master's degree in Economics from the Prague School of Economics.

Lucy Qian Liu is an economist in the Middle East and Central Asia Department at the IMF, and was in the Fiscal Affairs Department while this book was being written. She holds a Ph.D. in Economics from Queen's University in Canada.

Edouard Martin is a senior economist in the Middle East and Central Asia Department at the IMF, and was in the Fiscal Affairs Department while the book was being written. Previously, he worked in the French Ministry of Finance.

Paolo Mauro is Chief of a Fiscal Operations Division in the IMF's Fiscal Affairs Department. He was previously a division chief in the Research Department and has held various operational positions in the IMF. He is a highly cited author of journal articles on topics including corruption, sovereign bond spreads, exchange rate regimes, and growth-indexed bonds. He recently coauthored *Emerging Markets and Financial Globalization*, Oxford University Press. He obtained his Ph.D. in Economics from Harvard University.

Sandro Momigliano is Chief of the Public Finances Division in the Structural Economic Analysis Department at the Bank of Italy. He has published journal articles on fiscal policy, fiscal multipliers, and structural analysis of public finances.

Taisuke Nakata was in the IMF's Fiscal Affairs Department while this book was being written. He is an Economics Ph.D. candidate at New York University. Previously, he worked as an assistant economist at the Federal Reserve Bank of Kansas City. He holds a B.A. in Economics from the University of Chicago.

Junhyung Park was a research assistant in the IMF's Fiscal Affairs Department while working on this book and is now a Ph.D. student in economics at the University of California, Los Angeles. He holds a B.A. in Economics from the University of Virginia.

Pietro Rizza is an economist in the Structural Economic Analysis Department at the Bank of Italy. He holds a Ph.D. in Economics from Boston University and has previously worked as a consultant at the European Commission, the European Central Bank, and the World Bank.

Cemile Sancak is a senior economist in the Fiscal Affairs Department at the IMF. She has published on the impact of the business cycle on revenues and the determinants of long-term growth. Previously, she was an economist at the Federal Government of Canada and a lecturer at Carleton University, Ottawa, Canada. She holds a Ph.D. in Economics from Carleton University and a Master's degree in Economics from Queen's University, Kingston, Canada.

Keiko Takahashi is an economist in the Fiscal Affairs Department at the IMF. She previously worked on macroeconomic and fiscal policy at the Ministry of Finance and the Cabinet Office in Japan. She holds a Master's degree (M.Phil) in Economics from University of Oxford.

Kiichi Tokuoka is an economist in the Asia and Pacific Department at the IMF. Previously he worked for the Japanese Ministry of Finance. He obtained a Ph.D. in Economics from Johns Hopkins University.

Irina Tytell is a senior economist in the European Department at the IMF. She had previously worked in the Research Department at the IMF and the IMF Institute. She holds a Ph.D. from Cambridge University, an M.Sc. from the London School of Economics, and an M.A. from the New Economic School in Moscow.

Ricardo Cicchelli Velloso is Deputy Division Chief in the IMF's Fiscal Affairs Department, where he coordinates fiscal operational support to several IMF member countries. He has led technical assistance missions on fiscal transparency, fiscal risks, and fiscal rules. He previously held various positions in the IMF, including Resident Representative in Peru. Prior to joining the IMF, he worked in Brazil's Applied Economics Research Institute and taught at the Federal University of Rio de Janeiro. He holds postgraduate degrees in Economics from the University of California at Berkeley and Federal University of Rio de Janeiro.

Mauricio Villafuerte is Deputy Division Chief in the IMF's Fiscal Affairs Department. He previously worked at the Ministry of Finance and the Central Bank of Ecuador. He specializes in fiscal and monetary policy issues in natural resource–dependent countries and has published on fiscal policy management and fiscal institutions. He pursued his doctoral studies in Economics at the University of California, Los Angeles.

Irina Yakadina is an economist in the European Department at the IMF and was in the Fiscal Affairs Department while this book was being written. Prior to that, she taught at the IMF Institute. She obtained a Ph.D in Economics from Pompeu Fabra University in Barcelona and holds a Master's degree in Economics from the New Economic School in Moscow.

Index